EUGEN ROSENSTOCK-HUESSY
Studies in His Life and Thought

EUGEN ROSENSTOCK-HUESSY
Studies in His Life and Thought

Edited by

M. Darrol Bryant and Hans R. Huessy

Toronto Studies in Theology
Volume 28

The Edwin Mellen Press
Lewiston/Queenston

Eugen Rosenstock-Huessy: Studies in His Life and Thought
edited by M. Darrol Bryant and Hans R. Huessy

This is volume 28 in the continuing series
TORONTO STUDIES IN THEOLOGY
Volume 28 ISBN 0-88946-772-2
TST Series ISBN 0-88946-975-X

The Edwin Mellen Press
Box 450
Lewiston, New York
USA 14092

The Edwin Mellen Press
Box 67
Queenston, Ontario
CANADA L0S 1L0

Printed in the United States of America

TABLE OF CONTENTS

Eugen teaching at Dartmouth College in New Hampshire
where he taught from 1935 until his retirement in 1958.
c. 1953.

Acknowledgements

The task of putting together a collection of essays is one that involves the collaborative efforts of many. Here I wish to acknowledge some of those who contributed to this task. First, I wish to thank Principal Ian Campbell of Renison College, Waterloo, Ontario, who generously supported the conference on Eugen Rosenstock-Huessy where these studies were first presented. The assistance of the Principal, and the staff of the College, was exemplary throughout and made our time together in Waterloo enjoyable and fruitful. Secondly, a grant from the Social Sciences and Humanities Research Council of Canada (#443-820063) helped to defray travel costs for the participants. Without such assistance the participation of many would not have been possible. Thirdly, I wish to thank the Rosenstock-Huessy Foundation of Norwich, Vermont, and the Office of Research, University of Waterloo, for their contributions towards the costs of preparing this volume for publication. These grants will allow the work of the conference to reach a wider audience.

In the four years since the conference many people have contributed their advice, counsel, and expertise to readying this material for publication. But I want to especially acknowledge the continual support of Freya von Moltke without whom the many difficulties that inevitably accompany a project like this could not have been overcome. Moreover, her knowledge of German life in this century combined with her familiarity with the content and spirit of Rosenstock-Huessy's life and work saved me from many errors. She also supplied several of the photographs that appear in the volume. The other photographs were provided by Hans Huessy. Carol Kieswetter input these essays and graciously made the changes that were later introduced. She was constant in her attention to detail and cheerful in her handling of revisions. Susan Hodges Bryant and other friends in Waterloo offered valuable editorial suggestions and checked the manuscript for errors when my eyes had become dulled by too much familiarity with the text. I want also to thank the contributors to the volume who have patiently endured the many delays that attended this project. Their willingness to rework their initial presentations was much appreciated. Finally, let me thank my co-editor, Hans Huessy, whose advice and assistance was invaluable. I am deeply grateful not only for his support and assistance but also for his willingness to collaborate with me in this project.

Without the support and assistance of all these people–and others I neglected to name–this project would not have been possible. I am grateful for their assistance but acknowledge that the errors that remain are the responsibilities of the editors, especially this one.

M. Darrol Bryant

Introduction

M. Darrol Bryant and Hans R. Huessy

The studies in this volume explore varied aspects of the life and work of Eugen Rosenstock-Huessy (1888-1973), a little-known but highly significant figure whose life and writings were forged in the tumultuous events that have convulsed our century and are transforming our world. Whether or not the readers of this volume will come to share our conviction of the significance of Rosenstock-Huessy must await the outcome of their encounter with him, but it is our hope that these essays will serve to encourage a larger number of people to examine for themselves this neglected writer. This situation of neglect–benign, accidental or deserved– poses the burden of this introduction, namely to set the context for a fruitful engagement with the *essays* that follow and the *figure* whose life and thought they explore. Thus we wish here in this introduction to introduce both the circumstances that surround the essays that follow and the life and thought of the figure with whom they are all engaged. First, then, let us turn to the circumstances that surrounded the genesis of these papers and their appearance in this volume.

The Originating Context

The essays in this volume were initally prepared for a conference held at Renison College, University of Waterloo, Waterloo, Ontario, in June, 1982, on Rosenstock-Huessy: His Life and Work. This conference, attended by over fifty participants from North America and Europe, had three major purposes. First, it sought to bring together those who had been influenced, in different ways, by the life and work of Rosenstock-Huessy. The result–due to the variety of relationships the conference participants had to Rosenstock-Huessy–was a rather unique gathering. Some of the participants had known Rosenstock-Huessy intimately as father, grandfather or as a close friend. Some had been his students at Dartmouth College where he taught from 1938 to 1957. Others had participated in Camp William James, a work camp

Rosenstock-Huessy helped to found in the early 1940s. And still others knew him only through his writings which they had encountered at various points in their lives. This variety of relationships to Rosenstock-Huessy, his life and work, was evident in the papers that were presented at the conference and is retained in the studies included in this volume. They include essays by his family, friends, students, and, as Professor Berman noted, his "co-workers". This is not only a distinctive feature of this volume, but a highly appropriate one given the range of Rosenstock-Huessy's own life and writings.

Secondly, the conference marked the first major attempt in the English-speaking world to explore the significance of Rosenstock-Huessy for contemporary intellectual life. Rosenstock-Huessy remains a little-known figure despite a bibliography that contains hundreds of items (see the companion volume *Eugen Rosenstock-Huessy: A Complete Bibliography*). Nonetheless, people in a range of disciplines and areas of intellectual endeavour have found in his writings important contributions to their own work. At the conference itself the range of Rosenstock-Huessy's work was reflected in the variety of backgrounds and disciplines from which the participants came. In our midst were to be found teachers of law, history, sociology, religion, psychology, social work, literature, speech communications, theology, philosophy, and environmental studies. This range reflected the astonishing scope of Rosenstock-Huessy's own work and perhaps offers a clue as to why he is often ignored: few can match his range of vision since most within the academic world work within specialized disciplines with methodologies that recoil in the face of challenge to their own narrowness.

Thirdly, the conference sought to celebrate and make better known the life and work of a person who had, in varying ways, touched and inspired those of us who participated in this event. Unlike many academic conferences that unfold as if the ideas being examined and assessed had emerged untouched by human lives– immaculately but undivinely conceived–this conference acknowledged the events in Rosenstock-Huessy's life out of which his writings were born. The great watershed in Rosenstock-Huessy's own life was the First World War and he never failed to acknowledge that his writings emerged from the suffering it has been the fate of this century to endure. Thus in the conference we paid attention to some of the circumstances and relationships that touched deeply Rosenstock-Huessy's life and work. This dimension of the conference is also reflected in this volume. But this feature of the original conference is also reflected in the fact that these studies are characterized by a concern to appropriate Rosenstock-Huessy's thought and to indicate its relevance to several fields of study. Many at the conference were aware that Rosenstock-Huessy's own work is often difficult, sometimes obscure, and perhaps flawed in many ways. But this more critical evaluation awaits a further stage in the process. Right now the more pressing need is to make his work better known, and it is our hope that these studies will contribute to that end.

It is, then, from this conference and the confluence of factors indicated above that these essays are drawn. The contributors were asked to revise their contributions in the light of the discussion that surrounded them in Waterloo, but then we had to make further selections. The selection of papers for inclusion in this volume was governed by three interacting considerations. First, which papers best illuminated aspects of Rosenstock-Huessy's life and thought? Secondly, which collection of essays best illustrated the range of Rosenstock-Huessy's own work? And thirdly, which essays best exposed the fruitfulness of Rosenstock-Huessy's thought for our contemporary intellectual work? Among the essays that follow, then, are contributions that address themselves primarily to one or another of the above questions and that, taken together, address themselves to all three considerations. But before the reader is given a preview of what lies ahead, it is necessary to say something about the life and work of the subject himself: Rosenstock-Huessy. In this way, the reader may gain a brief overview of the man and his life as the context for reading the more specific essays included here.

Rosenstock-Huessy: A Sketch of His Life and Work

Eugen Rosenstock-Huessy was born into an educated Jewish family in Berlin in 1888. He was the fourth of seven children. His father was a banker and his mother a woman of considerable intellectual accomplishment. Both of them passed on to their son a love of books. From an early age he exhibited a gift for languages and a fascination with speech. While yet in his early teens he translated Egyptian poetry from the sayings of Ptah-Hotep for his sister's birthday. He read widely in the classics of Western civilization and was drawn to historical writings, especially military history. While still in his teens he quietly entered the Christian church and received baptism. Upon graduation from the gymnasium, he entered the university and completed his doctoral studies at Heidelberg at the age of twenty-one in 1909. His thesis focused on jurisprudence, but he explored a whole range of historical and philological questions as well. In his brief essay "Biblionomics or The Nine Lives of a Cat," written in the late 1950s, Rosenstock-Huessy recalled some of his early investigations with Karl Hampe in Heidelberg.[1] He recalled his studies "on a forgery of the name of Dante by a later Humanist," one on the whereabouts of "St. Francis of Assisi's last will and testament," as well as on "various other legal antiquities." While at Heidelberg, he also studied under the great jurist Otto Gierke, who was also the editor of the series in which his first book, *Herzogsgewalt und Friedensschutz* appeared in 1910. In 1912 he became a Privatdozent at the University of Leipzig as a result of his study of constitutional history, *Konigshaus und Stamme.* This work Rosenstock-Huessy called his "first totally inspired book."[2] Received at the time with skepticism, it is now recognized as the standard work on the subject of territorial kingship in the twelfth century. Thus at twenty-four he had joined the ranks of the professoriate as a legal historian.

His career at Leipzig was cut short by World War I. At the outbreak of the war in August 1914, he married Margrit Huessy, a Swiss from Sackingen, Germany, and from that union came his full name, Rosenstock-Huessy. The outbreak of war was to alter his life in ways he could not have imagined. He held an officer's rank and served in the German army for the duration of the war. Much of his time was spent at the front near Verdun. While at Leipzig, one of his students had been Franz Rosenzweig, in whose life both Eugen and Margrit came to play vital roles. The important correspondence between Rosenstock-Huessy and Rosenzweig on Judaism and Christianity was to become well known. This correspondence, as well as his own reflections from this period, abundantly testify to Rosenstock-Huessy's growing conviction that the war marked a watershed, or better, an end, in Western civilization. No longer could it be business as usual. What was being tragically enacted in the war itself marked a crisis that was consuming the very spiritual and institutional foundations of the modern era. The war brought about, Rosenstock-Huessy was convinced, the end of an age, and significantly, marked the beginning of a new era. But, as Rosenstock-Huessy, was to remark later, "this recognition of the breakdown of the old standards was communicable to a few friends only. From 1915 to 1923 this group of friends felt as though living

---

1. Eugen Rosenstock-Huessy, "Biblionomics or the Nine Lives of a Cat," in *Biography-Bibliography* (New York: Private Printing, 1959), pp. 15-16.
2. Rosenstock-Huessy, "Biblionomics," p. 15-16.

on Patmos."[3]

After the war, then, Rosenstock-Huessy did not return to the university, nor did he accept invitations to work on the constitution for the Weimar Republic or the great religious periodical, *Hochland*. Instead, he went to work for the automobile manufacturer Daimler-Benz. Here, and later as co-founder of the Akademie der Arbeit in Frankfurt, he furthered and developed adult education projects that he had conceived and tried behind the trenches at Verdun, but this time it was adult education for workers. For this work and his later contribution to the development of the work camp idea, he is considered one of the founders of adult education in post-war Germany. Throughout the twenties, he published prolifically, slowly developing his vision of post-world war society through essays and subsequently in book-length publications. He also continued his legal writing, but now focused on *Industrierrecht* (industrial law).

Out of the "Patmos" circle–a group that included Franz Rosenzweig, Hans Eberhardt, Ehrenberg and Victor von Weizsaecker among others–there emerged a journal, *Die Kreatur*, that published the work of those who had been deeply affected by the epocal floodtide of change. Karl Barth, the young Swiss theologian who was to become a major voice in Protestant theology, Martin Buber, the remarkable Jewish philosopher whose work became well known, the young von Weizsaecker, whose scientific work sought to place medicine on a new anthropological foundation, the Catholic writer, Joseph Wittig, who was to become an important friend of Rosenstock-Huessy, were among those who wrote for the new journal.

In this circle of creative ferment, his life unfolded. In 1923, after the birth of their first and only child, Hans, Rosenstock-Huessy reluctantly agreed to return to university life because, as he remarked, "no legal basis of existence was open except this academic position."[4] Nonetheless, while at the University of Breslau from 1923-1933, he continued many of the initiatives begun after the war. He remained active in the field of adult education and he organized work camps in Silesia that brought together students, workers, and farmers on projects of social revitalization. In these efforts, Rosenstock-Huessy sought to rebuild, if not create anew, the rent fabric of a society devastated by the war.

3. Rosenstock-Huessy, "Biblionomics," p. 16.
4. Rosenstock-Huessy, "Biblionomics," p. 18.

When his Roman Catholic friend Joseph Wittig was excommunicated, he collaborated with him in writing *Das Alter der Kirche*. The
first version of his *Soziologie I, Die Krafte der Gemeinschaft*, also came
from this period. The scope of this legal historian had grown to
include the whole panorama of humanity in time. History,
psychology, sociology, religion, industrial life, and politics drew his
attention. And at the heart of it all was his abiding preoccupation
with speech: the lifeblood of society and the body of the spirit.
Articles and books poured forth year after year.

With great prescience, Rosenstock-Huessy had anticipated the
catastrophe that was to unfold in German society. Thus despite the
fact that his great work *Die Europaischen Revolutionen und der
Charackter der Nationen* had been published and did much to establish
his growing European reputation–it was rewritten and published in
the United States in 1938 as *Out of Revolution, Autobiography of
Western Man*–he immediately resigned his post at Breslau when Hitler
came to power. He then, as he said, "immigrated into" the United
States. After three years at Harvard, teaching in several different
departments including philosophy, German, and theology, he joined
the faculty at Dartmouth College. Here he taught as a professor of
social philosophy until his retirement in 1957. The move to the
United States involved great changes for Rosenstock-Huessy as he
sought to appropriate the spirit and character of American life. As
was indicated above, he was not content to simply translate his work
into English. Instead, he sought to reformulate it in accord with the
inner transformation his immigration entailed.

While at Dartmouth, Rosenstock-Huessy purchased land across the
river in Norwich, Vermont, and there built the home in which he
was to remain until his death in 1973. Together with Margrit and
their son Hans, Rosenstock-Huessy's life unfolded in a ceaseless
round of intellectual and social activity graced by the tranquility of
beautiful Vermont. Four Wells, the Rosenstock-Huessy's Vermont
home, was at once the locus of his domestic life and a place to meet
with other European immigrants and new American friends and
colleagues. It was in the 1940s remembered by one of his students
who had participated in Camp William James as "a command post
for a coming new world." It was also the place where
Rosenstock-Huessy kept the horses he loved so well and which he
continued to ride daily until two years before his death. He even
became something of an area talking-point as he rode from Four
Wells to Dartmouth during the late thirties and through the war
years, tieing up his horse on the grounds of the College and going in

to lecture. His boundless energy continually devoured the record of the historical past and the news of the day and brought them into novel configurations both in his writings and in his life.

The consequences of the Depression and the gathering clouds of war led him to address himself to the necessities of social regeneration and reconstruction. His work-camp experience was now transfigured and reappeared in the founding of Camp William James in Vermont. It sought to overcome the limitations of the Civilian Conservation Corps (CCC) by providing a focus of service to society for all young men and women and not just jobs for those who were unemployed. Moreover, the name, Camp William James, evoked the memory of one who had sought a "moral equivalent to war." The year following the end of the Second World War saw, thanks to the prodding and assistance of George Morgan, an expert on Nietzsche and later a distinguished diplomat in the U.S. Foreign Service, the publication of Rosenstock-Huessy's vision of Christianity, *The Christian Future, Or the Modern Mind Outrun* (1946). Here the themes of the Word, service, and a vital faith are orchestrated into a moving vision of the future. And the following years saw the appearance of his *The Multiformity of Man* (1949), a much expanded *Soziologie* (1956-1958), *Die Sprache des Menschengeschlects* (1963), and his *Speech and Reality* (1970), a book that summarizes his grammar of speech and society.

Rosenstock-Huessy was, by all accounts of those who knew him, a brilliant man of great passions, often fiery. He never rested content within the artificial boundaries that separate disciplines from one another in the modern university, nor with the often specious distinctions and assumptions characteristic of the modern intellectual. He insisted that "the heart of man either falls in love with someone or something, or it falls ill." And he declared that history was an affair of passion, not the cool, unfolding of reason. At the same time, his insights allowed him to speak of the larger unities of Western culture and the whole world. He turned time and again to speech as the living voice of the human journey from the beginning to the end of time. His wide-ranging vision coupled with his attention to the nuances of speech combined to generate insights that both startle and inspire his readers. W.H. Auden, the English poet, acknowledged his indebtedness to Rosenstock-Huessy for his insights into speech and language, and others lauded his historical insights and his penetrating vision. In their introduction to *I Am an Impure Thinker,* a collection of Rosenstock-Huessy's essays, Freya von Moltke and Clinton Gardner summarized his contribution in the following way:

> His impurity is intended to redirect our thought, to give us a new orientation to our world. Reorientation, indeed, is perhaps the best single word to describe what Rosenstock-Huessy is up to. His writings and life have been devoted to grasping the strands of history which led up to the World Wars and to reweaving from these strands a new fabric of thought and action which will enable us to cope with the changed times in which we live.[5]

The foundation of the reorientation Rosenstock-Huessy sought is to be found in his grasp of speech as "the life-blood of society." While it is impossible to adequately summarize this central theme of his work (aspects of Rosenstock-Huessy's insights into speech and language are explored in virtually every essay in this volume), it is perhaps helpful to indicate three features of his speech-thinking. For Rosenstock-Huessy, speech, in all its dimensions, is *fundamental to the life of human beings and societies.* It is in our names and naming, hearing and responding, speaking and listening that we, as human beings and societies, are being made and remade. Secondly, the speech that makes and remakes life is *multiform in relation to its functions and the fronts of life to which it is addressed.* For Rosenstock-Huessy, we are faced backward and forward in time, and inward and outward in space. He summarizes this human situation and condition as "the cross of reality." And on this cross our speech and language is multiform as it addresses the fronts of life: *subjective* on the inner front, *objective* on the outer front, *trajective* in relation to the past, and *prejective* in relation to the future. All of these forms of speech are necessary to personal and social well-being. Thus–and this is the third point–*the human situation is best approached through a grammatical method that respects this cruciform nature of language and reality,* a method that can simultaneously see unities, differences and patterns over time. That method attends to what is being said–and the form of speech used in its saying–as the vital clues to how we are continually being made and remade, changing or failing to change, falling apart or holding things in balance, over time. As creatures of time, our speaking is not timeless but either too early or too late and occasionally in the fullness of time. With his grammatical method, Rosenstock-Huessy discerned patterns and processes across time that have provided the calendar of epochs and ages that are the story of humankind.

---

5. Freya von Moltke and Clinton Gardner, "Introduction," p. x, in Eugen Rosenstock-Huessy, *I am an Impure Thinker* (Norwich, VT: Argo Books, 1970).

But we are perhaps anticipating too much since it is, in part, the burden of the following essays to uncover some of the creative consequences of Rosenstock-Huessy's work. Here we want simply to emphasize that Rosenstock-Huessy's work was designed to lead us more deeply into personal and social transformation. His work did not aim simply at adding new bits and pieces to a growing pile of information, but to restoring his readers to life-giving relationships with the imperatives of our time. Such an effort is surely audacious, but for Rosenstock-Huessy it was a personal necessity. We stand at a crossroads. And here the writer is called to something extraordinary as he wonderfully expressed it in the closing words of *Out of Revolution: Autobiography of Western Man,*

> My generation has survived social death in all its variations, and I have survived decades of study and teaching in scholastic and academic sciences. Every one of their venerable scholars mistook me for the intellectual type he most despised. The atheist wanted me to disappear into Divinity, the theologians into sociology, the sociologists into history, the historians into journalism, the journalists into metaphysics, the philosophers into law, and–need I say it?–the lawyers into hell, which as a member of our present world, I never had left. For nobody leaves hell all by himself without going mad. Society is a hell as long as man or woman is alone. And the human soul dies from consumption in the hell of social catastrophe unless it makes common cause with others. In the community that common sense rebuilds, after the earthquake, upon the ashes on the slope of Vesuvius, the red wine of life tastes better than anywhere else. And a man writes a book, even as he stretches out his hand, so that he may find that he is not alone in the survival of humankind.[6]

It is something of the character, range and vision of this "outstretched hand" that we have sought here to indicate. But we can only offer this sketch at this point. What we have sought to do is provide the reader with a background for the reading of the essays that follow, knowing full well that the complete portrait of Rosenstock-Huessy's life and work remains to be written.

Previewing the Essays

The studies in this volume range broadly as befits their subject: Rosenstock-Huessy's life and work. They begin with an address given

6. Eugen Rosenstock-Huessy, *Out of Revolution, Autobiography of Western Man* (Norwich, VT: Argo Books, 1969), p. 758.

at the Waterloo conference by a student of Rosenstock-Huessy's, Harold Berman, then Professor of Law at the Harvard Law School and now of Emory University. Berman speaks of the suggestive significance of Rosenstock-Huessy's work for the history of law in the West. Rosenstock-Huessy's approach to history rested in the conviction that humankind had to be viewed as an interrelated whole in which each society and epoch is both an event within the unfolding of the human story and a contribution to its eschatological destiny. For Berman, law in the West, beginning with the Papal Revolution of the twelfth century, illustrates this basic conviction of Rosenstock-Huessy. There is, Berman contends, a pressing necessity to retell the narrative of the formation of the Western legal tradition as a unified story, punctuated by the successive revolutions in Western history that both criticized and renewed the legal tradition, grounded, as that tradition is, in the conviction that law "is rooted in the cosmic order of the universe." Thus Rosenstock-Huessy's historical vision has provided Berman with the inspiration for his own work on the history of law.

The next two essays focus on aspects of Rosenstock-Huessy's personal and intellectual history. Harold Stahmer, from the University of Florida, focuses on the origins of Rosenstock-Huessy's Christianity in the years from 1902-1916, and Raymond Huessy, a grandson of Rosenstock-Huessy and a New York set designer, turns his attention to Rosenstock-Huessy's relationship with Joseph Wittig, a friend and colleague from the 1920s on. Stahmer situates Rosenstock-Huessy within the ferment of German intellectual life at the beginning of this century. He notes the importance of his exchanges with Franz Rosenzweig, who was to emerge as one of the great Jewish theologians of the twentieth century, in the formation of Rosenstock-Huessy's understanding of Christian faith. For Rosenstock-Huessy, revelation is understood as *orientation;* his Christianity is a way of being situated and oriented in time where the Word is not a timeless abstraction but crucial speaking and thinking and living. In a complementary vein, Raymond Huessy examines the relationship between his grandfather and Joseph Wittig, a Catholic theologian and priest who was excommunicated in the 1920s but restored to the Church shortly before his death. The friendship between Wittig and Rosenstock-Huessy resulted in collaboration on *Das Alter der Kirche* where, Raymond Huessy observes, "in writing about the Church whose age is past, they honour the church as the community of all believing souls, they defend the spirit of all times against the spirit of any one age, and look forward to the una

Sancta, taking shape in the Church's daughter, Society." Huessy's moving account of Wittig's life illustrates dimensions of Rosenstock-Huessy that would be missed if we focused only on his writings.

The essay by Clinton Gardner, businessman, author and long-time student of Rosenstock-Huessy, explores the intellectual roots of Rosenstock-Huessy's speech thinking. Gardner argues that an important influence on Rosenstock-Huessy and other speech-thinkers like Martin Buber and Franz Rosenzweig was the nineteenth-century philosopher, Ludwig Feuerbach. While avoiding Feuerbach's reductionist tendencies, these twentieth century speech-thinkers were inspired, argues Gardner, by Feuerbach's "prophetic call for an end to idealistic philosophy...and his vision of a higher social science based on grammar." Further, Gardner sees the significance of Rosenstock-Huessy to lie in his *social translations,* a la Feuerbach, of the insights of religion into a higher sociology. For example, Rosenstock-Huessy understood the social content of the doctrine of the Trinity in ways, Gardner argues, that generate transforming insights into social grammar and processes.

We then return to the larger historical themes articulated in Rosenstock-Huessy's work in the essay by Stanley Johannesen, a historian at the University of Waterloo. Writing critically as a historian of the American experience, Johannesen sees the significance of Rosenstock-Huessy's writings on America to lie in their setting the American story within the wider context of the history of the West. When approached in this way, both the continuities with that longer tradition and the distinctive new configurations of American history emerge. Moreover, Johannesen noted, Rosenstock-Huessy sets before us a "rigorous standard by which any claim for a spiritual character in a race of men must be judged." Thus Rosenstock-Huessy's work has important methodological consequences for the study of history, a theme that we saw earlier in Berman's address.

As we noted above, much of Rosenstock-Huessy's work was directed towards understanding the psycho-social processes that make for social life and death. Central here is Rosenstock-Huessy's focus on "speech as the life-blood of society" and its attendant grammar of social life. For Rosenstock-Huessy, we are creatures who find ourselves in social time and space, named and addressed. And as we respond, we come to be as persons (I's) who make common cause with others (We's) and then leave our mark on the intergenerational fabric of life. These psycho-social dimensions of Rosenstock-Huessy's work are examined from a number of different perspectives in the next seven essays in the volume. They begin with the important study by Eugene Tate, a sociologist from St. Thomas College in the University of Saskatchewan who argues that Rosenstock-Huessy's work constitutes an "intellectual breakthough" beyond the Cartesian assumptions of modern communication theory. Tate, after reviewing communications theory, impressively outlines the elements in Rosenstock-Huessy's insights into speech that would lay the foundation for a new social theory based upon the view that "communication, not thought, is the basis of all human existence." According to Tate, Rosenstock-Huessy points the way to an understanding of speaking-and-listening that has revolutionary consequences for communication theory and for our understanding of life in society.

Related aspects of Rosenstock-Huessy's work are explored in Duncanson's essay on life in a rhetorical culture. Duncanson, from the Department of Speech at the University of Minnesota at Morris, draws on Rosenstock-Huessy's insights into the nature of speech to analyze the ills and strengths of contemporary society. Citing the dangers of a rhetorical culture that loses sight of principles and becomes bewitched by process, Duncanson sees in Rosenstock-Huessy a "third way" to regenerate the collectivity. That way centers in the recovery of vital speech in the service of "preserving and creating our families, communities, and planet." The contribution of Rosenstock-Huessy to illuminating our social landscape is further pursued by Patricia North in her study of labour and the spirit. Though holding a doctorate in the history of religions, North earns her livelihood in seafood processing plants in Oregon. It was in this context that North first encountered the writings of Rosenstock-Huessy, especially his *Multiformity of Man.* She draws upon Rosenstock-Huessy to illuminate her experience in the canning factory and, by implication, that of other workers in the industrial sphere. Rosenstock-Huessy's analysis of the modern forms of production grew out of his intimate acquaintance with workers in many spheres, often sharing their burdens and labour. And this contemporary worker, Patricia North, finds in his work confirmation and illumination of her own experience.

The social ideas of Rosenstock-Huessy were, in part, forged in his experience of founding work camps both in Europe and North America. It is this aspect of Rosenstock-Huessy's life that is examined in Terry Simons' study of "the bridge builder in quest for community." Simons, a geographer and natural resource and policy consultant, looks at Rosenstock-Huessy's ideas on history and education and shows how they led directly to his involvement in adult education and in work camps that aimed at the inter-generational renewal of social life. These are, Simons notes, important aspects of the legacy of Rosenstock-Huessy.

In the midst of the diversity that characterizes these essays on social aspects of Rosenstock-Huessy's work, the discerning reader will also notice the emergence of underlying continuities. Those continuities involve the centrality of vital speech to the life of society, a centrality that should be equally present in our thinking as in our practice of social renewal and regeneration. For Rosenstock-Huessy, it was the vital speaking and listening of persons and communities across generations that constituted the heart of society. Often this fundamental insight is lost in sociological thinking that is bewitched by numbers and in social programs and initiatives that are likewise centered on a social mathematics. For Rosenstock-Huessy, it was full-bodied life on "the cross of reality"–the inner, outer, backward and forward front of life constantly confronting us as societies, communities, and persons–that should hold our attention and our hearts. The next three essays in the volume, the essays by Hans Huessy, Cynthia Harris, and Richard Feringer, turn our attention to the psychological implications and educational dimensions of Rosenstock-Huessy's work.

Hans Huessy, an *emeritus* member of the faculty of psychiatry at the University of Vermont, outlines the psychological implications of his father's work that lead to "a new method for the study of man which can avoid the present Tower of Babel of the various segregated social science disciplines." Huessy stresses those aspects of his father's work that can overcome the "object-subject, organic-psychological" dilemmas of contemporary psychiatry. His exposition of the implications of Rosenstock-Huessy's grammar of human experience is complemented by Cynthia Harris' study of Rosenstock-Huessy and Fritz Perls, the founder of gestalt psychology. Cynthia Harris, a psychiatrist in Connecticut and friend of both Rosenstock-Huessy and Fritz Perls, argues that Rosenstock-Huessy "created a world view for our time. He fashioned a vision of the past and a sense of the future which serves the vital, irreplaceable function of framing our daily-weekly-hourly-instant-present, of enhancing its excitement and meaning and leads us to undertake words and thoughts and deeds of which we would otherwise have no inkling." At the same time, she brings the therapeutic insights of Fritz Perls into the discussion as offering a practical correlate to Rosenstock-Huessy's more universal vision.

This bringing of Rosenstock-Huessy's work into direct contact with our work in various cultural spheres and institutions is also reflected in Richard Feringer's "letter" concerning the grammatical method of Rosenstock-Huessy and the psychology of learning. Feringer recounts his experience with students at Western Washington University where he teaches. He demonstrates the relevance of Rosenstock-Huessy's social method in "re-establishing order in the thinking of my students." In a situation where knowledge is increasingly fragmented and the student torn–a situation familiar to many of us in education–Rosenstock-Huessy's method has, Feringer saw, "the fullness to accept knowledge from all disciplines...and still offers an integrating order." This interest in the educational consequences and usefulness of Rosenstock-Huessy is not incidental. Indeed, Rosenstock-Huessy argued that education, the process of teaching/learning, was integral to the new methods he was proposing since here we see a basic transaction taking place: the linking of speakers and hearers across generations and epochs. And it is precisely this process that builds social peace.

The centrality of the Christian faith to Rosenstock-Huessy's life and work has already been alluded to. While Rosenstock-Huessy asserted that his was an orthodox faith, it was never conventional. Indeed his Christianity was marked by passion and inspired daring in his life and in his thought. The last five essays in the volume explore different aspects of Rosenstock-Huessy's Christian sensibility and the inspired insights into the life of humanity in time that emerged in his writings. The essays in this section open with one by Richard Shaull, the Princeton theologian of liberation, who found in Rosenstock-Huessy "someone who seemed to share my assessment of the present historical situation looked at the world from the perspective of Christian faith, defined in eschatological terms, and at the same time encouraged me to think theologically in a new way." Out of his experience in Brazil, where Shaull lived and worked in the 1950s, he was led to seek a form of historical practice and theological reflection adequate to the crises of our time. And it was Rosenstock-Huessy who became his "guide on a lonely journey." Similarly, Dale Irvin, a student of theology at Union Seminary, reflected on the fruitfulness of Rosenstock-Huessy in relation to his experience in the Philippines. For Irvin, the significance of Rosenstock-Huessy lay in his call for "the revolutionary creation of a new form of humanity." This means, Irvin contends, that we have to understand mission in our time as dialogue between persons in the different faith communities that make up our world. It is thus important to see, as these two essays suggest, that Rosenstock-Huessy's faith was deeply engaged with history and the imperatives of our time. We encounter in Rosenstock-Huessy an incarnate, timely faith that knew the secret that life can grow out of social death.

However, Rosenstock-Huessy not only exemplified a vital and living faith, but he also addressed himself to themes that are of central importance to contemporary Christian thinking. William Strickland, a biblical scholar and philosopher from Appalachian State University, focuses on Rosenstock-Huessy's interpretation of the gospels and demonstrates how Rosenstock-Huessy's commitments to the Spirit and "the creating power of language which changes humankind" led him to reject that presumptuous historical criticism that places itself above the Scriptures. Instead, Rosenstock-Huessy showed how the gospel writers are not alternative voices, but that they together constitute a witness to, or a song of, the unifying power of the Word. Casting his vision more broadly, M. Darrol Bryant, a teacher of religion and culture at Renison College, exhibits the relevance of Rosenstock-Huessy's work to contemporary Christian life and thought. In an exposition of what Bryant calls "the grammar of the spirit," he argues that in Rosenstock-Huessy we see how "the truth of faith opens out to the truth of reality, to a grammar of the spirit that expresses the truth of faith in social and temporal terms." Thus in Rosenstock-Huessy we have transcended the "sacred/secular" antithesis that has plagued contemporary Christian social thinking. Rather it is on the "cross of reality" that the fullness of faith and the fullness of the world meet each other.

A fitting conclusion to the essays in this volume is provided by Bas Leenman, a Dutch disciple of Rosenstock-Huessy who for many years ran a half-way house in Vermont. Leenman returns to the theme of the unifying power of the Word against the background of the unfolding of generations from the beginning to the end of time. Leenman argues that Rosenstock-Huessy ushers us and all the great representatives of our race to our "places in the conversation of humankind between Alpha and Omega." Thus Rosenstock-Huessy's faith transcends the boundaries of denominationalism–and even religion–while recognizing the contribution of each and all to the full life of the Spirit. This account of the visionary aspects of Rosenstock-Huessy well portrays a major reason for the gratitude felt by all the contributors to this volume for Rosenstock-Huessy's life and work.

As we indicated at the outset, it is our hope that these essays will lead the reader to turn directly to the writings of Rosenstock-Huessy. The bibliography exhaustively compiled by Lisa van der Molen and published separately as *Eugen Rosenstock-Huessy: A Complete Bibliography* is the companion volume to these studies. It will make the task of turning to Rosenstock-Huessy's writings that much easier for the reader who is now brought full circle to the beginning: the life and thought of Eugen Rosenstock-Huessy.

Renewal and Continuity:
The Great Revolutions
and the Western Tradition

Harold J. Berman

I am grateful to have been drawn into this circle of co-workers with Eugen Rosenstock-Huessy. I am grateful to those who have challenged him as well as to those who have appreciated him. I think *he* needs to be challenged; and *we* need to challenge him, and not only to appreciate him.

This conference has certainly exemplified the diverse character of his life and work as well as its unity. We here have had many different kinds of relationships with him, both personal and intellectual. I was his student at Dartmouth and took his courses in social philosophy. I wrote my thesis under his guidance. I took a so-called topical major, in public opinion, which was in fact a combination of sociology, history, and philosophy. And for some years thereafter he was my mentor and guide. Although I was only occasionally in touch with him for the last fifteen or twenty years of his life, his writings always were, and remain, a very strong influence on me. They are a major source of inspiration for my own work, especially in legal history and legal philosophy, but also in my life generally.

I referred to us here as co-workers with him. Of course, that also means co-workers with those in whose footsteps he followed, and were an influence upon him. Part of his style was to refrain from quoting, or referring to, those who had had the greatest influence on his own work and were his own mentors and guides. I think that was a fault. It took me many years to discover how much of his thought came from Augustine, Abelard, Edmund Burke, Hegel, Savigny, Nietzsche, Rudolph Sohm, and many others. He was steeped in the scholarly literature of the past and of his own time. I think that it would be very helpful to us not only to study his works but to study their relationship to the works of others. He had his own reasons for not wanting to identify himself with other traditions of scholarship, with which he was in fact associated. But that should not bar us from doing so.

Several people have emphasized that we are not here to master and repeat Rosenstock-Huessy's thought. That would contradict his own injunction, which has been quoted at this conference, that each generation has to act differently precisely in order to represent the same thing. The same thing that we are here to represent, I would say, is the retranslation of the Christian tradition for the people of today, for people living between the second and third millennia of the Christian era. But I would add that not only must each generation act differently in order to represent the same thing, but that *within* each generation different people must act differently while at the same time making common cause with one another.

Tonight I would like to tell you about my own historical research in order to shed light on the work of Rosenstock-Huessy. I would like to present my work as a confirmation of the insights of Rosenstock-Huessy. Of course you may disagree with me that my work does in fact confirm his method since my method is quite different from his in many respects. But I think it does confirm the validity of many of his substantive discoveries.

I start with several Rosenstockian postulates. First, history is periodic in its course; it is patterned. Second, it shows a purpose in its development. And in that sense I think he would say that history is revelation; history is a revelation of our destiny. God is a God of history. Therefore if we study our history we should try to find in it the purposes of it. And we *can* find in it purpose and pattern and periodicity. And third, I start, as he started (and perhaps I learned it from him but I also learned it from my own experience), with an intuition of the end of an era. This is something that cannot be proved. The end of an era cannot be proved scientifically. You either have an intuition of it or you do not.

Now we have three generations linked by the fact that they have lived through, or are living through, a world war. That is, we have the generations of those who lived through the First World War, those who lived through the Second World War, and those today who live in dread of a third world war. All three have had a common experience that supports an intuition that an age has ended, and that we are at the beginning of a new age.

The old metaphors have died, or are dying, or are threatened with death. And here I count law and religion. Law and religion have, indeed, furnished the main metaphors of the age that is now coming to an end. Archibald MacLeish wrote some powerful lines about this:

A world ends when its metaphor has died.
An age becomes an age, all else beside,
When sensuous poets in their pride invent
Emblems for the soul's consent
That speak the meanings men will never know
But man-imagined images can show:
It perishes when those images, though seen,
No longer mean.

I think that because the age is ending we are able to discern its beginnings. In the middle of an era, when the end is not in sight, the beginning is also hidden from view; and then history, as Maitland put it in the opening pages of his *History of English Law,* has the appearance of a seamless web. But now the entire life of our civilization is stretched out before us. Our entire past is there and we can uncover its origins because we know what it is whose origins we seek.

The era that is ending is the era that originated in the late eleventh and the twelfth centuries, the era of what Rosenstock-Huessy called the Papal Revolution. Incidentally, some other historians have also called it that, without acknowledging Rosenstock-Huessy's authorship of the phrase. And a great many leading historians support the insight, which he was among the first to have, that our modern Western political institutions and ideas, our theology, and our legal systems–had their origins, or re-originated, in the Papal Revolution.

Because we are now emerging from a revolutionary period, we can see more easily the revolutionary periods of the past. That is, of course, what he envisioned in the First World War. He saw the World War as a revolution and then saw the history of the West in terms of a series of revolutions. And I start at that point, though I do not follow him exactly in the analysis of the various revolutions.

Each great revolution has been followed by a long period of evolution; and that evolution has taken its most significant form, it seems to me, in the development of law. Each of the revolutions produced new law; each transformed the legal order. And so the Western legal tradition is punctuated by a series of revolutions. And this is his insight which, as I say, I take as a starting point. Rosenstock never presented the history of Western law in a systematic way and, I think, did not pay enough attention to it in his writings, though he referred to it from time to time in his great book *Out of Revolution.* But the basic postulate is there: that Western history from the eleventh and twelfth century on is characterized by these alternating periods of renewal and continuity. Violent revolutionary upheaval is followed by a continuous period of peaceful development, something like the phenomenon of death and resurrection.

We have had in the past, in the West, the resources to accept these catastrophic upheavals and to build on them and not to fall victim to despair over them. At the same time there has been an apocalyptic element present under the surface even of the evolution. And this element breaks forth again periodically in new revolutions.

I will make some more detailed comments about that and then I will try to face the question raised by many here, perhaps most dramatically by Richard Shaull, concerning the significance of this kind of historiography, this kind of knowledge or insight into history, for our situation today–the significance of, you might say, the *academic* knowledge of it.

The story which I want to tell very briefly is the story of how the Papal Revolution created the first modern legal system, which was the canon law of the church, and laid the foundation for the secular legal systems that rose up in the wake of the canon law. You will recall from *Out of Revolution* that the Papal Revolution, starting in 1075 and culminating about fifty years later, was a revolution for what was then called the "freedom of the church," that is, a revolution against the domination of the clergy by emperors, kings, and lords and for the establishment of the Church of Rome as an independent, corporate, political and legal entity under the Papacy. The church, now viewed above all as the clergy (and this was the first great split between the clergy and the laity in the history of the church), would work for the redemption of the laity and for the reformation of the world through law, in the direction of justice and peace. That was the great idea of the Papal Revolution.

Another side of the movement was that secular political and legal authority would also be enhanced, the power of the kings and emperors and the cities that were springing up at that time would be enhanced. There are other sides to it as well: enormous economic expansion, colonization of eastern Europe, the Crusades, a new orientation of Europe. This was a total upheaval. Indeed, it was called at the time a Reformation–the Gregorian Reformation (after Pope Gregory VII). I think it can safely be called a revolution even in the Marxian sense of a "total revolution."

The reason the Western legal tradition was formed in this context was that the Church accepted and proclaimed a limited jurisdiction, namely, over "spiritual causes." The word "spiritual" is used here for ecclesiastical. In fact these "spiritual causes" included all matters affecting church property–and the church owned one third of the land in Europe; it included all crimes committed by the clergy; it included crimes committed by laymen *against* church property and *against* the clergy as well as many other types of crimes committed by the laity–ideological crimes such as heresy and blasphemy, sex offenses, and many others; spiritual causes also included legal questions of marriage and family relations, wills, all contracts where the parties pledged faith, and a host of other matters. Thus the Church, operating for the first time through professional courts, with appellate review by the papal curia in Rome, exercised an enormous jurisdiction. In doing so, it developed in the late eleventh and twelfth centuries, for the first time, a sophisticated system of canon law, with professional jurists, with the first legal treatises. You may recall that the first European university, Bologna, was founded at that time–in about 1087–for the express purpose of studying the legal texts compiled by the Roman Emperor Justinian, which had just been rediscovered–not accidentally–after more than five centuries, and which furnished much of the vocabulary needed for the systematization both of the canon law and of the secular law.

There was one single ecclesiastical jurisdiction, one single body of canon law, applicable throughout the West. But the secular authority was divided. In the first place, there were the emerging royal jurisdictions of the various kings and dukes. Then there were thousands of chartered cities and towns that were founded in the period from 1050 to 1200, each with its own government and its own law. And there was a systematization of feudal law, as well as a newly emerging mercantile law that governed the greatly expanded trade both overland and across the Mediterranean.

The dualism of ecclesiastical and secular jurisdictions, and the pluralism of secular jurisdictions, created an enormous competition, out of which came not only rule *by* law but also the rule *of* law. Each jurisdiction was checked in its claims by other jurisdictions. That is, I think, an essential feature of the Western legal tradition which lasted, in one form or another, in spite of the revolutions that have punctuated it, for eight or nine hundred years. The rule of law was founded not only on plural jurisdictions but also on the duality of the secular and the spiritual, which implied a belief that history itself requires redemption of the secular, a redemption of mankind, and that law could play a role in that redemption.

God was a God of justice and a God of Law. "God is himself law," the *Sachsenspiegel* says, the first German law book, written in 1220.

"God is himself law, and therefore law is dear to him." That was a century after the Concordat of Worms had settled the Investiture Struggle. Nevertheless, it was a direct expression of the philosophy of the Papal Revolution. You can find this over and over again in all the countries of Europe, and in all the cities.

Our tradition is rooted in that belief, and in the manifestation of that belief in dual secular and spiritual jurisdictions, and plural secular jurisdictions, and in the very idea of the secular in its modern meaning (which of course is not Harvey Cox's secular city at all–nor is it St. Augustine's; it is rather the secular realm of Christendom). This secular realm was responsible for the control of violence and for justice, especially justice in the realm of property and other economic matters. This was a redeemable part of the world. And this was the program of the church, both the organized church and the whole society viewed as a church.

Another part of the Western legal tradition comes from the belief in the progressive redemption of the world through law. Included was the idea that the law itself has an autonomous character. For the first time in the West, law was viewed as separate from theology and economics and politics; for the first time there was something identifiable which could be called law, which had its own professional guardians called lawyers, and which had its own literature. There were no law books in Europe before, no treatises on law, though there were sometimes collections of laws. There wasn't really legislation in the modern sense before the twelfth century. The first systematic legislation was in the church. Thereafter kings, too, began to issue laws as a regular matter. At the same time law books came to be written, law began to be studied in the universities, and a profession of jurists emerged. And it was their task to guard and develop over generations and centuries a *body* of law. The idea was that the law formed a body, an integrated whole. And that it grew and developed over generations. This is the nature of the Western legal tradition.

The paradox is that this came out of a revolutionary upheaval that disrupted and interrupted the continuity of the past; and that this belief in continuity was maintained even though the tradition was punctuated periodically by revolutions which threatened to destroy the whole legal order. A good example of this strange and marvelous idea that law grows and develops over centuries, perhaps the most vivid example, is the Constitution of the United States. It is genuinely believed by Americans to be something that grows and develops over generations and centuries. That is a very mystical idea.

The Founding Fathers wrote a constitution. They said, for example, there shall be no cruel and unusual punishments. It never occurred to them that this principle might eventually be applied to capital punishment or to harsh prison conditions. Little by little, over generations, people interpreting the Constitution filled the phrase "cruel and unusual punishment" with different content. But it is not *any* content; it is content that has developed, not out of the concept as such, but out of the whole institutional life and growth of the country. The understanding is that these old legal concepts have to be adapted to new circumstances. That idea originated in the canon law of the eleventh and twelfth centuries. The popes were continually issuing new decretals, deciding new cases, making new laws; in doing so, they sought to preserve the continuity with the past. In 1140 Gratian wrote the first great legal treatise, the first systematic comprehensive analysis of a body of law ever written, characteristically called "The Concordance of Discordant Canons." His pupil, Huguccio, added to it, developed it. For example, Gratian had said that a pope may be deposed for heresy (an extraordinary statement!), and Huguccio added that when Gratian said "heresy" he did not mean *only* heresy, he also meant other things *like* heresy, including moral offenses, such as fornication. Thus law was conceived as something that can be expanded, something that grows and develops over generations.

Nevertheless, periodically in European history, starting with the Reformation in Germany, and then going on to England in the seventeenth century and the French Revolution and then the Russian Revolution, there have been upheavals in which the whole continuity has been destroyed. People said, "Kill the lawyers. Get rid of this legal system. It does not fulfill the vision that underlies it. It is failing to realize its ideals and purposes. We have to start over." These upheavals settle down and the old law is restored, but it is not the same old law any more. Part of it is the same, part of it is changed. There has been a new birth, a rebirth, of legal consciousness.

I have attempted to write a history of Western law which will overcome the nationalism which dominates legal historiography even to this time, and even the historiography of the so-called Middle Ages. My first volume shows the formation of the Western legal tradition in the period of the Papal Revolution.[1] A second volume will be on the impact of the national revolutions–German, English,

---

1. See Harold J. Berman, *Law and Revolution, The Formation of the Western Legal Tradition* (Cambridge: Harvard University Press, 1983).

French, and Russian. This of course follows the pattern of *Out of Revolution.* And the third volume will be on the crisis of the Western legal tradition in the twentieth century.

I am still not sure whether to put the Russian Revolution in Volume Two or Volume Three. That is a question I would be happy to have advice on. In many ways the Russian Revolution looks like one of the traditional national revolutions, which has reformed the Russian legal system and adapted it to a new age of socialism, planned economy, and a collectivized, mobilized society. On the other hand, the Russian Revolution may be viewed as part of a total and lasting breakdown of the Western legal tradition and its replacement by something else. It may be more outside of Western history than inside it.

The style of my book is not the style of Rosenstock-Huessy. I try to make everything extremely simple and extremely lucid–so that even I can understand it. I want it to be read by law students and law teachers. I cite Rosenstock-Huessy frequently, together with others who support the points I make. I give abundant citations and try to spell the story out at great length, and to make it clear, so that readers will be able to accept it without undergoing a conversion before they can really relate to it. The hope is that after they read it they might then be ready for such a conversion, because the story itself is of very extraordinary power.

If people would just accept the story it would not be necessary to give any theory at all. Nevertheless I do take up the theoretical implications of the story at considerable length, to the dismay of the publisher, because I think that the prevailing theories of society that most educated people now hold–the prevailing assumptions about history–are simply contradicted by this story. This story cannot be explained in Marxian terms of a feudal period followed by a capitalist period, and it cannot be explained in Weberian terms of political domination or of various types of law.

It seems to me that Marxian and Weberian concepts now predominate among people who think at all about the history of the West. That is, most people who have general ideas about history are either Marxian or Weberian. I find that most law students, for example, after having had a college education, are either Marxian or Weberian. That is, they believe either in economic or political determinism. They believe that the reason we have a legal system is so that the people who are in control may effectuate their control. These are conceived to be either economic controls or political controls. Furthermore, there is a great belief in models, and in ideal types, which Weber preached; this goes along also with the Marxian idea. Weber is very brilliant in distinguishing various types of law: "formal rational law," where there is a whole system of formal rules that enable people to calculate the consequences of their acts, which is very useful, he said, for capitalism (although the English, strangely enough, never adopted the formal rational system—Weber could never explain that); "traditional law," where you look back to the past and try to maintain it, which Weber associated with feudalism; "charismatic law," where the charismatic leader gives the law, or the judge is the oracle of the law (Weber treated English law as charismatic law). And then he presented another type of law, which does not exist anywhere yet, but which he thought might come in with socialism, which is the "substantive rational" type. "Substantive rationality" is, basically, fairness and equity; it does not go by formal rationality, that is, by syllogistic logic. I am sorry to bore you with this; what I want to emphasize is that Weber's mode of analysis allows you to ask whether a legal system is "formal rationalistic," or whether it is "traditional," or whether it is "charismatic," or whether it is concerned with "fairness and equity." This is an improvement, in my opinion, over the Marxian mode of analysis, which allows you to ask whether a legal system is "feudal" or "capitalist" or "socialist." But the Western legal tradition in its formative period combined all these different types or models—and went beyond them. And the story of the origins of the Western legal tradition is, in itself, a refutation of Marxian and Weberian theories that now dominate Western thought—theories that I believe are essentially destructive.

It is important, I believe, to remind educated people that our legal tradition is rooted not only in political and economic conditions but also in religious faith, that it is rooted in a belief in a God of justice, in a belief that there is a cosmic order which is lawful. Historically, that is how our law came to be what it is. The skeptic must be asked to face that historical fact. It will help him to understand the route by which he arrived at his skepticism. And perhaps he may experience, together with that illumination, a certain nostalgia, which may even be a precondition of what I spoke about before, not very delicately, as a conversion. At least it may be a source of revitalization of legal consciousness.

I would like to bring to people who are concerned about our legal system an awareness that our entire legal tradition is now in crisis. Why is it in crisis? It is in crisis because we no longer believe that law is rooted in the cosmic order of the universe. We think today that law is an instrument or device by which people in power get their way, effectuate their will, or that it is a rationalization of economic interests, or that it is some other type of means or instrument for achieving some non-legal ends. That law is an end in itself, that law is justice, that law is rooted in the Ten Commandments and in the Word, that the summary of the law is love of God and neighbor, that "the weightier matters of the law," to quote Jesus, "are justice and mercy and good faith"–these elementary truths have been replaced by a superficial instrumentalism.

I would hope that the kind of history I have recounted, the kind of story, would help us to recover the sense of law that went with it.

Rosenstock-Huessy never told this story. He told the story of the Western revolutions, and of the political and social orders that came out of them. But for some reason he never told the story of the Western legal tradition. He did not tell the story of the canon law and its rivalry with royal and urban and feudal law. He did not tell the story of the impact of the Protestant Reformation on the codification of criminal law. In dealing with the English Revolution he did say something about the English common law, but it was very loose. He did not deal with the Napoleonic codes, which expressed the spirit of the French Revolution. I do not know why he neglected the impact of the Great Revolutions on the Western legal tradition, since he was, after all, a legal historian by training and for many years a teacher of legal history at Breslau University.

Perhaps the reason he turned away from legal history is connected with his reason for turning away from academic traditions generally. His historical writings fully use the academic apparatus. In their factual exposition they meet the highest standards of scholarship. Yet they are addressed primarily to a non-academic audience, and they speak a language that is almost ununderstandable to most professional scholars.

Although I can share Rosenstock-Huessy's revulsion against the sterility of much that goes on in the world of academic scholarship, I do not think it is right to live in the university and not speak a language that is understandable to one's colleagues and students. On the other hand, I recognize that something is missing when that language is spoken. Most often what is missing is the very sense of crisis which is evoked by the story that has to be told.

And so I come to a question that is crucial for us in evaluating the work of Eugen Rosenstock-Huessy: is the university a place where one can confront and really deal with the crisis of our time? Must one abandon the university, whether physically or spiritually–must one revolt against it, as Rosenstock-Huessy did more than once–or can one find within it, and within its traditions, a community that will both accept and transcend the past?

Let me close by relating that question specifically to my own work. Is the university a place where I can confront and really deal with the crisis of the Western legal tradition in the twentieth century? Beyond that, is it a place where I can effectively teach that the Western legal tradition has been cut off from its historical roots; and even beyond that, where I can help to found a new legal tradition applicable not only to the West but to all humanity? Is the university a place where I can both teach and act out the idea that the peoples of the world must achieve on a universal scale that which the peoples of the West once achieved for themselves–a common legal language based on a belief in law as part of a common destiny? Saying that in a university is very different from saying it elsewhere. Saying it in the classrooms of a law school means teaching international commercial law (letters of credit, for example, which are the same all over the world; international joint ventures between business organizations of East and West, or of North and South; and a host of other "technical" matters); it means speaking about the emergence in the sixteenth and seventeenth centuries of a new law of nations out of the supranational law of the church, and the emergence in the twentieth and twenty-first centuries of a new supranational law of the world out of the law of nations; it means participating in the world of ongoing scholarship in the fields of international law, comparative law, legal history, and legal philosophy–a world that is hostile to the very term "crisis."

If I risk that hostility, yet share in the common educational and scholarly tasks and in the common language of the university, am I not building in a constructive way on the inspiration of Eugen Rosenstock-Huessy? And does not my very different approach confirm the validity of his approach? And does it not also offer a hope that the university may play a part, as a community, in living out the third millennium of the Christian era?

Christianity in the
Early Writings of
Eugen Rosenstock-Huessy

Harold M. Stahmer

The Crucifixion is the fountainhead of all my values, the great divide whence flow the processes most real to my inner life, and my primary response to our tradition is one of gratitude to the source of my own frame of reference in everyday life.

A friend and former colleague of Rosenstock-Huessy's, T.S.K. Scott-Craig, recently described him as a "revolutionary conservative." I found that interesting because it coincided with an increasingly strong conviction on my part that his views on Christianity could be characterized as those of a "revolutionary orthodox Christian."[1]

What I have attempted is to draw upon selected events and relationships in Rosenstock-Huessy's early years (1902-1916) to introduce the reader to certain key elements and themes that emerged during this period that had a profound effect upon the shape and quality of Rosenstock-Huessy's Christian faith and subsequent writings.[2] One of the many problems in understanding Rosenstock-Huessy's diverse interests is the extent to which one can discern unifying threads woven throughout his writings that explain or relate, for example, his Christian thinking with his sociology, his works on history and revolutions, adult education, work camps, and, last but not least, his "grammatical thinking" and his "Cross of Reality." What I offer here suggests that in Christianity Rosenstock-Huessy found a "standard," an "orientation" that provides a framework or background for many of his major interests and, specifically, that the origins of his "Cross

1. Some illustrations from *The Christian Future* (1946) that bear upon the issues treated here are contained in a short appendix at the end of this essay.

2. I wish to express my deep gratitude to Dr. George A. Morgan for his critical comments and suggestions and for making available to me material from his Index of key concepts and themes in Rosenstock-Huessy's writings that Dr. Morgan has been working on for more than ten years. The information contained in Dr. Morgan's files is basic to any scholarly treatment of Rosenstock-Huessy's writings.

of Reality" and "grammatical or speech-thinking" are integral components of his Christian commitment. Of special interest may be Rosenstock-Huessy's remarks about "soul," "cross" and "church" in his 1916 correspondence with Franz Rosenzweig (1886-1929) and the extent to which these themes provide possible linkages with other elements in his writings.

In 1958 at age seventy Rosenstock-Huessy was awarded an honorary degree of Doctor of Theology at the University of Münster and hailed as the J.G. Hamann (1730-1788), the "Magician of the North" (Magus des Norderns), of the twentieth century. The association with Hamann is one way of introducing the reader to Rosenstock-Huessy's views on Christianity since each was a devout Christian who lived under the "spell of language" and "time." For each man the word as "speech" (in Hamann's vocabulary, "verbalism") was the *via media* between the Scylla and Charybdis of philosophical and theological discourse, the vessel that gave life and meaning to their Christian faith. Compare the following statements from both men:

> And this temporal character of my thinking is in fact the Alpha and Omega from which I grasp everything afresh. Speech reflects this mode of procedure, even for someone who has been influenced by philosophy. For that reason I prefer to talk about speech rather than about reason.
>
> Rosenstock-Huessy to Franz Rosenzweig
> (10.28.1916)

> I know of no eternal truths save those which are unceasingly temporal.
>
> I speak neither of physics nor of theology; with me language is the mother of reason and revelation, its Alpha and Omega.
>
> With me the question is not so much: What is reason? but rather: What is language?[3]
>
> J.G. Hamann

Rosenstock-Huessy's serious preoccupation with Christianity began about 1904 at age sixteen. By his own admission, Rosenstock-Huessy's decision to become a Christian was not a partic-

3. Cf. Stephen N. Dunning, *The Tongues of Men: Hegel and Hamann on Religious Language and History* (AAR diss. ser., 1979); also, Harold M. Stahmer, *"Speak That I May See Thee:" Studies in the Religious Significance of Language* (Studies in the works of J.G. Hamann, Eugen Rosenstock-Huessy, Franz Rosenzweig, Martin Buber, and Ferdinand Ebner) (New York, 1968), pp. 68-147.

ularly momentous one at the time. Rosenstock-Huessy once told me that he converted to Christianity at "about age sixteen." However, in an unpublished manuscript written in longhand entitled "The First Year of the Academy of Labor (1921)," he indicates that it was the year 1907 when he was nineteen that he became a Christian. "Als ich 1907 Christ würde,....."[4] I have no evidence to suggest that Rosenstock-Huessy's decision to convert to Christianity came about suddenly or that it was due to a personal crisis or single major event in his life. My conversations with him, with his son, Dr. Hans R. Huessy, with Mrs. Freya von Moltke and others, leave me with the impression that his path to baptism was gradual but, in many ways, also an inevitable development.

The year 1902 marked the beginning of his scholarly preoccupation with language and philology, but it was not until his battlefield experiences during World War I that he realized that from 1902 until 1912 he had begun to "live under the banner of speech." His involvement with language during this period was one that involved his learning "to mix all the essences and tinctures of philology."

The events that brought each of these commitments together and made them driving forces in his life are associated with meetings such as the one with a group of young historians and philosophers in Baden-Baden in 1910. It was apparent to the members of such groups that they were facing an impending world catastrophe of the first order. It was equally apparent to them that the leading intellectuals in European universities were so involved in departmental and professional squabbling that they had divorced themselves from the deeper issues of the day. The philosophers present were especially concerned that academic philosophy was unable to address the spiritual needs of individuals. According to Rosenstock-Huessy, "...the whole world of the educated was embodying a *spiritual* lag." And, unfortunately, this "breakdown of the old standards was communicable to a few friends only."[5] Among those at the Baden-Baden meeting were at least three individuals who were to figure

---

4. Discovered and made available to me by Mrs. Freya von Moltke.

5. I have found the following works especially valuable in my attempt to understand the cultural, intellectual, and spiritual climate that shaped and influenced Rosenstock-Huessy's life. Fritz K. Ringer, *The Decline of the German Mandarins: The German Academic Community, 1890-1933* (Cambridge, 1969); Konrad H. Jarausch, *Students, Society, and Politics in Imperial Germany: The Rise of Academic Illiberalism* (Princeton, 1982); George A. Morgan, *What Nietzsche Means* (Cambridge, 1941, Harper Torchbook, 1965); Fritz Stern, *Gold and Iron: Bismarck and Bleichröder* (New York, 1979); Fritz Stern, *The Politics of Cultural Despair: A Study in the Rise of the Germanic Ideology* (Berkeley, 1974); and Jacob Katz, *From Prejudice to Destruction: Anti-Semitism, 1700-1933* (Cambridge, 1980).

prominently in Rosenstock-Huessy's life in varying degrees, either individually or as members of the Patmos group (1915-1923) that they later helped create and, subsequent to that, as contributors to the journal, *The Creature (Die Kreatur)* (1926-1930). The three persons he met at that meeting were the young historian and Hegel scholar, Franz Rosenzweig, and his two cousins, Hans and Rudolph Ehrenberg. Meetings such as the one in Baden-Baden that focused on the spiritual malaise of the times were, in retrospect, occasions whereby many of the participants began to undergo dramatic changes in their life styles and professional orientations. In some instances, as was the case with these four participants, earlier relig-ious affirmations and scholarly and scientific training were trans-formed and mobilized into forces that were to dominate their lives and writings and project them into unexpected roles of spiritual and intellectual leadership. Such individuals were, literally, seized, called forth by the crises of the hour, and each was to undergo a series of profoundly meaningful private and public metamorphoses. Rosenstock-Huessy has described his own odyssey in his "Biblionomics or The Nine Lives of a Cat" *(Bibliography/Biography*, 1959); in his Foreword to his *Soziologie* (vol. 1, 1956), in *Ja und Nein: Autobiographische Fragmente* (1968), and throughout portions of many other essays.[6]

Rosenstock-Huessy and Rosenzweig continued to meet after the Baden-Baden conference due in part to the latter's respect for this young law professor's intellectual powers and his fascination that this same person was a practicing Christian. According to Rosenstock-Huessy, "Franz, a very superior mind, frequents courses and seminars conducted by this younger man." And in a footnote, he added, "Franz's going to Leipzig was prompted...by a desire to...hear what a young, academically unorthodox *Privatdozent* had to say." Their meetings led to their well-known encounter the evening of July 7, 1913. They met, as Rosenstock-Huessy described it fifty years later: "Franz, a student of philosophy and history for eight years by that time defended the prevailing philosophical relativism of the day, whereas Eugen bore witness to prayer and worship as his prime guides to action." Rosenzweig's decision subsequent to that meeting to convert to Christianity and then his reversal of that decision and determination, instead, to "reaffirm" his Jewish roots, but "on a

6. Cf. Nahum Glatzer, *Franz Rosenzweig: His Life and Thought* (New York, 1972), pp. 1-85; Eugen Rosenstock-Huessy, *Judaism Despite Christianity* (University, Alabama, 1969), note especially the essays by Alexander Altmann and Dorothy Emmet, pp. 26-70; also, Harold M. Stahmer, *"Speak That I May See Thee,"* pp. 121-124.

different basis than before," has been discussed by many writers as
has their now classic exchange of letters on Judaism and Christianity
in 1916. The effect that these and other aspects of their relationship
had on one another was quite decisive. While most agree that 1913
marked the turning point in Rosenzweig's life that produced the
Rosenzweig now recognized as probably the most profound Jewish
thinker of the twentieth century, their meetings had an equally
profound impact on Rosenstock-Huessy's life and thought.[7]

For one thing, their encounters forced Rosenstock-Huessy not
only to defend and assert "publicly" his Christianity, but to do so in a
way that required his sharpening and actually testing the validity of
his convictions during a series of spiritually violent soul-shaking
encounters with a man whom he regarded as a worthy intellectual
and, later, spiritual adversary. Their relationship had several
profound consequences for the shape and quality of
Rosenstock-Huessy's Christian life and writings. For example, it
confirmed the importance of speech and "dialogue" as a way of
thinking and as a vehicle of spiritual as well as self-revelation.
Rosenzweig summed this up in letter number #17 of their 1916
correspondence when he wrote:

> I believe there are in the life of each living thing moments...when
> it speaks the truth. It may be that we need do no more than
> watch for the moment when this living thing expresses itself. The
> dialogue which these monologues form between one another I
> consider to be the whole truth.

Rosenstock-Huessy expressed the meaning of the dialogical
method in terms of its effect upon the biographies of the two corre-
spondents "as a junctim, the one provoking the other." It was for
him a three-part drama–the painful dialogue of 1913, the letters of
1916, and a robust epilogue in 1920, in the course of which "...Franz
and Eugen were existentially transformed." Rosenstock-Huessy
expressed doubt, in fact, that "any amount of documentation could
convince modern humanists...of the thesis that two men, Eugen and
Franz, exchanged life rhythms in the course of their encounter from
1913 to 1918." But "Eugen" is not troubled by this for:

---

7. Cf. Paul R. Mendes-Flohr and Jehuda Reinharz, "From Relativism to Religious
Faith: The Testimony of Franz Rosenzweig's Unpublished Diaries" (Leo Baeck
Institute Year Book XXII, 1977), pp. 161-174. Nahum Glatzer, *Franz Rosenzweig*, the
Altmann and Emmet essays in *Judaism Despite Christianity*, and my essay in *Modern
Judaism* (1984), "'Speech-Letters' and 'Speech-Thinking': Franz Rosenzweig and Eugen
Rosenstock-Huessy."

After all, the twelve apostles, the four evangelists, St. Francis and St. Dominic, and many, many other groupings represent examples of the interpenetration of "individual" lives. Even Hawthorne and Herman Melville got under each other's skin. *Franz and Eugen did exchange with each other certain fundamentals of their life rhythm, in mutality,* (sic) *and—must it be added?—*quite unintentionally, in total unconsciousness. Individual purposes or intentions were subordinated to a large extent to a process of recreation or transformation brought about by a most unwanted, even abhorred, exposure to each other.

The year 1916, for example, marked a reversal, in fact, in the pace of their respective lives. Up to that time "Eugen had been in a hurry:" he was by then "established; was married, had published two books and was well-recognized and respected in the academic community; while 'Franz' seemed to have procrastinated" in his development. But after 1917 this "delaying" and "hurrying" reversed itself. Rosenstock-Huessy, in his own words, "...was, so to speak, requested to delay, to postpone, to procrastinate," while his alter-ego, "Franz" accomplished in the remaining twelve years of his life what others could never have achieved in longer life times.[8]

Closely related to this discovery about the impact of these kinds of dialogues on one's life was Rosenstock-Huessy's recognition of the powerful role that letters can frequently play in one's life. In his *Biblionomics* he wrote, "...the reader may see...that the printed word was not radically different to me from the words spoken or written between friends. Fittingly, letters have played an immense role in my life. The letters printed in Franz Rosenzweig's volume of letters are a good example of their role in my own existence. *Many good books got started as letters.*"[9] The best example of this in Rosenstock-Huessy's own life is his "speech letter" *(Sprachbrief)* to Rosenzweig at the conclusion of their 1916 correspondence in response to Rosenzweig's invitation: "If you want to write to me about particular matters, please write to me about The Languages" (Letter #21). Rosenstock-Huessy's lengthy editorial comments about this request are most informative:

It was in response to this request from his friend that Eugen composed a lengthy statement on "Sprachdenken" ("speech-thinking"), representing a distillation of some of the fruits of his own "speech-thinking" since long before the war—indeed, since 1902. This *"Sprachbrief"* ("Speech-letter"), written in 1916,

8. *Judaism Despite Christianity,* pp. 171-172.
9. Rosenstock-Huessy, *Bibliography/Biography* (New York, 1959), pp. 22-23.

proved to be the first draft–and last one, in all save minor details–of Eugen's *Angewandte Seelenkunde (Applied Knowledge of the Soul)....*"[10]

Rosenstock-Huessy's insights into "dialogue" and the role of "letters" are crucial for understanding the "interior" or "private" dimensions of a life lived under the spell of the word as speech and are a central element in his Christian faith. Of more "public" importance for his Christianity, however, is his understanding of "Revelation" which forced Rosenzweig to recognize and admit the relativism inherent in his own philosophical position. Revelation, for Rosenstock-Huessy, was essentially "orientation." Three years later Rosenzweig, by then the formidable and "stubborn" believing Jew, asked Rosenstock-Huessy (Letter #11) to "...please explain to me your present idea of the relation between Nature and Revelation." In his response (Letter #12), Rosenstock-Huessy stated that "Revelation means the linking of our consciousness...with the union between earth and heaven that transcends the world." It is the opposite of Nature which Rosenstock-Huessy equates with "natural understanding" viewed by Cartesians as the "hub of the universe."

It is in the renunciation of "natural human understanding," seen in this central role that "revelation to, in, and for us (is) possible." Those familiar with Parts One and Two of Rosenzweig's *Star of Redemption* (1921) and his essay *Understanding the Sick and the Healthy* (1921) should be fascinated by the fact that the elements of Rosenzweig's treatment of the relationship between "philosophical reason" and "revelation" are already anticipated in Rosenstock-Huessy's response to him in this 1916 letter. "Natural understanding" is "luxuriating thinking"; it knows no limits, no bounds; it is conditioned neither by time nor by speech.

> You can believe in your autonomy. The Kantians believe in a senseless exaggeration of the autonomy of thought. The actual fact of seeing, on the contrary, testifies only to the autonomy of the married couple, speech *and* reason. For self-confidence of reason and trust in speech are both equally essential to a man who wants knowledge.

Revelation is "that bond from heaven to earth which makes space stable, like a rock of bronze, through the concept of the *Above.*" The natural mind cannot master time and space because it clings to its "concrete base, the intellectual arena," fearful that "the naive ego" will be destroyed. Without an absolute standard outside itself, human

10. *Judaism Despite Christianity*, p. 170.

speech degenerates into stagnant conceptualism. That standard that heals human speech and releases the mind from its self-imposed bondage is "the Logos doctrine of the Saviour."

'The Word became Flesh'–on that proposition *everything* indeed depends...the Christian revelation is the healing of the Babylonian confusion of tongues, the bursting open of the prism, *but also the sign on the tongues, speech that is now informed with soul. Since then, it has become worthwhile to think again, because thought has a standard outside itself, in the visible footsteps of God.*

And Christ redeems not only the pagan from his fear that his "naive ego" will be destroyed, but "the boundless naive pride of the Jew" as well. Hence, Rosenstock-Huessy's dissociation from Rosenzweig's view of Christianity as that of "Judaizing the pagans."[11]

In the next letter (Letter #13), Rosenstock-Huessy states that "All revelation is something that gives us a *standard....,*" but one that is outside ourselves. That standard, like "the Christian kingdom" is "not of this world, *nor is even the kingdom of the Christian priest*" (i.e. the Church). Almost twenty-five years later in a letter to John C. Bennett, then Professor and subsequently President of Union Theological Seminary, Rosenstock-Huessy reiterated the importance of this "standard" and characterized not only Revelation, but the general thrust of his thinking as basically "orientation." "Since we all have to make our special contribution within one great cosmic work-shop, I may perhaps mention my specialty: orientation."

Other key elements in Rosenstock-Huessy's subsequent writings found in the 1916 correspondence with Rosenzweig that bear upon the development of his understanding of Christianity are his use of "Four," "The Fourfold Division of Reality," and "The Cross of Reality" in connection with his "calendar thinking." The other important theme discussed is the significance of the French Revolution of 1789 in their exchange about the "Johannine Age" or "Age of the Spirit."

In his first letter to his friend, Rosenstock-Huessy acknowledged that he had "at last taken the saving step into a *system*" as one "soaked in the ideas of Schelling, Hegel, and Fichte." He later admitted also the influence of Schlegel, especially his *Philosophy of Life, Philosophy of Language,* and *Lectures on History* in connection with the development of his Johannine millenarian writings.

This particular letter and, in fact, the entire correspondence with Rosenzweig confirm the change, the new orientation beginning in

11. *Judaism Despite Christianity,* p. 122.

1915 that the War and other factors brought about in Rosenstock-Huessy's life and thought. He begins by telling Rosenzweig that "for the first time without any reservations...I am at one with you in scholarly research," but that Rosenzweig may not now be at one with him when the latter realizes that Rosenstock-Huessy has thrown away his "professional mask" ("To be jurist and historian has been burdensome to me for a long time,") and now appears before Rosenzweig "in the part of a philosopher." "Now that I am boldly philosophizing in my work, and not only in the privacy of my thoughts, I must write to you in this capacity, too." Rosenstock-Huessy's mood is one of "exaltation"; he is about to express for the first time what has been growing within him, he can no longer refrain from sharing it with his friend. One senses the excitement as he divulges his new way of philosophizing to Rosenzweig.

> Since I am at this very moment sitting in your own house, in the mood of exaltation...I must take the risk...of divulging to you this constellation of stars– *doctor haruspici* (Examiner of entrails, omen-taker). So, Master Examiner of Entrails, I am certainly not yet delivering myself up at your table of guinea pigs and rabbits, but I warn you: the dragon's seed is springing up in your own house.[12]

In this correspondence Rosenstock-Huessy divests himself of a conventional German academic prose style and adopts a style that even those quite familiar with Rosenstock-Huessy's subsequent writings find alternately unconventional, difficult, complex and, at times, explosive, if not bombastic and often overwhelming. "But," as W.H. Auden said in his Foreword to Rosenstock-Huessy's *I am an Impure Thinker*, "let the reader persevere, and he will find, as I did, that he is richly rewarded."

In 1916 at age 28, "philosophizing" for Rosenstock-Huessy is summed up early in his first letter to Rosenzweig (May 29, 1916) in

---

12. *Judaism Despite Christianity*, p. 78. Dr. George Morgan believes that the change in Rosenstock-Huessy's prose style actually began in 1915 and is reflected in "Kriegsteilnehmer aller Länder vereinigt euch St.-George-Reden" (1915) which appears as the first essay in Volume II of Rosenstock-Huessy's *Die Sprache des Menschengeschlechts*. Dr. Morgan also regards his 1916 correspondence with Rosenzweig as the major source for Rosenstock-Huessy's subsequent writings on "revolutions." In his autobiographical essay, Rosenstock-Huessy acknowledges Rosenzweig's influence in "promoting" the "metamorphosis" in his scholarship that led to his fascination with "revolutions." "It is clear to me today fifty years later, that in 1913 I planted the *germ* of the *"Star"* in Franz; and conversely the metamorphosis of my own esoteric works, from a kind of St. George-and-the-dragon approach into the worldly form of revolutions, was promoted thanks to Franz's grounding in the methods of scientific historical investigation." *Ja und Nein: Autobiographische Fragmente* (Heidelberg, 1968), p. 171.

the following way: "I philosophize in the form of a calendar." He then indicates the centrality of *four* to his "calendar" way of thinking. "Apart from the calendar–that is, the rhythm of time–my thoughts are haunted by a struggle against the *three*. I am all for the *four*, two squared as the foundation of all comparison, relation, and relativity." These remarks are largely appreciative responses to his telling Rosenzweig how much he enjoyed reading his friend's discovery of an essay by Schelling, "The Oldest Program of a System for German Idealism," that had been preserved in Hegel's handwriting and attributed to Hegel. In the next letter, Rosenzweig inquires whether his correspondent is aware of Hegel's use of "the number Four" in his dialectic and especially in Hegel's *Philosophy of Nature* and indicates that Rosenstock-Huessy's "transition to a written system" does not surprise him because he had always regarded his adversary as a "philosopher." In ,a lengthy letter (Letter #18) to Rosenzweig, Rosenstock-Huessy then outlines his "calendar thinking" in terms of the "Cross of Reality" as a scheme which he believes his friend will view, unfortunately, as "very dry and incomprehensible."[13] Nevertheless, Rosenzweig did respond and Rosenstock-Huessy took seriously his friend's critical comments (Letter #19) about his treatment of history and revolutions and accepted many of Rosenzweig's insights into the meaning of the French Revolution of 1789 and its bearing upon the Johannine Age. In *Ja und Nein: Autobiographische Fragmente*, Rosenstock-Huessy wrote:

> It is clear to me fifty years later, that in 1913 I planted the germ of the *Star* in Franz; and conversely, the metamorphosis of my own esoteric works, from a kind of St. George-and-the-dragon approach into the worldly form of revolutions, was promoted thanks to Franz's grounding in the methods of scientific historical

---

13. Those familiar with the centrality of the "Cross of Reality" to Rosenstock-Huessy's later writings–i.e. his two volume *Soziologie* and his "grammatical thinking" should know that the "Cross of Reality" as presented in this correspondence (cf. Letter #18, 26 November 1916) bears little resemblance to the way in which Rosenstock-Huessy applies it in his later writings. The context in 1916 is concerned almost exclusively with "calendarical" and "historical" concerns. It is as if Rosenstock-Huessy discovered the "Cross of Reality" metaphor in 1916 and then refashioned it between 1916 and 1924 when *Applied Knowledge of the Soul (Angewandte Seelenkunde)* and 1925 when the first volume of his *Soziologie* appeared. The usage is connected because we know, for example, that *Angewandte Seelenkunde* originated as a "speech letter" (Sprachbrief) to Rosenzweig in response to the latter's request at the end of their 1916 correspondence that Rosenstock-Huessy write to him about his views on "language." Scholars that have an opportunity to examine Rosenstock-Huessy's unpublished correspondence may shed light on how this change in usage evolved.

investigations.

In Letter #16 Rosenstock-Huessy discusses the beginning of the Johannine Age in terms of the emancipation of the Jews after the French Revolution as part of "...the process of the self-destruction of the European tradition, which has removed the dogma of the stubbornness of the Jews just as it blotted out the Christian Emperor." Later on he presents his views on the status of Christianity in Western history subsequent to the Middle Ages.

> The Middle Ages translated Christianity for the cities, the bishoprics, the communities, in a word for the centers-of-government; the Reformation translated it for the homes-of-the-people. Not in vain did Luther put the married woman in the place of the hated priest, and always extol her. *Today, the task is to translate Christianity for the single isolated individual who can be anything; Jew, Christian, Pagan.* The Fourth Estate, in the sense of the moral proletariat, did not exist up to 1789, among either Jews or Christians.

In Letter #19 Rosenzweig responds with his own comments about 1789 and the Johannine Age. It reads, for the most part, as if it had been written by his alter-ego, Rosenstock-Huessy. But then the nature of their relationship, as we have noted earlier, was such that each had no qualms about developing a thought or insight for the other.

> ...since 1789 the Church has no longer a relation to the "State," but only to "Society." The reason and meaning is that the Church has entered on its final (and to use Schelling's expression) Johannine epoch; that is, it has become without substance. Christianity has only now, since then, become a complete miracle; the Church of the Word (the epoch of Peter, and, since 1517, of Paul) were still things you could actually grasp through the realities that carried them, namely, the hierarchy and the Bible.

Then, Rosenzweig proceeds to introduce their discussion about the status of the Old Testament and Church history in the Johannine Age:

> But now the Church is everything; that is, it is no longer constituted as some particular entity, and it no longer has as its foil a particular reality beyond itself, by which it defines its own particular nature. There is no longer any instituted paganism, nor "Greek" wisdom, nor "Roman" empire; there is only Christianity. That is what the followers of John's Gospel wanted from the beginning, and yet it did not happen, because wisdom and empire had not yet fulfilled their time....This is why, as you so rightly say, the earlier real

periods, the Church's own history, assume the significance of an Old Testament, Christianity now has the proof of its reality behind it. *And the Old Testament is something that will disappear. So you say, and so say I.* But why do you not say that it *has* disappeared? I answer, because it has not disappeared, but it *will disappear so long as this Johannine epoch of Christianity, which began in 1789, endures.*

In Letter #14 to Rosenzweig, Rosenstock-Huessy chides his friend for confusing the "Church of the Spirit"–*Christianity*–with the "Church of Tradition"–*Church*–and treating Christianity as if the period before Constantine was the "good time" and the time after, the "bad time." He asserts that this is the typical view of those who have no trust in the "whole" and therefore "can see nothing but bricks." He then goes on to describe the relationship between "Christianity" and the "Church" in terms of their respective functions. That of Christianity is to "insure the rebirth of the mystery" of the Incarnation while the function of the Church is to make it possible that this mystery "lives in individuals as personal experience." And throughout the ages and in each age the way in which the mystery is experienced must differ. Quoting Goethe, "Nature has neither kernel nor shell, she is everything at the same time." Thus, every Christian "experiences the dogmas of the Church as *martuus* (witness), as personal experience," in a *different way*, and the nearer one approaches the "historical incarnation of God" the fewer the institutional and dogmatic traces and barriers. The history of the "witnesses of the faith" *(martyria testimonia fidei)* consists of opposing propositions reflecting the personal experience of each individual. And all of these experiences are "in their ways equally naive and conscious (or knowing) (Bewusst)." Every living creature contains within itself, in addition to the power of life, the powers of "specifying difference" (differentia specifica), "of self-defense, self-preservation, in brief, of protection and discrimination"–i.e. the apologetic history of the Church in the first five centuries; her dogmas, doctrines, and councils. The alternative of the naive and sophisticated testimonies within the Church must exist within each age and throughout the life of the Church. John, for example, the first and greatest apologist, was a "quite naive and spiritual writer" who was overwhelmed by the power of the Word, while Paul, the Gnostics, and most of Protestantism reflected the "conscious" (or "knowing") element.

So you have both parties, Mystics and Protestants; within the Church both the Franciscan and Dominican are possible, which is to say that differences of emphasis between naive and conscious/knowing must remain within each individual man; just as every hale and healthy man has two legs, in the same way he must know how to be humble and how to be bold.

The Christian Church as "the fellowship of the mystery" contains these two "fundamental powers of the natural man, being willing to be this essential contradiction in terms (crux=church)...The Church is the eternal recurrence of the same."[14] This alternation and contradiction in individuals is also the means whereby the *secret of the Church is rejuvenated.* Thus, in addition to "Christianity" and "Church," there is the special role of the "individual Christian," the "living spirit:"

Who constitutes a third factor, the mystery of the microcosm, the infinity of the individual soul which gives rebirth to the whole macrocosm, though it functions nonetheless as a member of this great body. This possessing of the whole, and yet not possessing it, in the individual is the secret of the Church, and what distinguishes it from all merely objectified forms of mind (Stage, Art, Religion, in the liberal Hegelian sense).

The remaining portion of this statement is especially important. In the original German "speaks," "speaking," and "live" as they appear in the following passage are all underlined. Referring again to "the mystery of the microcosm, the infinity of the individual soul which gives birth to the whole macrocosm," he wrote:

...for it *speaks,* and allows the individual to *speak* and to *live* in the macrocosm, this is to experience consciously (*Erleben*–a word that you don't get in English, French, or Italian) the double mystery of member and of whole as the *crux,* whereas Law is essentially only lived, Art is essentially only expressed, and Religion, in the Hegelian sense, is, generally speaking, dozed over.

In the passage just cited the secret for the renewal of the Church as well as each individual member in it is the "crux," "cross." In the first passage he equates "crux" with Church and in the second, the Church is renewed through the "soul"–through "the infinity of the individual soul which gives birth to the whole macrocosm." If we include the earlier insights from Letter #13, then the fate of the individual Christian throughout his temporal life is one of constant alternation between his "un-Christian life"–his "natural" condition, and his "Christian life"–one that has experienced the *vita illuminata,* the blessed illumined life.

This formulation, with its emphasis on the "Cross" and the "soul," suggests that *the individual soul lies at the "center" of the intersection of the arms of Rosenstock-Huessy's "Cross of Reality" within the framework of the Johannine Age or Age of the Spirit.* This date, 26 November 1916, may well be the first time that we know of that Rosenstock-Huessy actually used the term, "Kreuz der Wirklichkeit" (Cross of Reality).[15] He also refers to "This 'Fourfold Division of Reality' (Vier der Wirklichkeit), this *crux cogitanda* (a cross to be thought about; figuratively, the most important matter for consideration) that can be thought in every moment, and which ought and must be thought, now works itself out up to the last detail." At this early stage in the development of his use of "Cross of Reality," it appears in conjunction with or as the umbrella term for his "Fourfold Division of Reality" which he presents as a blend of liturgical and historical calendars which, likewise, is appropriate within a Johannine framework. He also stresses the link between Revelation, the Incarnate Word, and the human speech of the soul in an equally Johannine fashion. And the way he distinguishes among "Christianity," "Church," and "soul" suggests the strong possibility that the way in which the soul renews the Church, according to the "differentiating principle," makes possible the creation of a "churchless" society. This is also consistent with the Johannine epoch. And his use of *crux* as both Church and Cross as applied to the soul is consistent with his later interpretation of the meaning of the historic liturgy of the Church both in his two-part essay, "Liturgical Thinking" and in *The Christian Future: Or the Modern Mind Outrun.* On the basis of his use of "crux" in these passages and the frequency with which Rosenstock-Huessy uses the word "crucial" in *The Christian Future* (1946) and especially in his later unpublished Tippett Lectures (1967), I suggest that those who refer to him as an "existential" thinker might more appropriately coin the phrase "crucial thinker." The term "crucial" appeals to me because of the blending of traditionally sacred and secular themes that *crux,* as he uses it, achieves. Somehow, "crucial" preserves that splendid intermingling of the Word, the Cross, Christianity, the Church, history, liturgy, calendars and time, as they blend and unfold against the panorama of the

---

15. However, in *Soziologie I* (1925 and 1956) the "soul" is the "forward" or "future" arm of the "Cross of Reality" while in *Angewandte Seelenkunde* (1924) the "soul" moves throughout all four arms of the "Cross of Reality."

three ages: Petrine, Pauline and Johannine. Implicit in my focus on and interpretation of these passages is a further fairly important conclusion; namely, that within the setting of the Johannine Age–wherein the meaning of terms like sacred and secular lose their meaning–"Christianity" and the "Word" represent the "Above," the "standard" that gives meaning to human thought and speech. *This "standard" and "orientation" may well be the conscious basis, framework, and method for what appear to many to be his "non-Christian" interests–i.e. history, revolution, sociology.*

In conclusion, beyond a suggestion that I find it useful to describe and introduce Rosenstock-Huessy as a "crucial thinker," I otherwise join ranks with those who find it unproductive to engage in discussions about whether or not Rosenstock-Huessy was an essentially "religious thinker," a "social philosopher," or a kind of "New Age Theologian." Kurt Ballerstedt's conclusion to his "Biography" of Rosenstock-Huessy expresses my own sentiments about the man and what motivated him and I offer his summary as a fitting conclusion to this essay:

> One who tries to compress the life work of a man into a single principle, a single thought, or a fixed goal, strangles him. Something completely different from such deadly abstractions is required when we try to name the source of Rosenstock-Huessy's insights, his strength of constant renewal, the power to be true to his own. That source is the Word of God become flesh in Christ.[16]

Appendix

Some Relevant Passages About Christianity from Rosenstock-Huessy's *The Christian Future: Or the Modern Mind Outrun.*

"The Crucifixion is the fountainhead of all my values, the great divide whence flow the processes most real to my inner life, and my primary response to our tradition is one of gratitude to the source of my own frame of reference in everyday life."

Eugen Rosenstock-Huessy (p. 102)

---

16. Kurt Ballerstedt, "Biography" in *Bibliography/Biography* (Eugen Rosenstock-Huessy) (New York: private printing, 1959), p. 38).

"Christianity is the founder and trustee of the future, the very process of finding and securing it, and without the Christian spirit there is no real future for man."

Eugen Rosenstock-Huessy (p. 61)

"The time span of the length of the Church goes from the beginning of the world to its end since the Church originated in her faithful from the start and shall endure until the end."

Hugo de Sancto Victore (opposite title page)

"For, we basically hold that from the beginning of the world to the end of times, no period exists in which there cannot be found those who trust in Christ."

Hugo de Sancto Victore (opposite title page)

"God looks at us and has looked at us before we open our eyes or our mouths. He is the power which makes us speak. He puts words of life on our lips."

Eugen Rosenstock-Huessy (p. 94)

"All things were made by the Word. In the beginning there was neither mind nor matter. In the beginning was the Word. St. John was properly the first Christian theologian because he was overwhelmed by the spokenness of all meaningful happening."

Eugen Rosenstock-Huessy (pp. 128-129)

"The average church-going civilizee realized, one may say, absolutely nothing of the deeper currents of human nature."

William James (p. 2)

"I believe that in the future, Church and Creed can be given a new lease on life only by services that are nameless and incognito."

"In the third epoch, beginning today, Christians must immigrate *into* our workaday world, there to incarnate the Spirit in unpredictable forms."

Eugen Rosenstock-Huessy (p. 124)

"Hence the third article of the Creed is the specifically Christian one: from now on the Holy Spirit makes man a partner in his own creation. In the beginning God has said, "Let us make man in our image" (Gen. 1:26). In this light, the Church Fathers interpreted human history as a process of making Man like God. They called it "Anthropurgy": as metallurgy refines metal from its ore, anthropurgy wins the true stuff of Man out of his coarse physical substance. Christ, in the center of history, enables us to participate consciously in this man-making process and to study its laws."

Eugen Rosenstock-Huessy (p. 108)

"The death and resurrection of the Word, the intermittence of the Christian faith, the ebb and renewed flow of its life, must not blind us to the essential unity of the story of salvation. The tree of everlasting life can grow only through successive generations of men reaching their hands to each other in one spirit across the ages. And *each generation has to act differently precisely in order to represent the same thing.* Only so can each become a full partner in the process of Making Man; only so can life be as authentic in the last age as in the first."

Eugen Rosenstock-Huessy (p. 130)

Joseph Wittig's Life in
Silesia, Vermont, and Elsewhere

Raymond Huessy

This essay was first written years ago disguised as a history term paper.[1] I learned then that I was incapable of writing a paper "on" my grandfather and Joseph Wittig. That left me this time with the humbler option of trying to say something "about" them. My academic career came to a close very soon after I wrote the first version of this essay, so I was a sort of pirate at the conference in Waterloo, as I am at the communion rail, and it is as a pirate that I am made bold to speak of my grandfather and the "great-hearted psalmist" Joseph Wittig.

Within the small world of Rosenstock-Huessy scholarship there has been a considerable amount of discussion of my grandfather's correspondence with Franz Rosenzweig. But few in that small world have paid tribute to the other men whose lives bore fruit in crossing his: the lathe operator Eugen May, who contributed his life story and work experience to *Werkstattaussiedlung*, Dr. Richard Koch, Werner Picht, and especially Joseph Wittig. It is understandable: Rosenzweig is an established figure in the academic world. Wittig, a priest, professor, and popular author, was the victim of gross ecclesiastical injustice (excommunicated in 1925 for refusing to renounce his work and unconditionally freed from the ban twenty years later without explanation or apology). Today Wittig is almost forgotten. Why bracket Rosenstock-Huessy with someone even more obscure than he is?

In *Höregott*, Wittig writes that the world is quick to honour the testimony of the spirit, less eager to acknowledge the testimony of the flesh and blood from which the spirit sprang, and generally

---

1. In the course of three days most of the people at Waterloo managed to reconcile the names "Rosenstock," "Rosenstock-Huessy," "Eugen," and despite a few raised eyebrows, even "Grampa Eugen." It took me over three years, and I worked hard at it. I had known Grampa Eugen years before I ever met Rosenstock-Huessy. In fact, Joseph Wittig entered my life at about the same time as Rosenstock-Huessy, and the combination has seemed only natural ever since.

unaware of the origin of the process in God's call. (If the world were not so fond of approaching things backward, we should have said "farewell to Descartes" long ago). Our small world has honoured the richness of spirit in the Rosenzweig letters. It is now time to acknowledge the flesh and blood struggle which brought Wittig and Rosenstock-Huessy together in spiritual co-respondence. The inward dialogue of the war years with its speculation on Church, State, University, and Synagogue was followed ten years later by battles with the State of Prussia, the University of Breslau, and a Church turned synagogue in its elevation of law over faith. In both cases the speakers' lives were renewed–distinctions of belief gave way to unanimity in faith. In *The Age of the Church,* Rosenstock-Huessy writes that the true church knows no division between Catholic and Protestant. The Catholic keeps order on the inside and endures chaos on the outside; the Protestant attempts to impose order on the world in order to grant his heart greater freedom. They are only the inward and outward faces of the same faith. Rosenstock-Huessy's works record the progress of the Spirit through time–an ordering of time to permit free growth into the future. His vision at Verdun saw the millennium of European history as a whole; his work with Wittig widened the span to two millennia, establishing the unity of the times from Golgotha to the present. Later he pushed the limits of our story back to Adam, to the day that speech formed the tribes. Wittig "kept order on the inside" by demonstrating in his stories how doctrine sprang from truths revealed in everyday experiences, in his care for individual souls, and finally by remaining Catholic in the face of general condemnation.

I must admit that when my father first tried to interest me in Wittig's *Jesus' Life in Palestine, Silesia, and Elsewhere,* I turned my nose up at it. In fact, since I could not possibly admit that there was a book on earth I had not read, I replied that I had looked through it and found it uninteresting. This was however at a time when I also found the "cannibalism" of communion "unacceptable."

Then, in the summer of 1971 I copied tapes of my grandfather's lectures from the Baker library at Dartmouth. Since no one knew what was said in any given lecture, I had to listen and take notes. I was swept away, and came back to Four Wells every day with the latest news from 1954 or 1956. In his first lecture in Comparative Religion, my grandfather took his listeners to task as moviegoers and sightseers, upbraiding them for coming to stare at other peoples' religions when they did not even know their own. And most of the rest of the course was spent dissecting the American religion–not what America does on Sunday, but what she lives by. So I met two obvious truths for the first time: every man lives by some personal faith, and whatever that faith may be, it is his religion, regardless of what religion he may profess.

That same summer Bianca Wittig came to America and spent a week with us in Norwich. Though we had little in common except our respect for my grandfather and fondness for my sister Paula, we became good friends. Anca's presence succeeded where my father's good intentions had failed, and I resolved to read *Jesus' Life*. After all, it was right there on the living room bookshelf.

Jesus' Life in Palestine, Silesia, and Elsewhere

Wittig calls his *Life* a gospel; if Christ continues to live on in us as he lived on in the apostles, he says, then we should be able to bear witness as they did to the re-creation of the world. Like all Wittig's work, the book has an autobiographical spine. In the course of retelling Jesus' life, Wittig relates the events which transformed his own; he uses them to show, in Rosenstock-Huessy's words, that "dogma is not an intellectual formula but a record and promise of life. It does not propose ideas for our minds to master; it tells actual events which master and transform *us* as they did the first Christians."[2]

Joseph Wittig was born in Neusorge in the Silesian county Glatz in 1879. His mother was a weaver's daughter and a weaver herself, his father a corpenter as his ancestors had been since the Thirty Years' War. Poverty was another ancient heritage, but when Heinrich May, a young priest who spent summers in Neusorge, said that Joseph should study for the priesthood, the money was found. The retired priest who had agreed to prepare Joseph for the entrance examination soon despaired of his ever learning enough Latin to pass, and so Joseph was sent to Father May. Over the winter they covered enough Latin, Greek, and Math for Joseph not only to pass the exam, but to enter *Gymnasium* in the fourth instead of the first year. Wittig tells the story of the exam as a footnote to Christ's selection of his disciples. Jesus' miracles of healing are accompanied by Wittig's accounts of life in the seedy streets behind the convent, and Jesus' teaching by stories of Wittig's time at the University of Breslau. His own story ends with his last temptation and ordination, but he goes on to tell of Christ's death and resurrection, and ends the book with Christ sending the apostles, and Wittig, out into the

2. Eugen Rosenstock-Huessy, *The Christian Future* (New York: Harper & Row, 1966), p. 98.

world with the words, "Heaven stands open!"

In one of the last chapters, Wittig reminds us that the church calls every believing Christian to the dignity of priesthood. If we are not stepchildren but true children of God, then Christ is our brother; when he promised the apostles that they should do greater things than he had, he included us as well.

I was surprised that so much of what he wrote of his own faith resounded in me. Having learned that every man lives by some sort of religion, I now saw the working of religion in one man's soul—how the experiences of his life led him to accept the Catholic faith as his own.

I finished reading *Jesus' Life* after an operation on my foot and then took myself, my hip cast, and my crutches to Germany where I visited Anca. (This is not the place to describe her hospitality; suffice it to say that I shared it with a one-legged librarian from Lublin and *her* crutuches.) That winter I threw myself into my major in extra-curricular activities, only to be brought up short in February by Grampa Eugen's death. I think my childhood died with him. I know that though I cried like a baby, staying to fill in the grave with my brothers and sisters was my first act as an adult. I decided to read his books and to start with *The Age of the Church*. I approached it with some trepidation; my grandfather's books were for greater minds than mine but, I thought, Wittig will see me through. And he did.

The Age of the Church

Rosenstock-Huessy wrote *Out of Revolution* in response to what he saw as the death of Europe. In the attack on Wittig's championship of simple faith, the two of them saw the death of the Church and wrote a book looking back on its era from the end. The first volume chronicles the church's growth from a church of souls to the cultural power that converted and unified the tribes of Europe. The second volume covers both the five centuries of "internalization" in which Church scholarship and Church law created the first modern state and the five centuries of "transfiguration" in which the spirit of the church entered the state, preparing the world for society, daughter of the church.

Theological and historical chapters alternate as the changes in the hearts and minds of believing souls work changes in the visible church. There are moving tributes to Wittig's (and Rosenstock-Huessy's) spiritual ancestors whose "failures" opened up new avenues to the life of the spirit—Cyprian, Abelard, and Paracelsus. The authors' voices also alternate, approaching their common goal in syncopated rhythm. The antiphony creates a unique voice for the book (as the effect of a single voice speaking over a span of time does for *The Wedding of War and Revolution* and *The Speech of Mankind*). It resembles conversation, but whereas in the course of the Rosenzweig-Rosenstock-Huessy correspondence the two men first discover their differences, in *The Age of the Church* the two authors bear witness to the discovery of their unanimity.

> We have both sat at the table of the church we speak of in this book...the outsider was invited in, and the insider turned out, so that both could see from inside and outside. We met at the door and knew at once that we were friends...as different as our languages were, they became one language.[3]

Though he recognized the historical role of the Christian Church in shaping his own world, Rosenzweig remained a Jew. In spite of his excommunication and his defense of the unity of the entire Christian family, Wittig remained a steadfast Catholic. He and Rosenstock-Huessy felt indebted to the *whole* of the Christian tradition. *The Age of the Church* is the history of the church as the community of believing souls, the defense of the spirit-of-all-ages against the spirit of any one age; it looks forward to the "una sancta" taking shape in society. As Rosenstock-Huessy was to write later, "In the future every man will have to be a Jew, a Christian, and a pagan...Man is...threefold in God's image."[4]

The third volume is entitled "Day-to-Day" and contains documents pertaining to the "Wittig case." The first entries are friendly notes about early works of Wittig's from his bishop, Cardinal Bertram. Even after the Easter story *The Redeemed* appeared in *Hochland* (April 1922) and a parish priest demanded that the Cardinal take an official position on the story and its treatment of confession, he only urged Wittig to be more scientifically exact in his treatment of doctrine. But a week later Cardinal Bertram asked Wittig to renounce the story and to resign as head of the Catholic student organization. In May a Dr. Gisler attacked Wittig as *Luther redivivus.* The Cardinal then wrote the Cathedral provost that the article "would probably cause serious deliberation at the Holy See" and that he would ask Wittig to make an "unambiguous declaration of his regret and complete submission to the teaching of the holy Catholic church."[5]

3. Eugen Rosenstock/Joseph Wittig, *Das Alter der Kirche* (Berlin: Verlag Lambert Schneider, 1927), vol. I, p. ix.

4. Eugen Rosenstock-Huessy, *Das Geheimnis der Universität* (Stuttgart: Verlag W. Kohlhammer, 1958), p. 53.

5. Eugen Rosenstock/Joseph Wittig, *Das Alter der Kirche*, vol. III, p. 15.

Wittig complied. He also answered Dr. Gisler with *My Redeemed in Penance, Struggle, and Defense,* published in Habelschwerdt, whereupon the Habelschwerdt authorities were instructed never to give any book of Wittig's the *imprimatur* without first consulting the diocese of Breslau. In the fall of 1923, the Cardinal agreed to sponsor a week of seminars in Neisse on condition that Wittig's invitation to speak be withdrawn. The Vatican served Wittig with a *grave ammonizione* for having published without the *imprimatur* (mistakenly: the book in question was not Wittig's and the two essays of his that were included had already been approved for publication in Catholic magazines). But the Cardinal informed the catholic theological faculty only of the *grave ammonizione.* In fact, he showed a remarkable eagerness to publicize each move against Wittig throughout the affair. He denied the *imprimatur* to *Jesus' Life* and saw to it that the *imprimatur* tentatively granted in Passau was withdrawn. Wittig finally decided to publish without it.

He repeatedly offered to retract any specific section of his work that was proven as odds with church doctrine, but refused to renounce his work *in toto* as it expressed a lifetime of faith. He begged the Cardinal to take some action in his defense, to lay the facts of the matter before the Holy See. He even furnished a Latin translation of one of his letters at the Cardinal's request, but it was never forwarded to Rome. The Cardinal refused to defend him, and he was never allowed to defend himself.

In July of 1925 Wittig's books were placed on the Index and he was ordered to retake the *professio tridentina* and the antimodernist oath. He refused, on the grounds that he had not broken his original oaths. In the ensuing uproar he felt that he had no choice but to take a leave of absence from the University.

Rosenstock-Huessy published an appeal attacking the Church for stifling the new growth of faith and prophesying that in its lovelessness the Church would become an empty shell–Religio Depopulata. When Wittig's leave of absence showed no sign of ending, Rosenstock-Huessy submitted Wittig's request for retirement to the government, which responded by dismissing him. Dismissal meant that Wittig would lose his rights as a faculty member and his salary. On May 14th, 1926, after several weeks of correspondence, the Prussian Ministry of State withdrew the dismissal and granted Wittig *emeritus* status. On the same day Cardinal Bertram gave Wittig ten days to take the *professio fidei* and the antimodernist oath and to submit a statement unconditionally renouncing all parts of his writings judged erroneous by the Holy Office. Until the Holy Office specified which parts of his work it judged erroneous, replied Wittig, he would renounce nothing. And he would repeat no oaths. The Cardinal published the excommunication decree in the official Church paper, and it was reprinted all over Germany. Wittig himself was never officially notified.

What had caused all the uproar? Anca gave me a copy of *The Redeemed* to read. The story asks: if Christ really redeemed us by dying for our sins, why aren't we happier about it? Why so much anxiety about sin and confession? Wittig remembers a sermon he once heard in a country church. Man is not responsible for *what* happens, says the preacher, *what* happens is God's will. Man is responsible for his intentions in what happens; if he acts in good conscience he is guiltless before God. Should he err, his own sincere repentance is the only condition for God's pardon; confession and absolution follow as outward symbols. We really are redeemed, says Wittig, if we will only believe it. The orthodoxy of Wittig's portrayal of redemption, the Church, and the universal priesthood have been painstakingly established in recent years.[6] The Second Vatican Council defined the Church in terms close to Wittig's. John XXIII is supposed to have said that if he had been Pope then, there would have been no "Wittig case." But in the 1920s a less expansive spirit reigned. Perhaps it is the nature of a bureaucracy to enforce the letter at the expense of the spirit of the law; but why didn't the Holy Office specify what Wittig should recant? The books in question are not theological treatises, but stories of rural life, full of love for the Church and, in the case of *The Redeemed*, trying to win back the disaffected who had left the Church. No point in *The Redeemed* was ever officially cited as contrary to doctrine; Dr. Gisler heard the echo of Luther's *sola fides*, but not of the unimpeachably Catholic Augustine's *ama et fac quod vis*.

A man of less integrity might have re-sworn the oaths and thought nothing of it, or simply agreed to be silenced. But Wittig could not. Certainly the Cardinal's silence, especially his refusal to clarify the matter of the mistaken *ammonizione*, prejudiced the Holy Office against Wittig, as his interference when the bishop of Passau found Wittig's book unobjectionable forced Wittig to commit the offense of which he had been falsely accused. At the first sign of trouble, and the possibility that the trouble might bring Rome's attention to his diocese, the Cardinal turned on Wittig. The tone of his letters changes quickly; by the time of the Neisse seminars, his

---

6. See Kampmann and Padberg's uneven *Der Fall Joseph Wittig, fünfzig Jahre danach* (Paderborn: Ferdinand Schöningh, 1975).

attitude had become one of obvious hostility (as it was to remain for twenty years). Why didn't he forward Wittig's Latin letter after he requested it? It is hard not to see the "Wittig case" as the result of a weak and insecure man holding an office in which a stronger man might have held up the machinery of bureaucratic injustice.

After graduating from college, I packed a knapsack of books and headed for Berlin only to discover that my supposed employers had no work for me. I still do not know how the misunderstanding arose. I was miserable, but, relying on the patience of my hosts, I stayed and read. I read most of my grandfather's books, his correspondence with Rosenzweig, Wittig's *Novel with God,* as well as Heine, Balzac, and the Bible. As I read *The Speech of Mankind,* I found myself saying "That's right" and "Of course" over and over again. Enough of what I read found confirmation in my own experience for me to accept the rest on faith. If the book had not been written for me, at least it spoke directly to me. And one day in November I reached the chapter on the "morbus graecus," the worship of genius and the abstract, only to realize with a shock that here I was not only spoken to but spoken of. I was sorely ashamed; I looked back at twelve years of my life with the strange conviction that an era had ended. Augustine writes that the seeds of his conversion were planted long before they sprouted into consciousness. The seeds of my awakening were sown the summer I met Anca and listened to the tapes, but the sprouts came only after three years of inner turmoil and a complete humiliation of my spirit. Ever since that November, I have believed in the resurrection.

Novel with God

The posthumous *Novel with God* describes Wittig's own night of the soul; it is a journal of the daily trials of life toward the end of the war, looking back in bitterness at the years since his excommunication. When he was driven out of the Church, he returned to Neusorge, built a house, and sent roots deep into the soil of county Glatz. He married Bianca Geisler, and they raised their children as Catholics. But though his house stood in the landscape he had described so lovingly in his books, he longed for his "true home" in the Church. By the time he wrote the *Novel,* Wittig was old, suffering from insomnia, depression, and eventually sleeping pill poisoning. He developed a horror of dying outside the church since a secular burial meant a Nazi funeral service. Cardinal Bertram, himself almost ninety, pursued Wittig with horrible dedication to the end: he agreed to receive Wittig into the Church on condition that he leave his wife and family and move to an area where no one knew his name or history. When Anca reminded the vicar apostolic of the diocese that other married priests had been permitted to take communion as laymen, he replied that Wittig was too visible to the Protestant community for the Church to permit it. In the bitter year 1945, Wittig turned against the image of an omnipotent God and saw God only in the weak and helpless. He saw that the God whose Church had condemned him, the *ens a se* of the theologians, was indeed dead.

The end of the war brought no relief. Never, he wrote, in all his family's generations of poverty had they known such degradation and want. Yet when the forced evacuation began, he could not bring himself to leave. Anca bribed the community secretary and they were allowed to remain in Neusorge even after the second and third transports had left. On March 9, 1946 they received a letter with a telegram inside: "Joseph Wittig free of excommunication." Free without condition. He had come "home," but only just before he had to leave the house which had been his refuge in exile. The family joined the last transport from Glatz, and arrived in Westphalia after nine days in a cattle car. They were sent on to Göhrde in the Lüneburger Heath, where, on the day before their move to a permanent home in Meschede, Wittig died. The last journal entry describes their isolation, twenty miles from "world, church, or school":

> I am finished with sorrow and speculation...God has fulfilled our bishop's words...God left me my family though I had to leave the house I designed and built with my own hands; God fulfills everything said or asked in his name. But then, before he died, the bishop too had to leave his house and domain.[7]

The book ends with a hymn of thanksgiving.

Though awed by Rosenstock-Huessy's spirit, I still mistrusted him because it seemed that he was asking me to abandon one system for another–his own. But the testimony of Joseph and Anca Wittig, and especially of Anna Henke, a truly wise woman who had been my grandfather's Breslau housekeeper, convinced me that there was more to what Rosenstock-Huessy offered than a mere system. The cross of reality is not some Procrustean rule to be applied to life, but a recognition of the form inherent in life, in the free responses of God's creatures. To act as a full human being is to decide in any hour whether to answer the call of the past or the future, whether

7. Joseph Wittig, *Roman mit Gott* (Stuttgart: Ehrenfried Klotz Verlag, 1950), p. 228.

to be inside or outside a given group; we have all experienced the procession from "hot blood" to "cold print" as the events of our lives were conjugated through us. My grandfather always insisted that a bride on her wedding day knew as much of the power of speech as he did. And so, armed against the Greek disease, I went to New York to become a set designer.

Höregott

When I returned to Meschede in January of 1979 to celebrate Wittig's 100th birthday, Anca loaned me her copy of *Höregott*, a book rightly subtitled "a book about spirit and faith." Höregott, the Wittigs' first child, died after only four days of life, but his story fills the whole book. It starts with Wittig carving a cradle for his unborn child, and then jumps back: to Wittig's first attempts to write, to the publication of *The Redeemed* and the end of his former life, to the new life offered him in Bianca Geisler's love, to the birth and death of little Höregott himself. The book ends with the child's funeral and Wittig's decision to tell the story.

Wittig was ordained in 1903, spent a year as chaplain in Lauban and two years on an imperial scholarship to the German Campo Santo in Rome. Enemies of his Breslau teacher Max Sdralek blocked Wittig's nomination as "ausserordentlicher" professor of church history, so he spent three years as a parish priest in Breslau. In 1911 he was named "ordentlicher" professor of church history, early Christian art, and history of Christian literature.

He had seen too much as a priest to be just a professor, and in 1914 he began writing for the magazine *Heliand* under the name Johannes Strangfeld. The pseudonym was intended to protect the Catholic theological faculty from embarrassment, but his style and humour soon exposed the author as a Wittig in sheep's clothing. Rosenstock-Huessy was right to call him a psalmist. His stories present the truths and comfort he found in faith, equally free of theological subtleties and the platitudes of conventional "religious" literature. The stories became popular, especially with the members of the Catholic youth movement, and at first even with his bishop.

The furor over *The Redeemed* was well underway by the time Rosenstock-Huessy arrived in Breslau in 1923.

> My wife and I accepted in that year the call to the University...as if it were a descent into the grave. We went only because no legal basis of existence was open except this academic position...The blemish, or at least the ambiguity, of such an acceptance was bitterly felt...the comradeship with Wittig gave me a sense of still

having a foothold on Patmos.[8]

Wittig writes that on the first evening he spent with my grandparents, my grandfather gave him a copy of *The Wedding of War and Revolution*. Whole paragraphs of the final prophetic chapter are reprinted in *Höregott:*

> God has reserved the most secret vessel of life, woman, and today he honours her, destroys the division into earthly and heavenly love, and calls woman as woman to his divine work of love on earth...The hour of the daughter and the beloved is come...The empty pride of our spirit, the empty pride of our blood, belief in Church and State fade away before the unity of spirit and blood in love.[9]

> [Rosenstock-Huessy] took care not to influence my path, but he saw my path. He was not, as some spirits claimed, my seducer but my comfort. He did for me what no other man could do because he had, as no other man today has, the faith that God's omnipotence begins with the impossible. He endowed me with goods which by their worth won me other friends–from among his friends, but also from among his enemies. [From 1926 to 1928 Wittig edited the magazine *Die Kreatur* with Martin Buber and Victor von Weizsäcker.] And as thanks God made my heart into a crucible for my friend's word and being.[10]

Rosenstock-Huessy's work warns us of the stifling power of the academic spirit; Wittig's life was a defense of faith against legalism and the intellect, a defense of religion against Religion, which finds its fullest expression in *Höregott*. For me the book is Wittig's great achievement: he reminds us of the promised freedom of the children of God–that there is no law, human or divine, to which God will not eventually create an exception–and offers his life as proof.

His destiny deserves our respect and commemoration, but beyond that, Wittig is a figure of particular importance for those of us who would become "crucibles for [his] friend's word and being." Though his life broke the academic mold, Rosenstock-Huessy still spoke to an academic audience. He was always ready to recouch the substance of his books in everyday language for a particular audience, but we are now left with his books, in which he tends to address an imaginary audience capable of following his intellectual leaps. If his vision of

8. Eugen Rosenstock-Huessy, "Biblionomics," in *Bibliography/Biography* (New York: Four Wells, 1959), p. 18.

9. Eugen Rosenstock, *Die Hochzeit des Krieges und der Revolution* (Würzburg: Patmos Verlag, 1920), pp. 286-287.

10. Joseph Wittig, *Höregott* (Gotha: Leopold Klotz Verlag, 1929), p. 333.

the cross at the center of time and man at the crossroads of each hour moves us, we must hope to find it a wider audience.

It is not a question of perserving him as a "known intellectual figure." When I asked a friend of mine who was studying to be a rabbi if he had heard of Franz Rosenzweig he replied, "Oh yes, Rosenzweig is one of the great Jewish philosophers of the twentieth century." He knew of Rosenzweig, but did not know the *meaning* of the name. When I was in Berlin in 1975, I read a doctoral thesis on Rosenstock-Huessy. In her introduction the author complained of the difficulty she had faced reducing her subject to a card file. The thesis itself seemed to be little more than a tabulation of "series of three" and "series of four" in his work, once again without any idea WHY certain things come in threes and fours, or even acknowledging why *he* thought so: that God is threefold, and human experience four-fold.[11] We have to achieve comprehension as well as recognition; ideally we should evoke a response. The temptation is to provide a schematic introduction, a "Cliff Notes" of method: four dimensions, five spheres, and so on, but to do so is to run the risk of producing another document like that thesis.

Here Wittig can help us: perhaps not with his own books, which speak of and to a world which has disappeared, but with his ability to express what he and Rosenstock-Huessy believed in simple language and to make it accessible by relating large truths to small particulars in his own life. In the *Age of the Church*, Rosenstock-Huessy wrote that Paul brought Christ to the Gentiles by living what Christ had taught and teaching Christ's life. Perhaps these men's lives can provide the spine for a retelling of Rosenstock-Huessy's message.

We are already the third generation to hear the voice of Rosenstock-Huessy. We inherit the benefits of the unsung labour of translation and preservation; we are the generation whose task is to become "we". But new visions are necessary for our future. A fourth generation is rising, and to them Rosenstock-Huessy and Wittig may be no more than names. We to whom they are still living voices must somehow accomplish for this coming generation what Wittig and Rosenstock-Huessy accomplished between the wars: the translation of the Christian tradition into the language of a new age.[12]

11. For Rosenstock-Huessy's own view of the necessity of "four" to encompass the experience of reality, see *Soziologie* (Stuttgard: W. Kohlhammer Verlag, 1956), 2nd ed., vol. I, pp. 266 ff.

12. Since Wittig's works are not well-known, it might be helpful to list his major publications: *Das Papsttum* (1913), *Herrgottswissen von Wegrain und Strasse* (1922), *Das*

From Theology
to a Higher Sociology:
The Promise of
Eugen Rosenstock-Huessy

Clinton C. Gardner

We wish to be simply that short piece of cable which overcomes, faithfully, the gap between yesterday and tomorrow. Without such an entrance through the narrow door of time, the Spirit dies.[1]

In those words Eugen Rosenstock-Huessy sums up the project which he and Franz Rosenzweig, along with a number of other friends, undertook shortly after the First World War. It was a retranslation of the faith, an attempt to find universal and secular words to articulate what earlier ages had described in religious language.

Sometimes Rosenstock-Huessy has been accused of being "an occasional thinker" *(ein Gelegenheitsdenker)*, someone with flashes of insight but no substantial, coherent achievement. What I wish to do in this essay is to challenge that notion. I think it is possible to state, very simply, that Rosenstock-Huessy embarked early in his life on one great project, the translation of theology into a higher sociology. Further, that he elaborated a quite specific new "method" for this "new branch of knowledge," as he called it *(ein neue Wissenschaft)*.

While there is no one book of Rosenstock-Huessy's that presents the kernel of his thinking, undeniably his most significant work is *Out of Revolution: Autobiography of Western Man.* In that book, and in his two other major works, *Soziologie* and *Die Sprache des Menschengeschlechts (The Speech of Mankind)*, Rosenstock-Huessy reveals

Schicksal des Wenzel Böhm (1922), *Meine "Erlösten" in Busse, Kampf, und Wehr* (1923), *Leben Jesu in Palestina, Schlesien, und Anderswo* (1925), *Die Kirche im Waldwinkel* (1924), *Das Alter der Kirche* (1927, with Eugen Rosenstock-Huessy), *Der Ungläubige* (1928), *Höregott* (1929), *Aussichten und Wege* (1930), *Das verlorene Vaterunser* (1933), *Chronik der Stadt Neurode* (1937), and his posthumously published *Roman mit Gott* (1950).

1. Eugen Rosenstock-Huessy, Soziologie, vol. II (Stuttgard: Kohlhammer Verlag, 1958), p. 613; originally in *Hochzeit des Krieges und der Revolution* (Wurzburg: Patmos Verlag, 1920), p. 242.

his "speech method" and his vision of a higher sociology which might one day take over the task of theology, and at the same time replace today's "objective" social science with a science that acknowledged imperatives. His project, then, is reminiscent of Ludwig Feuerbach's: the "exalting" of anthropology into theology.[2] By taking that direction, his work stands in sharp contrast to that of Karl Barth. Rosenstock-Huessy summed up his differences with Barth when he wrote, "Karl Barth and the dialectical theologians claim that God appeared only once."[3] In other words, Barth focused all our attention *down* again on the New Testament story. Rosenstock-Huessy, by contrast, *widened* our focus out, so that one perceived how the historical millennia before Christ related to the millennia after him. How tribes and empires, Greeks and Jews, had become dead ends at Year Zero of our epoch. How Christ and his apostles translated those dead ends into new beginnings, becoming in effect the narrow middle in the hourglass of history. How each generation since that time has made its own continuing and necessary retranslation of the faith. In *Out of Revolution* he shows how even the French and Russian revolutions are part of that retranslation, since they, like the Reformation and the British Parliamentary Revolution, are responses to the imperatives established by the Catholic church in the middle ages.

Metanomics and The Speech Method

In the course of *Out of Revolution* Rosenstock-Huessy makes clear that he hopes the reader will perceive the book as more than a history. What he is writing, he tells us, is "an attempt by which history and science, law and theology, are joined into an indissoluble unit."[4] His epilogue envisions this "indissoluble unit" as a future sociology for which he offers the name "metanomics." Strangely, he does not even footnote the fact that he first described this new science in his *Soziologie, Vol. 1* (published in 1925, rewritten and expanded in 1956). In that book he first proposed the "speech method" or "Cross of Reality" as the appropriate method for a new science of man. Unlike contemporary science which imagines that we live in the bland two dimensions of time and space, "metanomics" would start

2. Ludwig Feuerbach, *The Essence of Christianity* (Harper & Row, Torchbook, 1957), p. xxxviii.

3. Eugen Rosenstock-Huessy, *Die Sprache des Menschengeschlechts* (Heidelberg: Lambert Schneider, 1963), vol. I, p. 696.

4. Rosenstock-Huessy, *Out of Revolution* (Morrow, 1938; Norwich, Vt.: Argo, 1969), p. 193.

with the realization that we really live at the center of a cross, the high-tension intersection of two spaces–subjective inner self and objective outer world–and two times–our future and our past. And it would start with the related realization that society today lives under the imperative of peace.

Perhaps Rosenstock-Huessy did not bother to footnote his more methodological *Soziologie* in *Out of Revolution* because the latter so clearly demonstrated, and thus eclipsed, what was only a proposal in 1925. Actually, the very first essay in which he suggested a new social method was *Angewandte Seelenkunde (An Applied Science of the Soul)* written as a letter to Franz Rosenzweig in 1916 and later published in 1924. Rosenstock-Huessy began his letter by pointing out that the German *"Seelenkunde"* could be translated either as simply "psychology" or as the much richer "science of the soul." He proceeds to ask if there is not a "grammar of the soul" which the new science of psycho-*logy* is overlooking precisely because of its "logical" approach:

> Is there, then, a grammar of the soul? Now, since certainly the word comes from the soul, and the truest word from the depths of the soul, and since we measure the power of speech by the degree of the soul's emotion...just as the mind has logic, so will the soul undoubtedly have "word-consciousness" as its inner struc-ture...Grammar is the key which unlocks the soul. Whoever wished to gain knowledge of the soul must probe the secrets of speech.[5]

His own probing of those secrets in that essay, in *Soziologie I*, and *Die Sprache des Menschengeschlechts*, (now partially available in English in *Speech and Reality* (Argo, 1970) and *The Origin of Speech* (Argo, 1981), took a direction which, up to a point, relate his "speech-thinking" with that of both Franz Rosenzweig and Martin Buber. The latter's *I and Thou*, published in 1923, is of course the best known statement of a "grammatical philosophy." Buber reveals precisely the poignancy and meaning of the realm in between the *I* and *Thou*. What arises in our minds, he says, is not a reflection of objective reality but a "spoken" reality which our dialogue with others and the world creates. Up to that point he and Rosenstock-Huessy agree. But where Buber's approach discloses a two-dimensional reality, Rosenstock-Huessy asks us whether our reality is not really four-dimensional.

Buber opens *I and Thou* with the statement: "To man the world is twofold, in accordance with his twofold attitude. The attitude of

5. Rosenstock-Huessy, *Die Sprache des Menschengeschlechts*, vol. I, p. 752.

man is twofold, in accordance with the twofold nature of the primary words which he speaks....The one primary word is the combination *I-Thou*. The other primary word is the combination *I-It*."[6] Now what is remarkable about this famous formulation is that it is not really "bound to time and nourished by time," as Rosenzweig described his and Rosenstock-Huessy's "new thinking."[7] Buber says as much when he writes "the world of *It* is set in the context of space and time. The world of *Thou* is not set in the context of either of these."[8] Buber's *Thou* is "timeless," because it refers to the "inner space" which we create through subjective speech, be it prayer or openness in dialogue with another. But even his world of *It*, on close examination, is not time-bound in the sense of an anticipated future and a preserved past. Buber's *It* really refers us to our "fourth" dimension, the outer space of the world around us.

Rosenstock-Huessy describes his larger understanding of our speech universe as follows:

> The correct, truly "existential" sequence is not *I-Thou* but *Thou-I*. In [my] view, Buber's *I-Thou* carries either the implication of a parity between the *I* and the *Thou*, or still worse, the implication that the *I* precedes the *Thou* in human experience. *Thou-I*, in contrast, quite accurately reflects an important reality that virtually everyone experiences, in one way or another—the fact that one is spoken *to*, one is nominated and addressed as a *Thou* (by one's parents, if no one else) before becoming an *I*....The soul must be called *Thou* before she can ever reply *I*, before she can ever speak of *us* and finally *It*. Through the four figures, *Thou, I, We, It*, the word walks through us. The word must call our name first.[9]

Now we are at the heart of Rosenstock-Huessy's insights, for the four "persons" which we become as we go through any important experience—*Thou, I, We, It* (the last also meaning he, she, or they)—correspond to the four primary grammatical moods, in that same order: imperative, subjunctive, narrative, and indicative (the subjunctive, as we shall see, he relates to the subjective *I*). And the most critical insight is that all significant events in social or personal life unfold in precisely that sequence, with the imperative or vocative always the starting point.

6. Martin Buber, *I and Thou* (New York: Charles Scribner's Sons, 1958), p. 3.

7. Nahum Glatzer, *Franz Rosenzweig: His Life and Thought* (New York: Schocken Books, 1961), p. 199.

8. Buber, *I and Thou*, p. 100.

9. Rosenstock-Huessy, *Judaism Despite Christianity* (Auburn: University of Alabama Press, 1969), pp. 69-70.

The Cross of Reality

The realization that Rosenstock-Huessy is not simply presenting some fresh insights concerning speech, but is proposing a new social method, may not become clear until we arrange the four grammatical forms of speech and the four persons on a diagram of the Cross of Reality. Then we can see the relationships, the sequences, the polarities, and indeed the conflicts, between our four speech orientations. The Cross of Reality is diagrammed as follows:

2. Inner Space created
by Subjective Speech
Example: "I"

3. Past Time created
by Narrative Speech
Example: "We"

1. Future Time
created by
Imperative
or
Vocative
Speech
Example:
"Thou"

4. Outward Space (the
World) created by
Objective Speech
Example: "He"

A concise way of describing how the speech method or Cross of Reality *works* as a new social method is to say that it explores future and past time and inner and outer space with the same confidence that the objective method of natural science has explored outer space. The speech method achieves this larger orientation by assigning *equal validity* to each of the four forms of speech. The Cross then shows us that any significant phenomenon involving human beings will always include these four forms of speech and contain these four time and space orientations. Further, it reveals why these orientations are normally established in the sequence of 1. Imperative or vocative, 2. Subjective, 3. Narrative, 4. Objective.

That sequence of speech we find repeated throughout our lives. Imperatives or vocatives set up fields of force toward the future, callings which demand a response. But we do not act or reply immediately; we retreat to our inner selves, that private space nourished by the speech of religion and the arts. Here our mood is conditional, in grammatical terms subjunctive, because we ask ourselves such questions as: "what would happen *were* I to go in this new direction?" When we are ready to act, to enter the stream of history, we speak out confidently, asserting ourselves. Finally, whatever we have created becomes fully visible to everybody. Objective speech ends that particular sequence, leaving us ready to hear a new calling.

It is vital to understand that we–any individual, group, or society–live and speak at the *center* of the Cross. Whenever we speak purposefully, we move from the inner space of our self to the outer space of the world. *At the same moment* we move from time past to time future. Significant speech, high speech, is what changes the times and spaces in which we live. By speech we anticipate future time and remember the past; by speech we collect ourselves inwardly or make ourselves heard outwardly. Times and spaces acquire meaning for us because we speak them into our lives. They form for us the cross of our reality.

Rosenstock-Huessy sums up the role of high speech in the present era as that of sychronizing antagonistic "distemporaries," by which he means creating peace in society.[10]

The First Speech-Thinker

Now I should cite the testimony, seldom noted, of Rosenstock-Huessy, Rosenzweig, and Buber that *all three* felt indebted to Ludwig Feuerbach. As Rosenstock-Huessy expressed it, "Ludwig Feuerbach, one hundred years ago was the first to start a grammatical philosophy of man. He was misunderstood by his contemporaries, especially by Karl Marx."[11] Rosenzweig wrote of the speech method in his essay "The New Thinking": "Whatever *The Star of Redemption* (his widely acclaimed book of 1921) can do to renew our ways of thinking is concentrated in this method. Ludwig Feuerbach was the first to discover it."[12] Finally, Buber says: "I myself in my youth was given a decisive impetus by Feuerbach....Never before has a philosophical anthropology been so emphatically demanded."[13] It is intriguing that Feuerbach, generally considered "the spiritual father of Marxism," should also have been so important to the three "speech-thinkers."

When Rosenstock-Huessy, Rosenzweig, and Buber acknowledge their debt to Feuerbach, they certainly do not mean to appropriate his naive humanism. As Hans Ehrenberg, one of their friends and

10. Eugen Rosenstock-Huessy, *Speech and Reality* (Norwich, Vt.: Argo Books, 1970), p. 44.

11. Rosenstock-Huessy, *Speech and Reality*, p. 9.

12. Glatzer, ed., *Franz Rosenzweig, His Life and Thought*, p. 200.

13. Martin Buber, *Between Man and Man* (New York: Macmillan Co., 1965), pp. 147-148.

cohorts, expressed it, Feuerbach was "a true child of his century, a non-knower of death and a mis-knower of evil."[14] One might say that his successors reproached Feuerbach, not so much for a lack of faith as for being overconfident. In concluding that God, the Trinity and the word of God are "not foreign but native mysteries, the mysteries of human nature," Feuerbach implied that God's powers–or our highest powers–are *given* in the natural order of things.[15] Where Rosenstock-Huessy and his friends correct their predecessor is in their realization that these powers are *not* given–but *achieved*. We achieve them as gifts from the past, through what religion calls "grace."

Rosenstock-Huessy called us "the up-hill animal" because we *can* go uphill, not because we are genetically programmed to do so. Our ability to speak in a timely, true, and creative manner is not inherent in us but is something which must be constantly renewed in each generation. Our super-natural power is our ability to speak beyond our own self-interest, beyond our in-group's self-interest, to speak and act in the interest of all humanity–past, present, and future. By such speech we *change* ourselves and our times. But this super-natural is not the invasion by an other-worldly power of the this-worldly order, as religious language has often expressed it. There Feuerbach's insight, as expressed in *The Essence of Christianity*, was right on target.

What Rosenstock-Huessy and his friends found inspiring in Feuerbach was not only that "one-world" view. It was also Feuerbach's prophetic call for an end to idealistic philosophy, as brought to a head by Hegel, and especially his vision of a higher social science based on grammar, a science which would embrace both the natural sciences and theology. Further, they found in Feuerbach certain small but vital hints for establishing the new grammatical method.

This brings us back to Rosenstock-Huessy's enigmatic statement that Feuerbach "was misunderstood by his contemporaries, especially by Karl Marx." The critical hints at an entirely new way of thinking, a method based on speech, these men found in such formulations of Feuerbach's as:

> The single man for himself possesses the essence of man neither in himself as a moral being nor in himself as a thinking being. The essence of man is contained only in the community and unity

14. Feuerbach, *The Essence of Christianity*, p. xxviii. Ehrenberg is quoted here by Karl Barth.
15. Ibid., p. xxxviii.

of man with man; It is a unity, however, which rests only on the reality of the distinction between I and thou.[16]

Here, and in similar statements, Feuerbach began thinking in terms of our grammatical persons, laying the foundations for Buber's *I and Thou.* Feuerbach elaborates on speech itself when he writes:

A divine impulse this–a divine power, the power of words....The word guides to all truth, unfolds all mysteries, reveals the unseen, makes present and past and the future, defines the infinite, perpetuates the transient....The Word of God is supposed to be distinguished from the human word in that it is no transient breath, but an imparted being. But does not the word of man also contain the being of man, his imparted self–at least when it is a true word?[17]

Now the prophet of Marxist "materialism" sounds almost too theological, but he seems to be anticipating Rosenstock-Huessy's interpretation of "the speech of mankind" as what theology calls the Spirit. Feuerbach and Rosenstock-Huessy bring our comprehension of spirit down to earth. Contrary to the theological view, spirit is not above us. Nor is it immanent in all the world, as pantheism would have it. Instead, spirit is what we experience with every true word that we utter; it is all-creative human speech.

To elaborate a bit on that, when we lie, are cynical, or gossip, we abuse our powers of speech, and sin against the Spirit. When we merely chatter, our speech is in neutral–not much to do with the Third Person. But whenever we speak as representatives of all humanity–and this is the highest purpose of speech–our speech is precisely the action of the Spirit.

To sum up, what Christian theology calls the Holy Spirit, the Third Person of the undivided Trinity, a Person which is both God himself and yet an aspect of God, may also be something as common as the voice of God in each of us. And this Spirit in us may be nothing more remarkable than any word which we utter when we speak seriously and from our heart. What all religions call Spirit (for they all have this category) is simply the higher form of speech spoken by the whole human race and made audible in the words of every good man or woman.

16. Ludwig Feuerbach, *Principles of the Philosophy of the Future* (Indianapolis: Bobbs-Merrill, 1966), p. 71.
17. Feuerbach, *The Essence of Christianity,* pp. 78-79.

The Trinity in Secular Terms

Strangely, Feuerbach named just *two* specific "persons" in his secularization of the Trinity: "I and Thou" (He implied that the "third person" was the Spirit linking these two). But then Rosenstock-Huessy named *four* persons when he wrote: "The soul must be called *Thou* before she can ever reply *I*, before she can ever speak of *us* and finally *It*. Through the four figures, *Thou, I, We, It*, the Word walks through us." It was many years after I had read that in my studies with Rosenstock-Huessy that it finally began to dawn on me that he was talking about the action of the Trinity–without ever saying so. Then I realized that the *first three* of those four figures–*Thou, I, We*–correspond to the three persons of the Trinity: the Spirit's *Thou* inspires us in the imperative, the Son's *I* is our subjective reply, and we speak the Father's *We* as we participate in the narrative of creation. Finally, there is a fourth orientation: we also speak in the world of our daily experience–objectively.

As I pursued that train of thought, it seemed to me that the name "God" does not refer to "a being who exists" but to that trinity of powers which we assume as we speak our times and spaces into a whole. We represent and complete the Trinity's actions as we bring these divine powers down to the earth of the objective world. What religion calls the actions within the Trinity, or between the Trinity and worldly persons, are the same actions revealed by our daily, historical experience of speaking in the real world of times and spaces. The three divine Persons, which were once known to us as items of *belief*, could now be recognized as categories of being and becoming fully human. That means speaking beyond the limited frame of our "natural" body as the mammal *homo sapiens*.

To put it more succinctly, the name God may not refer to the *object* of our religious thought. It may refer to what we are capable of representing when we bring reality to full expression in the world. In that case, God does not "exist"; he only "speaks," and he speaks primarily in man.

What I have been writing above now cries out to be shown on the Cross of Reality. *Thou, I, We, He*–the Word walks through us. These four persons of grammar can be recognized as the three *Persons* of the Trinity, plus the world. Systematically expressed:

1.   The Spirit's imperative *Thou* beckons us toward the future. Vocative speech is the source of all new inspiration or revelation. This *begins* any experience.

2.   The Son's subjective *I* then turns us toward our inner self. Subjective speech makes us aware of our personal responsibility for

bringing our inspirations down to earth and thus redeeming the world.

3. The Father's *We* next ties us into our historical role. Narrative speech links us with our past, with all the generative powers of creation.

4. The world's objective *He* (she or they) records and analyzes the first three acts. Objective speech enables us to understand our first three orientations. What had seemed divine acts now seem mere facts. The experience is over, and we are free to be inspired again.

At the end of *Die Sprache des Menschengeschlechts*, Rosenstock-Huessy makes a remarkable statement that sums up those four steps:

> The Son establishes the proper relationship between the spoken word and the lived life. Words should be commands that are given and promises that are made. Life consists of commands that are carried out and prophecies that are fulfilled. This, we saw, is the real goal of all speech and ritual since man first spoke.[18]

Without mentioning the Cross of Reality, Rosenstock-Huessy has managed here to link it with the Trinity in terms of what happens as we listen and speak. "The spoken word," "commands" and "prophecies" are how we hear the Spirit's imperatives. "Promises made" and "prophecies fulfilled" are our subjective replies as Son. "Ritual" refers to the narrative ceremonies through which we repeat creation's story. And "the lived life" refers to how we embody in the world, and thus complete, the three previous forms of speech.

I hope it is clear that these formulations are not a Gnostic schematizing of the mysteries. If anything, they should emphasize why the Trinity will always remain a mystery, even when we understand it in a non-religious sense. Feuerbach did not remove the veil. For him the Trinity remained "the mystery of social life." Nicolas Berdyaev says the same when he writes: "The life of man and of the world is an inner moment of the mystery of the Trinity."[19]

The mystery remains in the sense that it describes an active process, and one cannot predict the outcome of such a process. At any time, between any two or three persons, in any group, new inspiration may take an unexpected turn. It remains the mystery of interpreting the strange past, experiencing the creative present, and having faith in the outcome of the unknown future. It is our participation in this process that separates us from the natural, objective

---

18. Rosenstock-Huessy, *Die Sprache des Menschengeschlechts*, vol. II, p. 903.

19. Donald A. Lowrie, ed., *Christian Existentialism: A Berdyaev Anthology* (Harper & Row, Torchbook, 1965), p. 53.

world, that makes us "the uphill animal."

A Third Language

My use of Rosenstock-Huessy's Cross of Reality to describe the Trinity in secular terms is only a suggestion of comparable translations between religious and secular language which one finds throughout his writings on history, sociology, psychology, and theology. His remarkable ability to speak both languages, particularly as expressed in *Out of Revolution,* gives us many fresh starting points, not the least being in the realm of Christian-Communist dialogue. One might describe his project as the search for a "third" language beyond those of religion and science.

That "third language," which Franz Rosenzweig described at its birth as "the new thinking," Rosenstock-Huessy saw as eventually becoming an essential "new branch of knowledge." As theology had served the first half of the past millennium, and as natural science had served the last five hundred years, so a higher sociology might serve to make peace among the many different people in our emerging global society.

The Problem of American History in
Out of Revolution

Stanley Johannesen

The essay that follows is an attempt to frame a Rosenstockian answer to a classical question in American thought: What is an American? Rosenstock himself addressed this question in *Out of Revolution,* but the section devoted specifically to the American historical experience is from many points of view unsatisfactory and incomplete.[1]

It was not Rosenstock's intention, of course, either to pose or to answer any question about the American identity from the usual standpoint of such questions in America, that is from an initial assumption of uniqueness, as though it must be assumed that the American character flows from radically new moral premises. Because Rosenstock's attention was mainly fixed on what he regarded as the central dramas of European revolution, and because his view of revolution entailed the idea that particular revolutions are revolutionary because they create new human types, he could scarcely have been impressed with this standard American claim. New men are not made in new worlds, but in the ripening experience of the old world.

About his view of the American experience, Rosenstock was unequivocal. He saw the newness of America rather in the light of spiritual infancy than in connection with the major advances of European civilization. "Birth is not rebirth"; "A far distant colony does not make a revolution merely by becoming independent. Cutting the umbilical cord of the new-born child is no revolution!" "Was the American Revolution," Rosenstock asks, "a true revolution, with revolutionary effects, effects that were permanent and that forecast a particular form of life?" No, the Revolution was an "opposition against the abuses of the last total revolution (i.e., the English Revolution)," and a "precursor revolution" which led directly to the French Revolution.[2]

---

1. Eugen Rosenstock-Huessy, *Out of Revolution: Autobiography of Western Man* (Norwich, Vt., 1969), pp. 643-686.

Rosenstock's view of the character of the American Revolution, beginning with one of his characteristic aphorisms, must be quoted in full:

> The sound of the axe is the natural philosophy of America....Facts, facts, facts, are the reality in a new world. Men, men, men, are the need of a pioneering group. It is not the salon, not a feminine culture, but bosses who run America. Not inspired writers but shrewd politicians, not genius, but self-made men, are what is wanted.
>
> Now all this does not vary greatly from the English type. The pioneer is necessarily harsher, coarser, more ruthless than the fighting gentleman; but he is by no means his antitype, as the Frenchman is. Thus no really new type was created by the American Revolution....A certain variation is attempted, but no really new variety of man is produced, based on a new aspect of the human soul.[3]

It is not difficult to quarrel with some of this. The American Revolution, for one thing, was an urban affair, the product of communities old enough to have surplusses of time and energy for cultivated activity. The Revolution was itself such an activity. Its leaders were clergymen and lawyers, students of history and law, men whose speech was formed not by the sounds of the frontier but by classical education. It is not without interest that Rosenstock's descriptive phrases are drawn from the rhetoric of reformist opposition to the political culture of late nineteenth-century America ("bosses," "politicians," "self-made men"), and from European romantic and conservative idealizations of elite culture ("the salon," "inspired writers," "genius"). The coarsening of social and political standards in the republic was real enough, but it happened much later than Rosenstock implies. Tocqueville described this coarsening, and ascribed it to the passion for equality he observed in Jacksonian America. Like Rosenstock after him, and many other European aristocratic observers, Tocqueville was fascinated and repelled by the American democrat; struck most of all, as an aristocrat, by what to him was the absence of government itself, and by the spectacle of a large society entirely devoid of cultural brilliance. But Tocqueville was near enough to the event to realize that the achievement of the Revolution, the autonomy of a republic based on Puritan political ideals and a slave economy, was precisely what was endangered by

2. Ibid., pp. 643, 657-658.
3. Ibid., p. 659.

rampant equality, something the Fathers had not foreseen. The culture of the frontier, insofar as one may speak of such a thing, did not create the Revolution; it rather subverted in some measure the republican institutions created by the Revolution.

Rosenstock comes closer to the truth of the matter when he remarks that the type of the American revolutionary bears a family resemblance to the type of the English Revolution, although the relationship is certainly not quite as Rosenstock says, one of crude imitation of the model. In fact the farmer-warrior ideal of the American Revolution, the ideal expressed, for example, in the name of the Society of the Cincinnati, is both Horatian and English in derivation. If it is not the culmination of the type, it is at least the last distinguished representative. We shall want to return, actually, to this Rosenstockian character, the "fighting gentleman," in his American embodiment, but we need first to say something more concerning Rosenstock's final verdict on the American as a social type: "A certain variation is attempted, but no really new variety of man is produced, based on a new aspect of the human soul."

To leave it at that is to allow Rosenstock the prejudices of high cultural self-consciousness without challenge: to allow that the answer to this question of human types–in Rosenstock's sense, a "really new variety of man...based on a new aspect of the human soul"–must be sought in the mimetic and creative self-realizing activities of cultural elites, activities in which individual, not to say egocentric, forms of argument and explanation take precedence over collective mentality. Collective mentalities have also their mimetic and creative self-realizing activities. Repetition and variation have everywhere in culture the potential for revolutionary transformation. What I should like to argue in the remainder of this essay is that there were processes of revolutionary change, mimetic and creative self-actualizing processes, in America, at levels of popular mentality, broader and deeper than the language of the revolutionary leaders.[4]

The human type that the American Revolution added to the stock of human types is the dissenter. Not the dissenter of English history: the dissenter as survivor. The variation that makes the Rosenstockian "new variety of man" is the dissenter as inheritor, the dissenter as an autonomous political personality. This is the figure caricatured by Tocqueville as the conforming democrat, and by

4. James Henretta, "Families and Farms: *Mentalité* in Pre-Industrial America," *William & Mary Quarterly* 35 (1978):3-32.

Rosenstock as the frontiersman. All caricatures that are effective, that stick to their prototypes, have a measure of truth in them. But these have obscured the specific spiritual quality of the American dissenter.

Here we must return to Rosenstock for direction. Rosenstock quotes John Adams in 1818 on the meaning of the Revolution: "The Revolution was in the minds and hearts of the people; a change in the religious sentiments of their duties and obligations."[5] So far, this is a serviceable description of the religious dissenter in America. It notices the religious basis of nationality, and it notices that the operative religious features are those pertinent to a condition of *felt* obligation. The American people switched their allegiance on the basis of religious *feeling*. The American is a man whose associations and duties are elected by himself, and one for whom the pattern of political association is derived from the pattern of his worship. Lest we miss this last implication Adams goes on to say that the change in religious sentiment was a change in the nature of colonial prayers!

But then Adams cannot resist boasting, and in the end contradicting himself. He goes on to say that the people one day ceased "to pray for the king and queen and all the royal family, and all in authority under them," and came rather to think "it their duty to pray for the Continental Congress and all the thirteen State Congresses." We may doubt that any but Anglican parishes did very much of the former, or that anyone did much of the latter at any time. The contradiction comes when Adams, so anxious to underscore the labours of the revolutionary leaders, makes it seem as though there had been no concerted and prior revolution of sentiment at all:

> The colonies had grown up under constitutions of government–so different, there were so great a variety of religions, they were composed of so many different nations, their customs, manners and habits had so little resemblance, and their intercourse had been so rare, and their knowledge of each other so imperfect, that to unite them in the same principles in theory and the same system of action, was certainly a very difficult enterprise.[6]

Rosenstock quotes this lengthy passage with sympathy and approval, and notes that "the warmth of the old prayers of the pioneers for their European homes could not simply be transferred to the Continental Congress." "To pray for Congress was a poor thing; it meant, in effect, that one no longer prayed at all." "Let us

5. Rosenstock-Huessy, p. 660.
6. Ibid., pp. 660-661.

keep in mind this hollow, incomplete religious situation and the sudden shrinking, the crippling of the idea of 'Commonwealth.'"

Contrary to Rosenstock, one might say that Adams and his colleagues in the legislatures and the public press used effectively the language of "Commonwealth" (Adams' "principles in theory," and "system of action," which he thought Americans slow to catch), because the religious situation was pregnant with Revolution. That is, Rosenstock is profoundly right to seize on the issue of prayer, and it may be that to pray for Congress is a poor thing, but it is a mistake to stop the inquiry into forms of prayer with this question of an appropriate substitute for the king in the prayers of Christians.

Even though we criticize Rosenstock's foreshortening of American history, his reading of the frontier democrat back into the English period of America's identity, and his serious underestimation of the strength of the native religious tradition in the colonies (he seems unaware of the Great Awakening, for example), we are deeply in his debt for setting before us rigorous standards by which any claim for a spiritual character in a race of men must be judged, if this char-acter is to be taken seriously in a universal history. Rosenstock himself believed that what the American Revolution created was a Noah's ark for the rescue of all the precious human types of all the revolutions past and to come. He further believed that this American ark was identified in the minds of post-Revolutionary Americans with Nature herself, that the names of "state," or "nation," or "empire," "reduce America's stature to the petty level of political institutions," and "swim on the surface of America's political talk."[7] Yet we must see that the problem of American history is thereby only pushed further back into the past. A Noah's ark argues a Noah, a figure able to disentangle himself from the ready-made formulas given to him by his birth and his society. Noah had to become a political type before he could build an ark. Noah was a dissenter before he was a patriarch. Any such figure who speaks a word of dissent in a new context, and creates a new world of it, is a revolutionary type in Rosenstock's sense. He passes muster by Rosenstock's own standards. Noah may or may not have prayed for his king, and those having authority under him. But the important part of his prayers, could we recover them, would lie in the revaluation of self implicit in the total gestural system of worship and work, the way word and action contrived to bind the self to a historical task. This is a self-actualizing and self-annointing process. Rosenstock feels that any such process is trivial that is not connected with the great work of

7. Ibid., pp. 660, 675 and 680ff.

the maturing of civilization, by adding to the stock of universal human types. But if America is in any sense a necessary repository of the types of man, as Rosenstock says it is, then the mentality which made this repository possible must be itself one of the great human types. This type is John Adams "people," who wrought "a change in their religious sentiments of their duties and obligations."

Lionel Rothkrug's recent study of medieval and early modern religious practices argues that Christianity as a religion was formed over the centuries by the work of converting, and then civilising, the populations of Europe. At the heart of this process lay succeeding definitions of community as expressed in attitudes towards the dead, and in practices that defined relationships between the dead and the living.[8] Extrapolating only very slightly from his argument, one may say that there have been two major "economies" that have dominated the spiritual vision of the Christianized West. One of these, that we conventionally call medieval, was an atemporal plenitude of souls, governed by a penitential apparatus that was largely public in nature. Some of its most visible features were the traffic in relics, and the monastic social ideal. This economy was superceded by an economy in which penitential concerns were privatized and came to fill a distinctive temporality–a time-world variously conceived in relation to pilgrimage, to purgatory, or to highly personal and subjective salvation-sequences involving "works," or penance, or to morphologies of salvation psychologically defined.

The magisterial myth-dogmas that have dominated orthodox Christian conceptions of time in this extraterrestrial mode are three: the extended but finite time of purgatory; the mysterious time of the history of God's decrees of election and reprobation; and the Christocentric time of redemption-justification. But even as penitential concerns were hived off of the spatial world occupied by social structure, that common-sense world of men took on its own temporal significance: In the flowering of interest in biblical prophecy; in dispensationalism; in apocalyptic and millennial thinking; and also in the formation of those communities of memory that re-created civic life in Europe in modern times.

An interesting problem for the Christian West, however, is the question (which worried Augustine in the opening books of *The City of God*), whether the revival of the culture of pagan antiquity is in

8. Lionel Rothkrug, *Religious Practices and Collective Perceptions: Hidden Homologies in the Renaissance and Reformation* (Waterloo, Ontario, 1980).

itself sufficient to recreate the moral basis of civic life. Such revivals of civic humanism have been significant enough in the history of the West, and the question of their importance to modern political culture has been raised again recently in the remarkable synthesis of J.G.A. Pocock, *The Machiavellian Moment,* and in his new edition of Harrington's political writings.[9] The argument is subtle and elusive, but the gist of it for our purposes is that the American Revolution, far from being the opening episode in an age of revolutions, was in fact the closing act in a long moral and intellectual quest that began with the great Florentine humanists, and continued in the thought of the neo-machiavellian James Harrington and his English followers down into the eighteenth century. The whole point is worth pursuing here, because the classical basis of American political culture is frequently emphasized by historians, and we want to put that into proper relationship with what we will argue is the Christian basis of American community.

The problem that the classical tradition addressed itself to, Pocock points out, was the apparent inevitability of the decline of political societies, no matter how auspicious their beginnings, or glorious the day of their zenith. It had been universally agreed in antiquity that this decline was due to the corruption of manners among a people, and the stultifying of political imagination in rulers. The question of polities really came down to a question of virtue. Classical writers were generally fatalistic. The theory, given its fullest expression in Polybius, was that the cyclical rise and fall of political societies was a kind of law of nature, which reform might arrest temporarily, but could not abrogate.

Machiavelli and his contemporaries considered the problem and gave initial form to the modern theory Pocock calls classical republicanism, the view that republics were of all polities most capable of successfully resisting the corrosive effects of time. Among other reasons were these: regular rotation of power in a republic permitted an accumulation of political experience over longer periods of time than the life of any prince; oligarchies in which virtue was the standard for political competence were more sure of maintaining those exemplary standards, even though there might be defections, than might a monarchy, however virtuous the prince; republics, being responsible to a political constituency, and holding power at the pleasure of that constituency, were capable of correction before

9. J.G.A. Pocock, *The Machiavellian Moment: Florentine Political Thought and the Atlantic Republican Tradition* (Princeton, 1975); Pocock, ed., *The Political Works of James Harrington* (New York, 1977), Introduction.

abuses had reached the fatal point.

There is no question that the American Revolution must be understood in the light of this tradition. A generation of historians have made it the leading intellectual interpretation of the Revolution. Bernard Bailyn, building on the pioneering work of Caroline Robbins, established that the leading source of authorities and precedents for colonial pamphleteers was a tradition of Old Whig, "country," and opposition writers in England who had opposed to the Hanoverian Whig commercial ascendancy in Parliament, a commonwealth, or classical-republican ideology, which they in turn had gotten from James Harrington and the Parliamentary apologists in the seventeenth century. Gordon Wood demonstrated the precise steps by which numerous American writers and politicians approached the radical solution of making the whole people the constituent body politic, and dividing power into a few manageable but mutually restraining departments.[10] What these historians, and their many students, have agreed on, is that the tradition focussed mainly on the issue of maintaining virtue in political societies, and that it perceived English government and society, since the brief experiment in commonwealth, to be approaching dangerously close to the point of no return in the Polybian cycle of corruption, decay and ruin. It was by means of such ideological filters that the American colonial publicists were able to perceive the relatively mild regime of George III as a despotism.

The tradition was in its deepest recesses a profoundly conservative movement. In its Harringtonian mood, the tradition identified political virtue with the mythical warrior-farmer of the ancient German constitutions, and of Harrington's *Oceana*–itself an idealization of the landed gentry of seventeenth century England who supported Parliament against the corruption of the "court." It was not difficult for the American farmer-lawyer-soldier-politician to see himself the resurrected avatar of this type, just as Rosenstock understands him to be. A certain pessimism in respect to untutored human nature–a pessimism of a quite traditional type–was balanced in the American founding fathers by the Enlightenment faith in science and common sense–this a Scottish importation–all of which resulted in a relatively elitist republicanism, a democracy with more faith in the power of

10. Bernard Bailyn, *The Ideological Origins of the American Revolution* (Cambridge, Mass., 1967); Robbins, *The Eighteenth-Century Commonwealthman...* (Cambridge, Mass., 1959); Gordon Wood, *The Creation of the American Republic, 1776-1787* (Chapel Hill, 1969). A guide to the vast and growing literature on this topic may be found in two review articles by Robert E. Shalhope in *William & Mary Quarterly* 29 (1972):49-80; 39 (1982):334-356.

self-correcting political machinery to retain political virtue, than in the voice of the multitude.[11]

The reconstruction of this pattern of thought, and the realization that it is connected in an important way with Florentine Renaissance political theory, and with the Machiavellian revival in the English republican tradition, accounts for a great many things about the language and spirit of the American republican movement.

But it also creates areas of misgiving. Not least because the exclusive stress on the revival of the intellectual problems of pagan antiquity seems to suggest that this in itself is a sufficient explanation for the moral and spiritual energy manifest in the pursuit of answers to those problems. It does not reckon with what must be taken for granted in the relevant texts: namely, a familiarity with the scriptures so profound as to amount to a *mentality*. The acute sense of the moral meaning of time, which made the revival of *these* antique problems crucial, is itself more biblical, and more Augustinian, than pagan. It is Christianity that insists time is linear; so that the Polybian problem takes on the critical and millennialist direction it has in the classical republican tradition. The account of the entire tradition needs to be recast in the light of the awakening of scriptural and patristic Christianity in late medieval and early modern Europe.

The extraordinary sensitivity of the founding fathers to questions of temporality in political society, and their ability to solve problems of long-standing and nagging difficulty in high Western culture, requires some explanation in light of the resolutely provincial, not to say rustic, character of this political leadership and intelligentsia. We do not want to exaggerate their isolation–as does Rosenstock–but the truth is they were not, taken together, worldly men. Nor does an extraordinary intellect or theorist stand out among them. The achievement was to a certain degree an achievement of culture, of a mentality broadly diffused.

One of the things that must be said about the English colonial societies in North America is that they were the first extensive society of Europeans to be made up nearly entirely of dissenters: every species of Old and New Dissent in Britain, with German sectaries and refugee Huguenots. And even those representatives of

11. See, for example, Garry Wills, *Inventing America: Jefferson's Declaration of Independence* (Garden City, 1978). But see also Ronald Hamowy, "Jefferson and the Scottish Enlightenment," *William & Mary Quarterly* 36 (1979):502-523.

the European state churches, including the Anglican communities in Virginia, in New York, and elsewhere, quickly evolved non-conformist, congregational attitudes, particularly in regard to the appointment of bishops. As Carl Bridenbaugh has demonstrated, there was probably no single issue uniting the colonists or preparing them more for revolution over a longer period of time than this matter of bishops.[12] Furthermore, the material, social and cultural life of the colonies was everywhere an expression of what in Britain would have been recognized as the culture of dissent.

Dissent was, by the eighteenth century, politically quiescent, but culturally radical. The dissenters were loyal to the Hanoverian monarchy, but they were people also with a heightened sense of the Christian evangelical imperative; their way of life was a rebuke to luxury, ostentation and cynicism; and they were close to the springs of biblical messianic and millennialist language. All these things produced a sense of expectation, a feeling that the time for true reformation was at hand. Nowhere was this more true than in America, where the rapid population growth was joined to conscious-ness of a maturing culture and an imperial destiny. The political opportunity for dissent was unique in America. Key cultural institutions–notably the universities–were able to foster an essentially dissenting worldview without labouring under the stigma of the excluded.

But dissent was a transatlantic culture that sprang from the heart of English cultural nationality at the moment of its formulation in the early seventeenth-century. And if we look at this culture in terms wider than the particular concerns of calvinistic Old Dissent, it should be clear that the dissenters over two centuries served the function of keeping the idea of English nationality from becoming, on its religious side, the ossified piety toward which "High" Anglicanism tended to drift. They also, as Donald Davie makes clear, kept scriptural Christianity on the track of public, civic and corpo-rate culture, and clear of the philistinism and sentimentality that came to mark low-church evangelicalism.[13] In short, if we are looking for a broad and convincing reason for why the relatively

---

12. Carl Bridenbaugh, *Mitre and Sceptre: Transatlantic Faiths, Ideas, Personalities, and Politics 1689-1775* (New York, 1962). See also Alison G. Olson, "Parliament, the London Lobbies, and Provincial Interests in England and America," *Historical Reflections* 6 (1979):367-386.

13. Donald Davie, *A Gathered Church: The Literature of the English Dissenting Interest 1700-1930* (New York, 1930). For a model study of the way in which dissenting culture molded a provincial society, usually understood in quite different terms, see Rhys Isaac, *The Transformation of Virginia, 1740-1790* (Chapel Hill, 1982).

esoteric tradition of classical republicanism took root as the dominant political culture of America, it may be that dissent had
prepared this ground by its attention to the millennialist understanding of national culture, and to the connection between personal
virtue and civic order, and that in America dissent was able to shed
its sectarian character and speak a biblical idea of nationhood in the
cosmopolitan language of classical republicanism.

Thus, we should not be surprised to see in such diverse characters
as Isaac Watts, the English lyric poet of the religion of dissent, and
Jonathan Edwards, the greatest American mind of his century and a
man whose intellectual life was entirely contained in the transatlantic
culture of dissent, the same intense preoccupation with millennial
language as the suitable language of collective piety. Neither of these
men is associated with the tradition of classical republicanism, and it
suggests something more of the complexity and inter-woven character of dissenting culture that Watts' hymns were better known in
America than any other religious language outside the King James
Bible, to the extent that many of his verses have become fixed as
anonymous folk-poetry, while Edwards was measured more at his
true worth in Scotland than in America, and never became a popular
religious hero.

The themes of Watts' hymns of course cover the full spectrum of
the concerns of the church and of Christian life. What is interesting
in the present connection, however, is the pervasive feeling for
religion as a journey of souls, for the vindication of the people of
God in time:

O God, our help in ages past,
Our hope for years to come;
Our shelter from the stormy blast,
And our eternal home.

This, and many of Watts' best hymns are paraphrases of the Psalms,
echoes of the Hebrew poetic of repetition and parallel contrasting
pairs of observation. Nonetheless, Watts made this poetic, and its
nationalistic burden, part of popular religious conceptions. His
hymns are studded with references to "nation"; to the coming
triumph of Christ's kingdom; to the witness of saints now dead to
the emergent kingdom of God. His last stanzas frequently point
forward, as do the second and last lines in the pair of couplets just
quoted, to hope in a collective future. There is little sentimental
individualism in Watts' hymns, even when they are most personal
and introspective. The vision of salvation is public, collective, and
inclusive throughout all times and places. The moral community of

saints, in Watts' hymns, is a democratized community of memory. It is not the elite dead who flourish in this exemplary pantheon, but the nameless "cloud of witnesses."[14]

In the broadest view, the religious culture of dissent refracted in Watts' hymns is a civilized and civilizing culture, in which revanchist millenarian and apocalyptic themes are effectively purged, and biblical temporal realism governs an economy of souls bound in the brotherhood of equal anticipation of the future, and therefore compassionate and hopeful in the present life.[15] The millennialism implicit in this–that the future Christ's kingdom is commensurate with the present life, that it shares the same temporal medium, and, through the witness of all saints, is built of the same ethical materials–is made explicit in the millennialist tradition occupied by Edwards and his student and spiritual heir, Samuel Hopkins. Edwards' millennialism has often been misunderstood as a somewhat graceless prophecy of American nationalism. Darrol Bryant has shown, in an unusually careful and valuable doctoral dissertation, that Edwards spoke for a vision of spirituality in which the promise of Christ's kingdom was to be built on prayer and spiritual unity, the assimilation of the Providential designs of God in all ages, not only the present one, and humility in the face of God's evident choice of instrumentalities that could not be anticipated in advance. Edwards' idea that a dispensation of divine providence had opened in New England with the Great Awakening cannot be read as an endorsement of whatever Americans would do in the future, or as foreknowledge of God's design for America.[16] Hopkins took this one step further, arguing not only that slavery was not an institution compatible with millennial expectation, but that things would proably get worse before they got better, and that his generation would not see the millennium.[17]

14. In general, see Horton Davies, *Worship and Theology in England*, vol. 3, *From Watts and Wesley to Maurice, 1690-1850* (Princeton, 1961).

15. I have developed an interpretation along these lines in, "Christianity, Millennialism and Civic Life: The Origins of the American Republic," *The Return of the Millennium*, ed. Joseph Bettis and S.K. Johannesen (Barrytown, N.Y., 1984), pp. 207-231.

16. M. Darrol Bryant, "History and Eschatology in Jonathan Edwards" (Ph.D. diss., University of St. Michael's College, Toronto, 1976.)

17. Joseph Conforti, *Samuel Hopkins and the New Divinity Movement* (Grand Rapids, 1981). More generally, Nathan O. Hatch, *The Sacred Cause of Liberty: Republican Thought and the Millennium in Revolutionary New England* (New Haven, 1977); and James W. Davidson, *The Logic of Millennial Thought: Eighteenth Century New England* (New Haven, 1977).

The millennim conceived in this way is of course essential to the assimilation of classical republicanism to scriptural Christianity. The millennium is the end for which the conquering of time in the civic life of men is important. Or, to put it another way, a population whose moral community is structured in hope and patience is prepared to believe it can solve the ancient problem of luxury and corruption. As a society of dissenters, Americans crossed that transitional line that had made Englishmen in the seventeenth-century torn between forms of voluntary and forms of involuntary community. In the dissenting church, as in republican, Harringtonian politics, everyone is a voluntary member, everyone assumes responsibility. It is sometimes said that Edwards had proven once and for all, in *The Freedom of the Will,* that calvinistic determinism was the only tenable Christian philosophy. But in a sense what Edwards achieved was the final demonstration of the paradox that election is finally a form of voluntary association. For where the heart leads, the will necessarily follows, and is indeed identical with the wish. With the distance between heart and will destroyed, the opposition between them is destroyed. *In*voluntary is an anomaly. Americans would similarly conclude that it was possible to conceive of America as an elect nation, and at the same time of Americans as free.

What was left to do in America after the Revolution was the complete democratizing of the moral community of the dead, the living, and the unborn. We may take a text from Thomas Jefferson, to set beside John Adams' "hearts and minds of the people." In a famous letter to Samuel Kercheval, of July 12, 1816, Jefferson argues for frequent revisions of the constitution on the ground that the deeds of the dead should not bind the living. "The dead?" he exclaims, "But the dead have no rights. They are nothing; and nothing cannot own something....This corporeal globe, and everything upon it, belong to its present corporeal inhabitants, during their generation." As the context makes clear, the ground of this attitude toward the dead is "the progress of the human mind." The dead who matter, the wise men of the past, would themselves approve of change, so that the Constitution may endure "from generation to generation, to the end of time."[18] The concrete remains of the dead, which is to say, of the elite dead, is not to interfere with the interests of all the dead and all the living, considered

18. *Thomas Jefferson: A Selection of His Writings,* ed. Saul Padover (Modern Library ed.), p. ?.

as one, in the perpetuation of civil society into a progressively perfected future.

Naturally, a full account of a human type in Rosenstockian terms–"a new aspect of the human soul"–must go beyond the elucidation of the environment of that soul, beyond the description of the spatio-temporal economy that governs the moral community. Even to flesh out the territory essayed here–the speech of a whole people caught in forms of prayer, of singing, of liturgy not even grasped as liturgy; the pattern of appropriation of the dead, and hope for the unborn, expressed in hymns so popular as to have become anonymous folk idiom; the precise tenses and moods of eschatological expectation in even the smoothest coinage of religious and political talk–would be a very large undertaking. Then there is the wider system of gestural life: the eschatological hope in the toil of the body, in the shapes of made things, in the exuberance of invention coupled with an exquisite tact in the handling of materials. Only a few scholars have ventured into this territory, so much of which is adumbrated in Rosenstock's "the sound of the axe is the natural philosophy of America"–provided only that we understand that "axe" in all its enormously complex relationship to landscape, to work, to the very style of a civilization.[19] Indeed, if "soul" can be made to mean anything in American English, it may be as an equivalent of "style"–stripped of its invidious and trivializing uses. Thus the material image we require for Rosenstock's figure of America as Noah's ark, is not the great wooden tub of the illustrations in the family Bible, but the Yankee Clipper, the fastest, most fragile and beautiful ship in the world. The dissenter as American is the artisan, the clerk, the merchant who is free to make things according to his own dreams and not according to the dreams of an elite patron. This is the other side of the dreary democrat, the side Tocqueville could not see because he was used to a different sort of brilliance. It is the other side of that equation that Rosenstock descried but weighted on the side of Nature. Rosenstock saw that the vast spaces of the new world called for a revolutionary rhetoric of appeals to the God of Nature and to a new human unity rooted in nature; he saw less clearly that this was not a triumph of acreage, but a triumph of human type. In order to conquer space the dissenter had first to conquer the weight of tradition, that is to say, the preponderance of

19. Each of these very different books deals in a significant way with these themes: Daniel Calhoun *The Intelligence of a People* (Princeton, 1973); John Kouwenhoven, *Made in America: The Arts in Modern Civilization* (Newton Centre, Mass., 1957); Leo Marx, *The Machine in the Garden: Technology and the Pastoral Ideal in America* (New York, 1964); Anthony Wallace, *Rockdale* (New York, 1976).

elite dead in the moral community of all souls. The American's God. is not only the God of Nature, who Rosenstock says is "deaf and dumb," but the God of Isaac Watts, who is *our* help, and *our* hope, in phrases that include a new pronoun of collective possession of both past and future. The American, in short, is the man who believes that the present is as good as any other time, and that he is as good as any other man.

Eugen Rosenstock-Huessy:
Revolutionizing Communication Theory

Eugene D. Tate

It is ironic that a scholar whose entire system is built on the reality of human communication should have been ignored for so long by communication scholars. Communication is central to his entire thought yet an analysis of the cumulative index of journals in communication shows not one reference to the work of Eugen Rosenstock-Huessy from 1915 to 1975. He has been ignored by the academic establishment because he calls one to take a radically new perspective on communication and human existence. Rhetoric and communication theorists are so enamored with the work of Aristotle and Descartes that an attack on the basic premises of their theory is unthinkable. Modern communication theory begins with the Cartesian principle that thought is the basis of all human existence. For Rosenstock-Huessy, *Communication, not thought, is the basis of all human existence!*

> Audi, ne moriamur. Listen, lest we die; or: listen and we shall survive is an a priori that presupposes a power in man to establish relations with his neighbor that transcend their private interests. The formula, by its own supposition, denies the Marxian idea of thinking as pure self interest; it also precludes the idealistic idea of thinking for the sake of thinking...By introducing the listener, the "you" that is expected to listen, something is achieved that science fails to do; the dualistic concept of a world of subjects and objects is abandoned. Grammar does not know of two but three persons, I, you, it...Human survival and revival depend upon speech.[1]

Four distinct schools of communication theory can be distinguished today. The first school, Rhetoric, is the most humanistic of the social sciences. Scholars in this perspective base their work on Aristotle or one of the more modern rhetoricians like Kenneth Burke.[2] The second school is the empirical perspective which seeks

1. Eugen Rosenstock-Huessy, *Speech and Reality* (Norwich, Vt.: Argo Books, 1970), pp. 24-25.
2. An informative history of communication theory can be found in Nancy

to develop an understanding of communication based on scientific research and observation.[3] This perspective was given focus by several scholars immediately following World War II. David Berlo's book, *The Process of Human Communication,* was one which helped focus this perspective in 1960. The third school, the phenomenological perspective of John Stewart[4] and Michael Hyde,[5] is based on the philosophy of Heidegger and Husserl. The fourth perspective is the Marxist perspective which has developed in Europe through the work of the Frankfort School. All four of these perspectives take as the starting point of their theory the Cartesian principle of thought as the basis of all human interaction. They all assume that in order to communicate one must first have thoughts, and it is these then existing thoughts that are verbalized during the act of communication.[6]

Harper, *Human Communication Theory: The History of a Paradigm* (Rochelle Park, N.J.: Hayden, 1979), or Ernest G. Borman, *Communication Theory* (New York: Holt, Rinehart & Winston, 1980). From a Canadian perspective see, Eugene D. Tate, "Developments in Communication Theory," *Canadian Journal of Communication* 7, no. 3 (1980-1981):57-71. See also Kenneth Burke, *Language as Symbolic Action: Essays on Life, Literature and Method.* (Berkeley: University of California Press, 1956); Kenneth Burke, *The Rhetoric of Religion: Studies in Logology* (Boston: Beacon Press, 1961); Wayne C. Booth, "The Scope of Rhetoric Today: A Polemical Excursion," in Bitzer and Black, eds., *The Prospect of Rhetoric* (Englewood Cliffs, N.J.: Prentice-Hall, 1971), pp. 93-114.

3. David Berlo, The Process of Communication (New York: Holt, Rinehart & Winston, 1960). See also Gerald R. Miller, ed., *Explorations in Interpersonal Communication* (Beverly Hills, Calif.: Sage Publications, 1976). Gerald R. Miller and Mark Steinberg, *Between People* (Chicago: Science Research Associates, 1975). Joseph Woelfel and Edward L. Fink, *The Measurement of the Communication Process: Galileo Theory and Method* (New York: Academic Press, 1980).

4. John Stewart, "Foundations of Dialogic Communication," *The Quarterly Journal of Speech,* 64 (1978):183-201. John Stewart, ed., *Bridges Not Walls: A Book About Interpersonal Communication* (Reading, Mass.: Addison-Wesley, 1973). Ronald C. Arnett, "Toward a Phenomenological Dialogue," *The Western Journal of Speech Communication,* 45 (1981):201-222.

5. Michael J. Hyde, *Communication Philosophy and the Technological Society* (University, Ala.: University of Alabama Press, 1982). Michael J. Hyde, "The Experience of Anxiety: A Phenomenological Approach," *The Quarterly Journal of Speech,* 66 (1980):140-141.

6. All communication theorists begin with the assumption that in order to communicate one must first have thoughts which are verbalized during the act of communication. A recent example of this assumption will be found in James M. Honeycutt, Mark L. Knapp, and William G. Powers, "On Knowing Others and Predicting What They Say," *Western Journal of Speech Communication* 47, no. 2 (1983):157-174. See also Colin Cherry, *On Human Communication: A Review, A Survey and A Criticism* (Cambridge, Mass.: M.I.T. Press, 1966), pp. 1-30.

I. Contributions of Eugen Rosenstock-Huessy to Communication Theory

The thought of Eugen Rosenstock-Huessy is an *intellectual breakthrough* of the greatest magnitude. Scholars rooted in the work of Thomas Kuhn[7] may be unfamiliar with the concept of intellectual breakthrough, since Kuhn requires that a new paradigm replace the old one. Kuhn's understanding of paradigm change requires continued communication between group and individual so that the group eventually accepts the new scientific paradigm. C.D. Axelrod, however, has shown that an intellectual breakthrough occurs with an estrangement between the individual and the group.[8]

> ...breakthrough begins with this estrangement–this relatedness to the tension between the individual and group. But they express this estrangement in a certain way; not by escaping or declaring indifference, but by attempting to generate more relevant and crucial possibilities for inquiry. They choose to struggle with the restrictive conditions of their membership in an attempt to renegotiate conditions suitable to their own experiences of theorizing. And in order to amend or dissolve the accepted paradigm, they articulate their critiques and provide a higher rationality–one that allows their work to reach an audience and to re-enter the community of discourse.[9]

The work of Eugen Rosenstock-Huessy, like that of Martin Buber and Franz Rosenzweig, meets the requirements of an intellectual breakthrough as defined by Axelrod. The work of Rosenstock-Huessy does not present a new paradigm for the social sciences. It is not confined to one academic discipline but ranges over all disciplines from Communication to Theology, Philosophy, History, Psychology, Sociology and Anthropology. In this respect it is threatening to the intellectual establishment with its organized areas of specialization.

> My generation has survived social death in all its variations, and I have survived decades of study and teaching in scholastic and academic sciences. Every one of their venerable scholars mistook me for the intellectual type which he most despised. The athiest wanted me to disappear into Divinity, the theologian into sociology, the sociologists into history, the historians into journalism,

---

7. Thomas Kuhn, *The Structure of Scientific Revolutions* (Chicago: University of Chicago Press, 1962).

8. Charles David Axelrod, *Studies In Intellectual Breakthrough: Freud, Simmel, Buber* (Amherst, Mass.: University of Massachusetts Press, 1979).

9. Axelrod, *Studies in Intellectual Breakthrough*, p. 69.

the journalists into metaphysics, the philosophers into law, and–
need I say it?–the lawyers into hell, which as a member of our
present world, I never left. For nobody leaves hell all by himself
without going mad. Society is a hell as long as man or woman is
alone. And the human soul dies from consumption in the hell of
social catastrophe, unless it makes common cause with others.[10]

In these words from *Out of Revolution*, Eugen Rosenstock-Huessy
expressed his experience of estrangement from the intellectual
community. He also located the source of the estrangement. A
generation which had been through the experience of World War I
could not accept the old paradigms of social science. Ludwig
Feuerbach and Soren Kierkegaard had provided a clue for persons
who understood the destruction of the intellectual community as it
existed prior to the War. Various scholars took different approaches
to the rebuilding of philosophy and the social sciences after the War.
Phenomenologists, following Husserl's example, withdrew into an
analysis of personal experience. Empiricists turned to statistics to
give reassurance about the stability of the world despite change.
Existentialists turned to themselves with an analysis of Being. Franz
Rosenzweig, Eugen Rosenstock-Huessy and Martin Buber turned to
the analysis of human speech and the reality created thereby. Since
the intellectual community understood the new paradigms suggested
by empiricists, existentialists, and phenomenologists, these new paradigms were accepted with continuing debate. These paradigms have,
after all, the same starting point as pre-World War I social science.
As Axelrod points out, Buber admitted he had no teaching and the
intellectual community could find no new paradigm in his work.[11]
Rosenstock-Huessy wrote, "I do not enlarge on the academic premises; I contradict them. Obviously this seems preposterous."[12] Franz
Rosenzweig explained the difference in these words:

In the new thinking, the method of speech replaces the method of
thinking maintained in all earlier philosophies. Thinking is timeless and wants to be timeless. With one stroke it would establish
thousands of connections. It regards the last, the goal, as the first.
Speech is bound to time and nourished by time, and it neither can
nor wants to abandon this element. It does not know in advance
just where it will end. It takes its cues from others. In fact, it lives

10. Eugen Rosenstock-Huessy, *Out of Revolution: Autobiography of Western Man*
(Norwich, Vt.: Argo Books, 1969), p. 758.
11. Axelrod, *Studies in Intellectual Breakthrough*, p. 69.
12. Eugen Rosenstock-Huessy, footnote in Rome and Rome, eds., *Philosophical
Interrogations* (New York: Holt, Rinehart and Winston, 1964), p. 32.

by virtue of another's life, whether that one is the one who listens to a story, answers in the course of a dialogue, or joins in a chorus; while thinking is always a solitary business, even when it is done in common by several who philosophize together. For even then, the other is only raising the objections I should raise myself, and this is the reason why the great majority of philosophic dialogues...are so tedious. In actual conversation something happens...For the thinker knows his thoughts in advance, and his expounding of them is merely a concession to what he regards as the defectiveness of our means of communication. This defectiveness is not due to our need of speech but to our need of time. To require time means that we cannot anticipate, that we must wait for everything, that what is ours depends on what is another's. All this is quite beyond the comprehension of the thinking thinker, while it is valid for the "speaking thinker."[13]

Here lies the crux of the estrangement. Eugen Rosenstock-Huessy and Franz Rosenzweig reject the Cartesian premise that thought is the basic reality of life. Speech replaces thought as the starting point for understanding human life in this new perspective. Every communication theorist to the present has accepted the Cartesian *Cogito ergo sum* as the starting point of his theory. Even John Stewart, who has sought to link phenomenology to communication theory, explicitly says that communication theory must begin with the Cartesian premise.[14] Eugen Rosenstock-Huessy rejected the Cartesian premise.

Both the credo ut intelligam and the Cogito ergo sum worked very well for a time. However, finally the Credo ut intelligam led to the Inquisition and the Cogito ergo sum led into an ammunition factory. The progressive science of our days of aircraft-bombing has progressed just a bit too far into the humanities, precisely as theology has dogmatized just a bit too much when it built up its inquisition. When Joan of Arc was questioned under torture, her theological judges had ceased to believe. When Nobel Prize winners produce poison-gas, their thinking is no longer identified with existence.[15]

13. Franz Rosenzweig in *Franz Rosenzweig: His Life and Thought,* Nahum N. Glatzer, ed. (New York: Schocken Books, 1961), 2d ed. rev., pp. 198-199.
14. "Motivated by the same desire that Descartes had to locate an apodictic foundation or absolute starting point for all thought, the phenomenologist begins with the indubitability of the cogitatio." John Stewart, "Foundations of Dialogic Communication, *The Quarterly Journal of Speech,* 64 (1978):186-187.
15. Eugen Rosenstock-Huessy, "Farewell to Descartes," *I Am An Impure Thinker* (Norwich, Vt.: Argo Books, 1970), p. 14.

This is what Rosenstock-Huessy meant when he said, "I do not enlarge upon the academic premises, I contradict them." His rejection of the Cartesian premise points to a social science totally different from that now present in our academies. For Rosenstock-Huessy one can develop a social science only on the analysis of human interaction through communication. Respondeo etsi mutabar–I respond although I will be changed. This formula is at the center of Eugen Rosenstock-Huessy's thought. A social science which is built on the Cartesian principle can only lead to a caricature of human beings.

> The abstraction and generalities that prevailed in philosophy from Descartes to Spencer, and in politics from Machiavelli to Lenin, made caricatures of living men. The notions of object and subject, idea and matter, do not aim at the heart of our human existence. They describe the tragic possibilities of human arrogance or pettiness, the potentialities of despot and slave, genius or proletarian. They miss the target which they pretend to shoot: human nature.[16]

Franz Rosenzweig illustrated the difference between the old social science and the new perspective with an analogy. He compared the Socratic dialogues–the old philosophy–with the new philosophy based on speech–the Gospels. In the dialogues of Plato, Socrates carries on a conversation with another person. The other person is allowed to talk but only as Socrates leads him. Socrates has thought out the topic in advance, initiates the conversation, and leads the discussant in the discovery of truth. Jesus, on the other hand, called for a response from the other person and did not frame the response for the individual ahead of time. He did not leave the disciples with prepared truths, but only with things which they did not understand until they lived into the new experience. The Gospels are full of indications that the disciples did not understand the words or actions of Jesus until after his death, resurrection, and ascension. Jesus called for a response from real people in real circumstances which reflection would later clarify.

> I do not know in advance what the other person will say to me, because I do not even know what I myself am going to say. I do not even know whether I am going to say anything at all. Perhaps the other person will say the first word, for in true conversation this is usually the case...I use the term "speaking thinking" for the new thinking. Speaking thought is, of course, still a form of

16. Rosenstock-Huessy, "Farewell to Descartes," p. 6.

thinking, just as the old thinking that depended solely on thinking could not go on without inner speech. The difference between the old and the new, the "logical" and the "grammatical" thinking, does not lie in the fact that one is silent while the other is audible, but in the fact that the latter needs another person, and takes time seriously...In the old philosophy "thinking" means thinking for no one else and speaking to no one else (and here, if you prefer, you may substitute "everyone" or the well-known "all the world" for "no one"). But "speaking" means speaking to some one and thinking for some one. And this some one is always a quite definite some one, and he has not merely ears, like "all the world," but also a mouth.[17]

This quotation from Franz Rosenzweig clarifies the difference between the traditional social scientific paradigm based on Cartesian principles and that proposed by Rosenstock-Huessy. How does one know what he or she will say until one is spoken to and a response is called forth? Meaning is created between persons in the response to one another.

Eugen Rosenstock-Huessy developed a social theory based on the reality of communication/response. Some of his insights are acceptable to modern communication theorists although others present a unique perspective because of his different starting point. Having rejected Cartesian psychologism Rosenstock-Huessy offered a different methodology for studying human behaviour–The Grammatical Method or Metanomics. "Speech sustains the time and space axes of society. Grammar is the method by which we become aware of this social process. Grammar, then, offers itself as the basis for the meta-ethics of society. We have called this new discipline not meta-ethics but metanomics of society, for the obvious reason that economics, bionomics, theonomy, deal with the laws (nomoi) of the different realms of science."[18]

Communication scholars would agree that one is changed through communication. Respondeo etsi mutabar–I respond although I will be changed–is a central premise of almost all modern communication theory. Communication scholars, however, do not take seriously the spontaneity of speech within the communication process through which reality is established between people. Rhetoricians have been concerned with discovering the arguments which will persuade the other person. Persuasion scholars, until recently, have been caught in the same trap. Emphasis is on the thought expressed in the message.

17. Glatzer, *Franz Rosenzweig*, pp. 199-200.
18. Rosenstock-Huessy, *Speech and Reality*, p. 43.

How to form the thoughts, the effect of various thoughts, the creation of new thoughts–these are the things important to modern communication scholars. The reality of speech, response, language, and listening, are what was important to Rosenstock-Huessy.

Modern communication theory reduces human interaction to facts, laws, or rules.[19] Human interaction is analyzed from many perspectives. Conflict is understood in these perspectives as related only to the choice of strategy which will cause one to win or as being solved by assessing the reward value in the strategy which has been chosen by one party. Rosenstock-Huessy demonstrated the futility of these approaches, or at least the limitations of such attempts, by taking seriously the act of speaking.

> The vulgar philosophy of language tells us that speech communicates one man's thoughts to another. But our opinions are ephemeral. If speech were intended to convey ideas, it would need as little power as possible. And it is true, our modern speakers lisp nearly tonelessly; they prefer to write form letters on a typewriter or send out mimeographed charts and statistics. They try to make as little noise as possible. They are right. Who am I that my opinions, thoughts or ideas should inconvenience anybody else? They live their faith in their philosophy of language. But their philosophy of language interprets secondary types of speech. It does not even try to interpret the monumental character of names. It believes with Kant that "time" is a form of thought.[20]

Modern communication theory suffers from a source bias which has been present in the development of the theory since Aristotle or earlier. Much of the emphasis in communication theory has been on what the source can do to persuade the receiver. I speak so that my thoughts, which I have prepared more or less carefully beforehand in a logical persuasive order, may persuade the other person that I am correct. The *I* precedes speech to the other person.

Eugen Rosenstock-Huessy affirmed that one cannot become an *I* unless one is first addressed by another as *Thou*. Only in response to the Thou spoken by the Other does one become an *I*, the inward, subjective, singular self. As we return the gift of having been addressed we form a duality, a *we*, as in marriage, the family, and other relationships in life. As one participates in the outside world,

19. Susan B. Shimanoff, *Communication Rules: Theory and Research* (Beverly Hills, Calif.: Sage Publications, 1980). Michael E. Roloff, *Interpersonal Communication: The Social Exchange Approach* (Beverly Hills, Calif.: Sage Publications, 1981).

20. Eugen Rosenstock-Huessy, *The Origin of Speech* (Norwich, Vt.: Argo Books, 1981), p. 81.

in the many groups which one becomes a member of, such as professional or business groups, one becomes known in the third person, a *she/he*. This represents the recognition and maturity which one obtains in the work world. This is the Cross of Reality which is central to Rosenstock-Huessy's thought and represents the four orientations of reality: inward, outward, future and past.

By taking speech seriously Rosenstock-Huessy has given the communication scholar a foundation for a new approach to communication. His method of analysis, metanomics, sometimes called The Grammatical Approach, provides an alternative to the traditional methodologies used in communication research. As Axelrod pointed out,[21] the scholar who establishes a breakthrough must provide an alternative to existing social scientific paradigms. Rosenstock-Huessy has not ignored the problem but has provided an alternative approach to the study of communication.

This new approach must begin with the a priori of response. A second a priori is a power in human beings to establish relationships with another person that transcend private interests. The analysis of communication/response through speech will then lead to an understanding of how speech "sustains the time and space axis of society." Language links one with those who have lived in the past, the present, and the future. "The energies of social life are compressed into words. The circulation of articulated speech is the lifeblood of society. Through speech, society sustains its time and space axis."[22]

It is not possible here to develop a complete outline of such an approach to the understanding of human life based on communication/response. It is only possible to suggest some directions in which such an approach might go. Such an approach will provide insights into all levels of human life. Traditional social sciences have been divided between the macro (societal) and micro (individual) analysis of human life. It often seems that while micro social scientists are willing to draw on the insights of persons working from a macro approach, macro oriented social scientists are much less tolerant of the micro approach. Rosenstock-Huessy moved freely from the macro to the micro and back again. Thus the perspective which he provided may be able to bridge the gap between the two extremes.

At the societal level, Rosenstock-Huessy's analysis of speech emphasized how speech patterns affect societies. Albrecht Goes's[23]

21. Axelrod, *Studies in Intellectual Breakthrough*, p. 69.
22. Rosenstock-Huessy, *Speech and Reality*, p. 16.
23. Albrecht Goes, "The Unquiet Night," reprinted in E. William Rollins and

affirmation that in order to destroy society one must first destroy the speech and language of a people is supported by Rosenstock-Huessy's analysis of the role of speech in society. In *The Origin of Speech* he discussed the four diseases of speech which affect society. War is caused by the limitation of speech to only those aspects related to the society and not listening to the foe. Revolution is extreme sensitivity to the slogans of the new order and destruction of the old society with its slogans. Tyranny is the repetition of the old, stock phrases and not paying attention to attempts to articulate a new life or social order. Crisis is not listening to the speech of people within the society or not giving direction to the society.

Speech includes listening and speaking, articulating and repeating. A healthy speaking group uses old terms for new facts (repetition), new terms for old facts (articulation), spreads out to new people (speaking), and includes every worthwhile speaker (listening). The two acts of listening and speaking extend the territorial frontiers of speech. We want to be able to speak to all and to listen to all. The two acts of repeating and articulating constantly extend the temporal frontiers of speech. We want to link up with all past and future generations.

All four acts are fraught with risk. More often than not, they miscarry. War, revolution, decadence, crisis are the four forms of miscarriage. In war people who think we should listen to them are excluded; in crisis people who think we should talk to them are not included. In revolution orders which expect to be honored are ridiculed. In degeneracy shouts which expect to be taken up remain inaudible.[24]

Reference to public opinion theory[25] may illustrate what is being discussed here. In revolution, what Galtung[26] has called the absolutist position is amplified. The old order is considered evil and must be totally destroyed. Any response to the old order, the old ways of speech and behaviour, is discouraged because the old must be totally destroyed before the new society can come into being. Public opinion theory takes a gradualist approach to social change. The old

Harry Zohn, *Men of Dialogue: Martin Buber and Albrecht Goes* (New York: Funk and Wagnalls, 1969), pp. 37-102.

24. Rosenstock-Huessy, *The Origin of Speech*, pp. 15-16.

25. The public opinion process is a conservative process of social change. See Bernhard Hennessy, *Public Opinion*, 4th ed. (Monterey, Calif.: Brooks/Cole Publications, 1981).

26. Johan Galtung, "Foreign Policy Opinion as a Function of Social Position," in J. Rosenau, ed., *International Politics and Foreign Policy* (New York: The Free Press, 1969), pp. 551 572.

order is tolerated, even encouraged, for the sake of social stability and allowed to die gradually. The old slogans, old ways of speaking and behaving are accepted and treasured until they are replaced by the new which have been growing slowly. Elsewhere[27] I have attempted to show that while United States history confirms the absolutist-revolution perspective, Canadian history confirms the gradualist position. Canadians still find meaning–utilize speech representing the pre-1867 reality–in the monarchy, the British parliament, etc. so that only in 1982 was the Constitution brought to Canada from Great Britain. There has been in the Canadian experience a willingness to honor the speech structures of the past and find meaning in them. As Galtung has shown, both the gradualist and absolutist perspectives have their own vocabulary.

Let us confront disease and remedy:

1. War as deafness, to peace as willingness to listen.
2. Revolution as shouting, to order as ability to formulate.
3. Crisis as muteness, to credit as willingness to entrust.
4. Decadence as stereotype, to rejuvenation as new representatives.[28]

Language, then, can serve the purposes of either war or peace, revolution or order, tyranny or representation crisis or trust, decadence or rejuvenation. An analysis of the speech patterns will enable the observer to examine how each are brought about through communication/response.

From the group, Rosenstock-Huessy moved to the individual. When an individual is given a name, he or she becomes a member of a group.

And this is the purpose of names. They intend to associate its carrier with other people. Names group. What is wrong with such a purpose? I may be associated with my background, my family, my playmates, or instead I may associate with my chosen associates of my later life. But associated I must be...But speech originates in a group through the names with which its members are addressed! Names are not words. With words we speak of things; we speak to people by names.[29] Words classify, but names orient. Words generalize, but names personify. Words dismiss living subjects into the realm of objectivity. Names pick up the little baby or the flower or the sun, and incorporate them into one society of

27. Eugene D. Tate, "Canada and U.S. Differences in Similar TV Story Content," *Canadian Journal of Communication*, 5, no. 2 (1978):1-12.
28. Rosenstock-Huessy, *The Origin of Speech*, p. 17.
29. Rosenstock-Huessy, *The Origin of Speech*, p. 77.

communication. Without names, communication would be impossible. For before two individuals may talk to each other in words about things, they must be mutually responsive, they must recognize each other as persons. Each must make more and more of a person out of his interlocuter by giving each other names.[30]

Names bring us into association with other people. Our name identifies us with a particular group of people, our family, and gives us a past. As we respond to our name we become oriented to the world and reality. Rosenstock-Huessy emphasized the historicity of human beings because of speech. An African student of mine once stated the African reality in these words, "I belong to my family therefore I am!" Rosenstock-Huessy understood that a name places one within a family which has a long history both past, present, and future. Names also have an imperative aspect since they call forth a response and demand a fulfillment from the individual.

But the real story of the human spirit always begins with our assimilating an imperative. We understand that we are meant, and in doing what our mother asks us to do we realize ourselves for the first time as our mother's–or our father's or our teacher's–"thou" and "you." I am a thou for society long before I am an I to myself.[31]

Most communication scholars would agree that the self-concept (I) develops through transaction with other people. There is a difference, however, between their understanding of the development of the self and that suggested by Eugen Rosenstock-Huessy. William Wilmot discusses the self-concept from a transactional viewpoint in his book, *Dyadic Communication*. Wilmot argues that our

self-concept is built by meanings we attach to all our experiences– those past and those which we are engaged in now–and the meshing of those meanings with our future aspirations. When we have a communication experience, the interplay between our expectations and how we see people reacting to us adds another element to our self-concept. It must be stressed that the meanings are constructed through selective perception, which is partially governed by our past experiences of social acceptance.[32]

Wilmot, beginning with this view of reality as an internal construction within the mind of the individual, continues by discussing the five step process of self-concept development. Thought constructs

30. Rosenstock-Huessy, *I Am An Impure Thinker*, p. 44.
31. Rosenstock-Huessy, *The Origin of Speech*, p. 90.
32. William W. Wilmot, *Dyadic Communication: A Transactional Perspective* (Reading, Mass.: Addison-Wesley, 1975), p. 44.

reality from past experience. This is interpreted by the other person who uses it as a base for action. The self-concept is then revised if there is incongruity between the past understanding and the perceived reaction of the other person. The self-concept of both participants in this transaction are "modified and grow out of the communicative exchanges." The self-concept resides within the individual.

For Rosenstock-Huessy the reality lies not in the thought one gives about self-image but in the response one makes to the speech of the other. Speech involves us in a multi-dimensional sphere represented by the four dimensions of the Cross of Reality. We respond to the imperative from the other person, thus being drawn into the future. The present moment is created through conjunction of the past and future. For Wilmot the past, or residual self-concept, interacts with the present to create the future self-concept. Through the Cross of Reality, Rosenstock-Huessy affirms that life is lived in all dimensions at once–inner and outer, past and future.

> The present, whether it be an hour, a day in our life, or a whole era, is not only created, but created by us; it does not simply happen to us, it is not a natural fact like space or a datum in nature, but a constant social achievement, and neither comes nor lasts except by our own making. Therefore, time is not a gift but a task; true presence of mind, the power to live in the fullness of time, is something that has to be won arduously and preserved by perpetual vigilance...When man rises above his future, which is the imminence of his death, and beyond his past, which is the reminiscence of his origins, he enters the present. From the conflict of end and origin, of death and birth, the present results for those who have the courage not to blink but face the abyss before and in back of them.[33]

Another way that Eugen Rosenstock-Huessy emphasized the restructuring of communication theory which occurs when the Cartesian principle is denied and speech is taken seriously lies in his attack on the Alexandrinian table of grammatical values, i.e. Amo, Amas, Amat, Amamus, Amatis, Amant: I love, you love, he loves, we love, you love, they love–or any of the grammatical lists we learned in childhood. By beginning with I love, Rosenstock-Huessy believed emphasis is placed on the willed action of the individual. Rosenstock-Huessy argued that this must be eliminated and a more "crucial" or accurate grammar instituted. The list he suggested is:

---

33. Rosenstock-Huessy, *I Am An Impure Thinker*, p. 94.

ama (amate).....love!
ame (ameus).....that I may love! (that we may love)
amatus..........loved (they love)
amavimus........we have loved

The Alexandrinian table treats all cases as being equal and of equal importance. Rosenstock-Huessy pointed out that amatur, he is loved, is an objective statement made by an observer. Amo, I love, is a statement which a person can make only for himself as he reveals his innermost thoughts to another person. It is not a statement that óne broadcasts to the world but one that is said privately to another or to one's family, in the same manner as one might say, "We are engaged to be married." Amas, you love, is a statement which can be made only by someone who knows you well enough to make it or stands in a relationship which bestows the right to make this observation. Amavimus, we have loved, can be said only by those persons who have been speaking and listening to one another. "To have spoken to each other is the indispensible base for our right or capacity to say 'We'!"[34] Amant, they love, is an impersonal statement which "can be said of any group and nation, big or small." It is impersonal and may be empirical. It is very different from the other statements made in the grammatical list.

> The crisis of our human relations has awakened me to the necessity of elevating grammar to the rank of a social science. Higher grammar tells us of our innate faculties of reason, authority, wisdom, experience. A higher grammar must reinstate the reality of speaking and listening people in place of the nightmare of a speechless thinker who computes a speechless universe. The Alexandrinian table of forms...will be discarded. It is the end product of a secondary process which has tried to obliterate the foundations of speech...The sentence "he loves," is justified if it is true and not false. But the sentence "I love," is justified if it is an act of faith and not shameless. The sentence "you love," is justified if it has a healing and not an insulting quality. The phrase "we love," is justified if it is based on experience of a common life and not on an abstract dogma.[35]

Another area in which one can find the emphasis of Eugen Rosenstock-Huessy differing from that of modern communication theory concerns his thought about reticence. Since 1970 there has been an increasing emphasis among communication scholars on silence, shyness, and communication apprehension. Several different

34. Rosenstock-Huessy, *Speech and Reality,* p. 110.
35. Rosenstock-Huessy, *Speech and Reality,* pp. 111-112.

explanations have been given to explain these phenomena. Zimbardo[36] points to culture which demands that people be quiet yet also demands superior social performance. McCroskey[37] developed the concept of Communication Apprehension to identify the anxiety syndrome which individuals experience when either anticipating or participating in oral, written, or musical communication. Gerald Phillips[38] has suggested the problem lies in the self-concept of the individual and the beliefs they hold about themselves. Michael Hyde[39] has defined shyness as "angst" arising from the ontological nature of Being. Hyde has been influenced by the writings of Heidegger.

Eugen Rosenstock-Huessy discussed the causes of silence from his perspective. In *Speech and Reality*, while discussing the problem of speaking about oneself, he discussed the risk which one takes when making a personal statement. To say what one is doing or going to do invites rejection or even destruction of the act. To say what one has done invites criticism and ridicule. Hence the most difficult sentence for a person to utter, said Rosenstock-Huessy, is "I love." This is a lifetime act which we do not wish people to interfere with or destroy. This risk is the first reason for silence among people.

The second reason for silence arises from the corruption of speech in the Alexandrinian Grammar. It has removed the understanding that "I" statements are different from indicative statements. This has caused people to objectify everything and the "timid soul," the shy person, "to overemphasize the subjective character of any sentence, and he will not even utter the most harmless sentence in the third person." Thus the ways of speech are confused and differences obliterated so that the one type of person, "the brazen intellect," neglects the real social life between speakers and listeners, objectifying everything.

Brazen objectivity and whispering shyness are social malaises which spring from an insecurity of grammatical distinctions. And they will abound, if grammatical distinctions have ceased to func-

36. Philip Zimbardo, *Shyness* (Reading, Mass.: Addison-Wesley, 1977).

37. James C. McCroskey, "Oral Communication Apprehension: A Review of Recent Research," *Human Communication Research* 4 (1977):78-96. See also James C. McCroskey and Virginia Richmond, *The Quiet Ones: Communication Apprehension and Shyness* (Dubuque, Iowa: Gorsuch Scarisbrick, 1980).

38. Gerald M. Phillips, "Reticence: Pathology of the Normal Speaker," *Speech Monographs* 35 (1968):39-49. Gerald M. Phillips, "Rhetoritherapy Versus the Medical Model: Dealing with Reticence," *Communication Education* 26 (1977):34-43.

39. Michael J. Hyde, "The Experience of Anxiety: A Phenomenological Investigation," *The Quarterly Journal of Speech* 66 (1980):140-154.

tion as expressions of social realities and states of emphatic living.[40]

There is a final reason for silence. Rosenstock-Huessy treated silence as a real social situation brought about because (1) one is alone, one lacks a person to talk to; (2) one has nothing new to say to the other, lacks authority, content, or something extraordinary to say; (3) one is in perfect agreement with another, there is no need for words; and (4) lack of relations due to embarrassment, misgivings, hostility, or no common ground for speech. "Social relations need a medium distance in space and time. Too great distances and too small distances, both are obstructive."[41]

Conclusion

The point at which the thought of Eugen Rosenstock-Huessy challenges traditional communication theory is at the very foundation of that theory, i.e. the acceptance of the Cartesian principle. This means that there must be a complete revolution in communication theory. Only Arnett,[42] among modern communication theorists, recognizes that meaning develops between people in communication/response with one another. Arnett has learned from Martin Buber, who, following Rosenstock-Huessy, rejected the psychological position of meaning existing within the individual.

Secondly, the communication scholar who joins Rosenstock-Huessy in rejecting Cartesian and Aristotelian philosophy will develop a theory which accepts the spontaneity of speech and rejects the traditional mechanical view of human nature. Such a theory will take speech seriously. It will examine carefully the structure of the language utilized in the communication transaction. Such a view of communication will take names seriously. This anti-mechanical revolt can now be found in the work of Harre and Secord[43] and to a certain extent in that of Kenneth Burke and Hugh Duncan.[44] The Symbolic Interactionists also have insights to offer since they understand symbolic interaction to be noninstinctual. However, to the extent that these theorists still accept the Cartesian principle of understanding behaviour to depend on norm and role specifications

40. Rosenstock-Huessy, *Speech and Reality*, p. 114.

41. Rosenstock-Huessy, *Speech and Reality*, p. 118.

42. Ronald C. Arnett, "Toward a Phenomenological Dialogue," pp. 201-222.

43. R. Harre and P.F. Secord, *The Explanation of Social Behaviour* (Oxford: Basil Blackwell, 1972).

44. Kenneth Burke, *Language as Symbolic Action*, and Hugh Dalziel Duncan, *Symbols in Society* (London: Oxford University Press, 1968).

which originate in thought, they will not comprehend what freedom Rosenstock-Huessy has offered the communication scholar. Few if any modern communication scholars are able to understand the individual as speaking-thinker, as defined l v Franz Rosenzweig and Eugen Rosenstock-Huessy.[45]

Thirdly, Rosenstock-Huessy's maxim Respondeo etsi mutabar, *I respond although I will be changed,* must become a central part of communication theory. F.H. Heinemann in his book, *Existentialism and the Modern Predicament,* criticized existentialism for attempting to place reality within the solitary Being. Heinemann affirmed, Respondeo, ergo sum! thus declaring that response to other people is what makes us human.

Eugen Rosenstock-Huessy has gone one step further. His maxim emphasizes the reality of change. Clinton Gardner argues that the word "although" emphasizes the pain which accompanies change.[46] In his essay, "The Quadrilateral of Human Logic,"[47] Rosenstock-Huessy supplemented the two Cartesian conjunctions "therefore" and "because" which objectify people with the two speech conjunctions "although" and "so that." Thus the old "I think therefore I am," "I will be measured because I exist," are corrected by the new "I hear so that I may come to exist," and "I respond although I will be changed." No logic predicts the "although," for this knowledge comes from common sense.

> Newness is not man-made. Manufacturing combines known things by "because," "therefore," and "so that." But that we may become changed men, although we suffer, although we have to suffer, aye, even to die, is incomprehensible to a Greek mind and yet it is the everyday experience of any living soul. In the respondeo, although I may be changed, the scientific mentality is transcended....It is by the strange conjunction of "although" that the new necessity overwhelms the most reactionary part of our organism, *id est,* our obstinate "consciousness."[48]

Fourth, the Cross of Reality, as developed by Rosenstock-Huessy should be an important part of communication theory. The Cross of Reality reminds the communication theorist that as one is addressed as Thou, one is able to become an I. As one responds, one begins to

45. See the debate between Arnett, who does understand this perspective, and Anderson, who accepts only a traditional view of communication and meaning, in the *Western Journal of Speech Communication* 46, no. 4 (1982):344-372.

46. Clinton C. Gardner, *Letters to the Third Millenium: An Experiment in East-West Communication* (Norwich, Vt.: Argo Books, 1981), p. 132.

47. Rosenstock-Huessy, *I Am An Impure Thinker*, p. 65.

48. Rosenstock-Huessy, *I Am An Impure Thinker*, pp. 66-67.

develop a self. As one returns the gift of having been addressed, we form a dual, a 'we', as in the family, in marriage, and in friendships. Finally, as one participates in the work world, one becomes known in the third person, a she or he. The Cross of Reality teaches that life is lived within four dimensions. The application of the Cross of Reality by Hans Huessy, Eugen Rosenstock-Huessy's son, to psycho-analysis[49] which defines emotional disturbance as getting stuck in one phase or dimension of life, is applicable to communication theory. Communication disturbance or failure may result from skipping one of the dimensions of life or getting stuck in one of them, thus being unable to communicate freely from all perspectives.

Rosenstock-Huessy, Hans Huessy, Clinton Gardner[50] and others have applied the Cross of Reality to many different situations. It is a useful tool for analysis and helps to further understanding of life. Above I have used the Cross of Reality to indicate the various dimensions of communication theory. One of the problems besetting communication theory is that scholars tend to emphasize only one perspective, ignoring or deriding all others. The Cross of Reality when applied to the study of human communication indicates that the communication scholar lives at the center, with all dimensions open to him or her. Those scholars who can escape the temptation to specialize in one dimension will be able to comprehend the totality of communication theory. They will be able to move freely among all the various aspects of communication because the Cross of Reality gives them a firm understanding of how all aspects relate to one another.

Fifth, metanomics when applied to the study of communication should help the communication scholar to escape from the necessity to create laws, rules, or a Grand Theory which will explain all communication behaviour. Beginning with the Cross of Reality, the communication scholar may learn that objectification of people occurs only at one level of theory development, that at other levels there must be a willingness to accept the spontaneity of true response.

Finally, a personal word: in 1957 I read the works of Martin Buber and was deeply affected by them. For almost twenty-five years I have read Buber and sought to bring his work to focus on the situations which I faced. As I read Eugen Rosenstock-Huessy, I have been aware of the similarities and the differences between these two seminal thinkers of our century. Both provide a breakthrough away

49. Gardner, *Letters to the Third Millennium*, pp. 131-132.
50. Gardner, *Letters to the Third Millennium*, pp. 131-132.

from the traditional philosophical and social scientific paradigms. Both men were deeply influenced by Ludwig Feuerbach and have tried to expand on his thought. Both learned from each other and from their mutual friend Franz Rosenzweig. Both share the insight that speech, response, the turning towards the other, is the most important facet of life.

Rosenstock-Huessy has emphasized the historicity of human beings. His grammatical analysis has led him to make important contributions to our understanding of human life. Yet, it seems to me, he works at the 'macro' level of human life and tells us little about the individual person in his or her daily existence with the exception of his emphasis on service to people in the Third Millennium.[51] Martin Buber was concerned with the meeting of two people. He was less concerned with the historicity of human beings. His application is more at the micro level of the individual person. He described the nature of the relationship between people which is two-fold depending upon the words spoken to one another. Rosenstock-Huessy described the fourfold dimensions of life, taking a wider viewpoint of relationships. Whereas Rosenstock-Huessy's grammatical method caused him to take the pronouns Thou, I, It, literally, Buber holds they are only descriptive terms for the stances which people take toward one another in the encounter. There is a tension between Buber and Rosenstock-Huessy, as seen in their comments to one another,[52] but I do not believe you can dismiss the one in favour of the other. This is not an either-or situation! Both have something important to teach which cannot be placed in the traditional language of the social sciences. We must stand between them learning from both, experiencing the tension which exists between their viewpoints.

51. Eugen Rosenstock-Huessy, *Planetary Service: The Way into the Third Millennium* (Norwich, Vt.: Argo Books, 1978).

52. Sydney and Beatrice Rome, eds., *Philosophical Interrogations*, pp. 31-35.

Mercenary or Pirate:
Life in a Rhetorical Culture

W. Thomas Duncanson

I. A Predicament

On an unpleasantly gray morning this spring a young woman, a student in my course "Interpersonal Communication," entered my office, obviously distraught, and asked if she might close the door so that we could speak in privacy. She fumbled about setting up a cassette tape player, saying that she would like for me to hear part of a tape I had required her to make for what would eventually be an interpersonal biography project. The barely audible taped voice of the student's biography subject spoke matter-of-factly about her childhood desires to kill a companion–a remark my student had laughed off, until the previous day when the subject had threatened to kill *her* if she ever revealed certain personal and family information which had been disclosed during the biographical interviews. Almost in tears, the young woman wanted to know if I thought the threat should be taken seriously, and what I thought she should do.

Though the threat seemed implausible to me, that it had disturbed my student to such a degree signalled that it deserved to be treated with utmost seriousness. Remaining calm, I made certain formal assurances and attempted to demonstrate my sympathy. The show of support was relevant but evasive; it did not answer the question I had been asked. What other information did I need to help this student? Objectively, the facts came from the young woman in a stream: age, sex, race, socio-economic status, and deviancies of the threatener. I sorted the factors and looked for a correlation, but the data was ambiguous. Dare I predict violence? Dare I *not* predict violence?[1]

I am grateful to my former colleague, Robert Hariman, of Drake University for suggesting extensive stylistic revisions in this paper, and more generally to Hariman, Allen Scult, and Jon Ericson for encouraging me to talk about values in a field which is sometimes inhospitable to such talk.

1. Dr. Carl P. Malmquist has found that behaviour change, "cries for help," object loss and threats to manhood among others are signals indicating the propensity for

We proceeded more slowly then: trajectively, subjectively, prejectively. "How long have you known this woman?" "How did you meet?" "Why did you choose to write about her?" "What do you do when you are together?" "What plans do you have to do things together?" "What had you hoped for from this relationship?" "What names, if any (co-workers, teammate, roommate, whatever), had you undertaken to live under together?" And then, "What are your options?" "What are the consequences of each option?" Slowly, obtaining and affirming each answer dialectically, together we established the trajectory of the relationship to this decisive moment. My student chose to not reward the threat, regained control in what was for her a grave crisis, and in the next few days lived out the choice with mostly good consequences. I too was moved, of course, from sympathy to commitment and vigilance. And I had Rosenstock-Huessy to thank for the epistemological versatility to get beyond "factors" and "correlations" to what was finally decisive and therefore ultimately of greatest assurance about the relationship of these two women.[2]

Yet for all of the very tangible progress my student and I had made that morning, I was extremely dissatisfied. I was worried that when most students go through the teacher's door they are not going to be joined in a decisive dialectic, but rather they are sort of "shopping" for advice and that that is precisely what they get. The student, patient, executive, or parishioner will shop teacher to teacher, doctor to doctor, advisor to advisor, priest to priest (or maybe even friend to teacher to doctor to advisor to priest) until either (1) they are told what they wanted to hear in the first place, (2) the truth somehow emerges and is understood, or (3) so much time is spent in consultation that the opportunity for meaningful

homicidal aggression, but in reality (though these factors are prominent in the make-up of killers) these and any other factors are always present in the population to a far greater degree than the homicide rate. Prediction is impossible. "Premonitory Signs of Homicidal Aggression in Juveniles," *American Journal of Psychiatry* 128 (October, 1971):461-465.

2. The genius of Rosenstock-Huessy was that with his motto *"Respondeo etsi mutabor"* he abolished social mathematics. With Rosenstock-Huessy we do not tolerate the assertion "I live in a 'high crime' neighbourhood." Instead we begin with the unquantifiable but symptomatic realities of affiliation and intimacy. We ask, "Do you always lock your doors?" or "Do you know your neighbours' names?" This is not mere personalism. It is personalism *and* formalism. For Rosenstock-Huessy's attack on social mathematics see "In Defense of the Grammatical Method," *Speech and Reality* (Norwich, Vt.: Argo Books, 1970), pp. 9-44. One account of his four-fold (objective, subjective, trajective, prejective) epistemology is contained in the essay "The Individual's Right to Speak," in *Speech and Reality,* pp. 155-189.

action passes.

Moreover, and in terms Rosenstock-Huessy had taught me in his writings to think,[3] I was unhappy because in the entire episode–from the biographical interviews, to the threat, to my student's tearful inquiry, to our dialectic, to her subsequent action–only the very most inconsequential thing of all had been accomplished *formally*, that being my promise to give the student extra time to complete her project and my assurance that she would not receive a penalty in her project grade for the gaps which would result because the interviews had been curtailed. We had not been able to expiate the sin in the confessional. We had not been able to dissolve the relationship in the court of divorce. We had not been able to consecrate the high seriousness of our talk at a public altar. We had not been able to incorporate our dialectical skills into a common stock venture. We had not been able to open a revised standard version of a sacred text and read about the immutable laws of trust. We had not even been able to conclude the episode with a lecture to the "Interpersonal Communication" class on the absolute truth about threats of violence. We had no way whatsoever to formally symbolize that we had chosen to stand in a new relationship to threateners; as far as our world was concerned we could be threatened again the very next day and we would again be mere, silent victims, undifferentiated from any other victims. It was as if our dialogue on trust meant nothing. The entire matter was to remain private, personal, informal–almost surreptitious and to be denied.

I sensed that my unhappiness about "shopping for advice" was probably related to my dissatisfaction with the almost total informality of the affair. Both are indicative of intolerable vulnerability–fallibility of intellect, weakness of will, absence of opportunity. Though it is desirable to accept a certain amount of vulnerability, it does not follow to say that such occasions as threats to one's life are merely personal and not within the sphere of formal social action. Surely life in the human collectivity should hold forth options between the effacements of privacy and the bowdlerization of publicity.

II. The Mercenary

I am by training and trade a rhetorician, a member of the ancient and dishonourable profession of teachers of public discourse. It is my task to know what is "effective" and what is "ineffective" public talk and why. It seems only reasonable to expect that my own profession

3. Rosenstock-Huessy, *The Origin of Speech* (Norwich, Vt.: Argo Books, 1981).

might provide some excellent advice on how to talk about threats or to threateners "effectively." So, I might investigate all of the works of my field, both ancient and modern, and I might even commission a study on the subject by my peers. If I did these things, this is what I might learn: topics one uses to invent an effective verbal response to a threatener, how threats function to alter relationships, techniques which may be used to curtail threat escalation, the semantic and non-verbal constituents of threats with special emphasis on disguise and passive aggression, a typology of threats by context, the likelihood of threatening and threat compliance by personality type, the influence of threats on third party behaviour, and the effectiveness of threats compared to other compliance-gaining strategies. Along the way I might be instructed in the intricasies of feedback loops, "watergate" models, balance and congruity, communicative competence, and enthymemic discourse. I might also be treated to some passages about the inherent evil of threats, the irrationality of *ad bacculum* discourse, the progressive differentiation or decay of relationships, the vulnerability of the self of the threatener, the inability of the dispossessed to answer threats, and the coercive nature of all language. In all, with diligence, it would be an impressive and not unuseful body of research.

At the conclusion of my study I would be able to advise my students, friends, children, or whomever asks how to (minimally and benignly) defuse or (maximally and malignantly) "pay back" a threatener. But why must we continue to be threatened? On this point my studies would be discouraging or even cynical. Threats, lies, compulsion, irrationality, and manipulation are "given" in human nature (in desire) and embedded in culture. To suggest otherwise would be immorally naive. But might we not redress the imbalance between the terrorist and the victim? *That* is a question of opportunity, and opportunity, it seems, lies beyond the scope of rhetoric.

The rhetorician cannot think before terror, hence cannot think beyond terror, and therefore rhetoric abets terror. Rhetoric as a discipline reacts to opportunity (and consequently shows up in the form of flattery under tyrants), but stipulates no preconditions or opportunities for its own being. To be sure, the rhetorician, whether engaged in bold demonstration or obsequious flattery, is always with us. Paradoxically though, in many cases it is the insinuations of flattery which are the true deeds of cultural heroism while the swaggering debate of the open forum is culturally negligent. Indeed, in the second half of the twentieth century in the West, the rhetorical (the bold public presentation) has become the predominant mode of cultural production and the consequences are at best a mixed blessing. One of my colleagues jovially professes: "Rhetoric is everything, and more." Ruefully, we understand that this is more a predicament than a natural description.

Ours is a rhetorical culture, and this has had a profound effect on the quality of our lives. A rhetorical culture is one in which (1) everything is arguable, (2) previous decisions may be revoked by new arguments, (3) successful rhetoric is its own qualification, (4) violence is condemned because it is evidence that a non-rhetorical process has taken the place of a rhetorical one, and (5) the popular conception of historical utility is the final measure of every act. Rhetorical cultures tend to have no first principle except, perhaps, the right to speak. Rhetorical cultures are a confusion of change, sweeping along on the acclamations of public opinion yet often stalled in comedic confusion. Rhetoricians have often flattered themselves that the teacher (almost a philosopher), the legislator, or the advocate before the bar is the fundamental rhetorical character. They do this in order to protect themselves against the charge that the rhetorician is the demagogue. The fundamental rhetorical character, however, is neither hero nor villain. The fundamental and irreducible character of rhetorical culture is the mercenary. It is the mercenary character of contemporary public life that separates the public from the private, diminishes opportunity by bleeding the formal, and ultimately gives the advantage to the terrorist over the victim.

Eugen Rosenstock-Huessy never spoke of "rhetorical" and "anti-rhetorical" cultures, yet he well understood that the West was gravitating toward rhetorical culture of a pure type–a mercenary life of blameless mercenary irresponsibility.

> Under the shades of the suburb's sidewalks, my words don't matter much. As long as my words made law in my work, the interlacing of my thoughts, words, and acts, decided over their being either good or evil. But nowadays, an advertising agency makes the young writer proclaim the latest hair tonic an eighth world wonder; why hold this against him? These words are not his own...."Sin has become collective. The same doctor or manufacturer or mechanic or teacher who is so tame and good and over-wrought that he has neither time nor opportunity to sin, belongs to one or more sinning groups. He belongs to a professional group, block, and lobby. They sin for him. And at home, he and his wife fall victim to all the drives in the community."[4]

---

4. Rosenstock-Huessy, *The Christian Future or the Modern Mind Outrun*, Torchbook ed. (1946; reprint ed., New York: Harper and Row, 1966), pp. 30-31.

In a rhetorical culture "successful rhetoric is its own qualification." So people have become habituated to domination in public forums by "hired guns." So many of our speakers are intellectual mercenaries that we doubt the sincerity of all speakers. Positions are taken and strategies are enacted. "Real speech" is driven into tormented privacy, and those who do speak without pay or at self-sacrifice are treated as messiahs, freaks, or as being engaged in mere catharsis. The distinction between public talk and private action is so acute it is never questioned in ordinary discourse.

Young men and women are profoundly altered when they are told they are "good communicators" and therefore can "get a job" writing and speaking for any corporation, trade association, influence group, or party in need. Similarly, when a young person is told she is not a very good writer or confirmed in her anxiety as a speaker, she abdicates the public in favour of the skillful mercenary. To say these signals of competence and incompetence make our best young people cynical is an historic understatement. When the graduate-to-be scanning the college placement bulletin says, "I suppose I could apply for this job in community relations with Behemoth Utilities, Inc.," something has snapped inside. When I put myself up for sale as a mouthpiece, I am a man without a country, or family, or party, or creed, or even mind to call my home. This is the homelessness of the mercenary not the refugee, and it is the curse of the American intelligentsia.

The proliferation of the intellectual mercenary has caused a marked shift in the nature of intellectual contest and therefore of judgment. The classical notion of intellectual conflict is dialectical: two ideas are said to directly "clash" in their mutual exclusivity. Today the dialectic of ideas has been superceded by competition for the auditor's attention.[5] That is, ideas, products, and allegiances "compete" for a finite amount of disposable "income"–dollars, time, praise. In 1925 in Green Valley, Illinois (population 500), there were two churches, Methodist and Presbyterian, and it made a big difference to my grandparents both for the here-and-now and (they thought) the afterlife whether they joined one or the other. We can be sure that the minister at each church went to some pains to point out the differences and that consequently the flock of each was fairly literate and articulate on subjects biblical and theological. Today, the two churches on the corner must make common cause against hobbies, social clubs, entertainment and sporting events, cable television, blue movies, workaholism, etc. *ad infinitum.* Today, their

5. See Jules Henry, *Culture Against Man* (New York: Vintage Books, 1963).

shrinking congregations can barely explain the difference between
Protestants and Catholics and know little of the Bible, but are fairly
well able to articulate the choices and pitfalls of popular culture.
Unfortunately, the mercenaries make the most of the blurring of
distinctions created by the "struggle for the attention of the audience," hence the sense of comparability one must enjoy to exercise
judgment in confidence is deteriorating.[6]

To say the mercenary intellectual "makes the most" of opportunities is both exaggeration and unnecessary condemnation. In reality,
the mercenary is never completely committed to his cause, is paradoxically reticent in hyperbole, is cautious in exaggeration.[7] To
facilitate the contest for the attention of the audience, the mercenary intellectuals hide behind the professionalism of specialist knowledge, what Rosenstock-Huessy called in a discussion of the journal-
istic presentation of reality a "Niagara of disconnected facts,"[8] as
well as the invention of fantastic possibilities.[9] That is, the mercenaries have hitched the *ethos* of science to the dream of transcen-
dence in order to obtain the attention of the multitudes. And
because mercenaries are paid for being confident in the fantasies
they create, they dare venture no self-criticisms, no suspicious
doubts, and no humble "NOs."

> He who will not curse the shortcomings of his profession as a
> lawyer, a teacher, a doctor, a priest, always will have to defend it
> beyond the health of his soul. The doctor who defends medicine
> as it is today, against all outside criticism, and nowhere bands
> together unselfishly with these same critics, must do harm to his

6. See Walter J. Ong, S.J., *Interfaces of the Word* (Ithaca: Cornell University Press,
1977), on the changing norms in strategies of judgment under changing technological
conditions.

7. Rosenstock-Huessy wrote almost favourably on the detached innocence of the
mercenary. See *Planetary Service: A Way Into the Third Millennium*, trans. Mark Huessy
and Freya von Moltke (Norwich, Vt.: Argo Books, 1978), p. 78.

8. Rosenstock-Huessy, *The Christian Future*, p. 5.

9. Of the traditional five canons of rhetoric (invention, delivery, arrangement,
style, and memory) "invention" has been seen as both the most characteristic and the
most philosophically interesting. Historically, rhetoric was thought to "invent" arguments along the lines of probability, e.g., "Is it probable that a smaller man would
attack a larger one?" However, probability is a calculation about possibility; and, especially beyond the context of the law court, the powers of rhetorical invention range
widely in the discovery of what is possible. In the late twentieth century we must say
that the invention and contrast of possibilities (fantasies?) is *the* prominent mode of
cultural production as opposed to other modes we experience but cannot say are
dominant: authoritative imposition, re-symbolization of existing features, dialectical
opposition, or emergence-unification. On rhetoric as possibility see Gerald Bruns,
"Allegory and Satire: A Rhetorical Meditation," *New Literary History* 11 (1979):121.

soul.[10]

Rosenstock-Huessy made the contrast absolutely distinct between the person who speaks from humility and the person who gives himself over to the fantastic in his essay "Hitler and Israel, or On Prayer." The "No" of humility is more basic than the mumblings of professional caution. It is the negation which marks the distinction between the possible and impossible, the purposeful and the purposeless, the human and the divine.

> Hitler's will and his God's will are nauseatingly one. The great art of speech has made Hitler crazy. Since he has the privilege of speaking, of inflaming the masses, he spellbinds. And so he hovers as a ghost from the abyss of paganism, a ghost of the days before God touched Israel's lips with his fiery coal: My will, O mortal, not thine, be done....

> We can't forget the Bible because the divine 'No' was created, in our speech, during those thousand years of Jewish prayer. And all the other departments of our linguistic faculty rest on this clear distinction between prayer, on the one side, and science, poetry, fiction, and law, on the other. If we do not pray with Israel, we cannot retain our Greek mathematics, our Roman law.[11]

Our scientists, our advertising writers, our host of "professionals" have no reply to Hitler; they differ from him in degree, not kind. Science and rhetoric admit to no limitation on their inventive capacities, and hence have only "technical" problems of adjustment but never any real problems of purpose.

Consequently, the masses of people, not selected for the job of professional spokesperson and bombarded by the "We are in control" of the mercenary professionals is as homeless as the mercenaries themselves. Theirs is the homelessness of the refugee. The concept of "merit" has run amok. As reasonable as it is that intelligence and diligence be rewarded with responsibility, responsibility-seeking must be equalled or surpassed by responsibility-taking or merit is a mockery. Societies become pathological as the dreams of their members depart from the consideration of consequences. Recall that in a rhetorical culture "successful rhetoric is its own qualification." No one is ascribed the status of "spokesperson" for the collectivity except at the moment they speak and are found agreeable. *Ethos* or "who may speak to whom about what on whose behalf" is granted

10. Rosenstock-Huessy, *The Christian Future*, p. 24.

11. Eugen Rosenstock-Huessy, "Hitler and Israel, or On Prayer," *Journal of Religion* 25 (1945):132.

grudgingly and withdrawn with fickle ease in a rhetorical culture. The speakers whirl across the stage crisis by crisis, fading with popularity or the even more fleeting "attention." The crisis comes when we ask "Who speaks for *you* on subject X to auditors Y" and the people cannot answer. *No one* is speaking for them about anything to anyone. They are "boat people" as surely as if they were afloat and leaderless, unclaimed and unable to make sensible claims about their allegiances. As the mercenaries, Rosenstock-Huessy's "brainy peppinjays,"[12] reel across the public stage, Richard Nixon's "silent majoritarian" knows well the homelessness of the refugee or the near total inability of society to produce elders.[13] Elders are meritorious, not in the brillance of youth at grabbing attention, but in the durability of their seriousness. True elders bare the unmistakable marks of the collectivity; if they err in orthodoxy, they do not do so out of flippant complacency. A society capable of producing elders, people with real *ethos* or the ability to speak to me and for me in matters of importance, is distinctly anti-rhetorical in that having a good argument is never enough. A good argument is a good argument because a person is willing to stay around and live with the consequences of that point of view. To do otherwise is to speak nonsense.

III. The Pirate

We have recounted the problems of rhetorical culture. We began with the problem of my student and myself, how Rosenstock-Huessy's four-fold typology of knowledge assisted us in discovering the decisive ground in our battle with a terrorist, yet how we lacked an opportunity to symbolize our mindfulness and decisiveness in a socially meaningful way, in a way which would put the terrorist at the disadvantage. We discovered that rhetorical studies could tell us much about answering the terrorist but not about the opportunities available in a society to speak. We learned that the rhetorician can insert himself in any political framework, that the principle rhetorical character is the mercenary. When rhet-

---

12. Rosenstock-Huessy, *Planetary Service*, p. 13.

13. I remember vividly the county political convention I attended in 1980 at which an elderly gentleman, the chairperson of the platform committee, protested in vain about platform revisions called from the floor. He stammered, "If you had been around as long as I have, you would understand these things...." He could not articulate what age entitled him to understand, so his age qualification and self-imputed status of "elder" was lost on the audience interested only in the merits of the argument no matter the source. The man was verbally trampled. See Rosenstock-Huessy on the production of elders. "Teaching Too Late, Learning Too Early," in *I am an Impure Thinker* (Norwich, Vt.: Argo Books, 1970), pp. 91-114.

oric is the ascendent mode of cultural production as it is at present in the West, the noetic economy of open persuasion and argument (rhetoric at its combative best and not its obsequious worst) alters the values, purposes, and even characters of a society. We concluded that a rhetorical culture may lose or dilute the very opportunities for public participation and common action on which it thrives. That is to say, the civil libertarian and civics textbook celebration of free speech may finally be absurd, inimical, and destructive. If defenders of rhetorical culture would step forward, what might they say?

First, they would be aghast, *reductio ad absurdum*, that free speech is anything other than a political absolute. But if the aspersions of fascism could be set aside, they might give their best argument–that rhetorical culture is always different *in kind* from fascism because it is always agonistic and never monolithic and the *process* of the competition of ideas assures the highest possible quality of life be made available to the greatest possible number of people. In a rhetorical culture the work of mercenary intellectuals may indeed be repugnant, but at least it is possible to hire the publicists, organizers, media advisers, and whoever else it takes to counter the villainy. Moreover, in this *process* free consumers buy the ideas and all the attendant consequences of the mercenaries and hence must become good shoppers. The great democracies, the argument goes, celebrate above all else, process, for it is process and not any particular product which is the highest good in human affairs.

We obviously must be very cautious in rejecting this line of reasoning, for after all our most fundamental grievance is with our lack of opportunity–the entrance point on public process. The rejection of democracy would not serve our interests. And yet a protest must be lodged against the celebration of process and the ludicrous "marketplace" metaphor. First, it is obvious to one and all that desire precedes process. Processes are established and maintained because they efficiently regulate and enable the satisfaction of desires. No process-absent satisfaction could endure. Indeed, the gravest weakness of process is hypocrisy, wherein actors reveal that satisfaction is more important than the process. Second, a single process or identical processes may be used for the counsels of the highest seriousness or may be subverted to triviality. Process requires the continuous investment of power and participation to remain viable. Third, processes are often if not usually inept and under continuous revision. Revision then becomes the ultimate process and a curious ultimate at that. Processes must respect *both* permanence and change and hence we must be maximally cautious in endorsing process *per se.*[14] The defenders of process must defend the *rhetorical* process or admit that it is the equal of, say, superstition or science in public life. Fourth, the "marketplace of ideas" is a singularly inept metaphor for community, one which forgets that competition is only *one* way of building community and also that the most splendid market is a nightmare for the impoverished. Rhetoric is a *skill* which guarantees no voice for the voiceless. Fifth, as we have seen, rhetoric is a skill which will adapt itself to changing public opportunities. Public speech and debate can be used to advocate the end of public speech and debate. In the main, rhetorical culture is about winning, not about the opportunities it will take to make life better. "Process" is no apology for the distortions and failures of rhetorical culture.

What would Rosenstock-Huessy have us put in its place? This, the revolutionary question, is the most difficult to ask of any great teacher. Rosenstock-Huessy would begin his answer, I think, by disavowing all so-called "idealism." He was not a constructor of utopias.

> Professor Walter A. Jessup frankly told me just before his death in an amazing conversation (with a son of William James, and myself), on the Moral Equivalent of War: 'We have invested many millions of dollars in one direction and now this is the trend. And you think that simply because you are right, you can change this trend?' He expressed the practical man's disgust with a hollow idealism which, while life is going actually in one direction materially every day, at the same time proclaims standards which point in exactly the opposite direction.
>
> Interim America is a fact; the factory is a fact. And therefore to the practical man these facts predict the future....
>
> But the practical man is impractical about the future....The practical man...embodies a philosophy of the past....
>
> That which simply goes on from the past as a trend is not 'future' in the full sense of this term....In human history the break with the past is the condition of any future. The relationship of any past and any future is never made by a trend, but always by a victory over trends. On the other hand, the idealist is only the fellow-traveller of the trend. He opposes his will to the trend, and no trend has ever been influenced by human will. Ideals are crushed. And idealists are rushed in the very direction which they deny.[15]

14. The reference here is to Kenneth Burke, *Permanence and Change*, 2d rev. ed. (Indianapolis: Bobbs-Merrill, 1954).

15. Rosenstock-Huessy, *The Christian Future*, pp. 32-33.

Rosenstock-Huessy contends that there is a third way, neither resigned nor rebellious. The third way is to *create* through sacrifice equivalent of the battlefront, if necessary, the world in which you want to live.[16] Those who have studied Rosenstock-Huessy have given much thought to the third way, speculating on whether or not it implies the abandonment of the institutions of school, community, and especially church as we have come to know them. Clearly his life and works bespeak of no such abandonment. What his life and works do signify, though, is a freedom and directness of thought and a willingness to take risks not ordinarily associated with our schools, communities, and churches. Rosenstock-Huessy was well aware of the hurt present in our "factory and suburb" culture. Rather than being the idealist and offering a vision of life which was the opposite of what pains us, he offered instead a new being, a new character, the pirate, who we can juxtapose against the dreaded mercenary of rhetorical culture to understand the direction out of our current cultural predicament.

Piracy is always for a minority. Like the mercenary himself, the pirate is distant from the *telos* of the reigning culture.[17] The pirate begins by loathing his culture, begins to build the world anew in *metanoia* ("from dead works").

> Metanoia is not an act of the will. It is the unwillingness to continue. This unwillingness is not an act but an experience. The words make no sense, the atmosphere is stifled. One chokes. One has no choice but to leave. But one does not know what is going to happen, one has no blueprint for action.[18]

Out of this sense of alienation and even revulsion piracy may begin.

"A pirate is a tempter," says Rosenstock-Huessy.[19] That is, the pirate "attempts" things others have not tried. Specifically, the pirate attempts "to assert oneself in the absence of the authorities."[20] Like the other great heroes of Rosenstock-Huessy, the argonaut (first to sail beyond sight of shore), the soldier, and the heretic, the pirate ignores her personal discomfort and risks life and fortune out of proportion to the probability of personal gain. As Rosenstock-Huessy makes clear in *Planetary Service,* in our era the pirate is most needed not in bringing noble deeds to the high seas but in establishing the

16. Rosenstock-Huessy, *The Christian Future,* p. 33 ff. and *Planetary Service* in its entirety.

17. Rosenstock-Huessy, *Planetary Service,* p. 78.

18. Rosenstock-Huessy, "Metanoia: To Think Anew," in *I am an Impure Thinker,* p. 189.

19. Rosenstock-Huessy, *Planetary Service,* p. 73.

20. Rosenstock-Huessy, *Planetary Service,* p. 74.

human relationships which will guarantee that the affiliation and epistemic pre-conditions exist for the continued and enriched existence of human life on planet earth.

Rosenstock-Huessy well understood that collectivities are created and maintained in formal naming. This authority, of course, eludes the pirate *except that in turning over our language to the rhetorical mercenaries, a void in authority has been created which is nearly as great as once existed on the high seas.* The future lies with those who would create and re-create the names which (1) are closest to encapsulating our individual, existential agendas, (2) reveal the bases of our common predicament and shared action, and (3) empower us to resist every force of indignity. Names must be founded or refounded which show the *seriousness* of our current crisis and the *enduring seriousness* of our hopes. It is not enough to know these names and meditate on their power. These words must be taken to the very people who trivialize the hopes, manipulate the crises, and mistrust the pirates. And the bearer of these names must not go forth as yet another martyred idealist but as a neighbour who insists on change, is willing to toil and sacrifice for change, who is willing to change for change, and yes, if necessary, die for change. The pirate acts on need (first things first); the mercenary acts on command. Both the pirate and the mercenary are called to "camp" in time of grave threat, and both go earnestly.[21] But the pirate (whether volunteer or draftee) sees in the campfire the single source of light and warmth for all, while the mercenary only sees the hearth of his home reflected there.

It is up to the pirates to create the planetary post-rhetorical culture. I cannot write here exactly what such a culture would be. However, we can suppose that *ethos* might be re-created in a stable body of elders, that the mercenary would fade as a major cultural character, that public life would regain stability and personal and public acts both would maintain some comparability under strong names. Hierarchy-creating names could bring order to the Niagara of news and information, and impatient fantasies might even be replaced by humble prayer and historical perspective. And most fundamentally the post-rhetorical culture might be founded on peace—not docility but the experience of the fruits of participatory order—rather than the bogus promises of "process."[22]

21. Rosenstock-Huessy, *The Christian Future*, p. 236.
22. Rosenstock-Huessy, *Planetary Service* concerns the prospect for world peace through piracy. More importantly, perhaps, peace is for Rosenstock-Huessy the value which makes all social science comprehensible. See "In Defense of the Grammatical Method," pp. 35-37.

And what might the pirate say to my student terrorized by her acquaintance? Not, I think, to build a new society in which terror is presumptively meaningless but to confront terror in its face and with all possible calm and dignity to deny its power. Therein the first step toward building a new collective order is taken. Piracy *is* opportunity and neither depends on being "given" an opportunity nor *post hoc* creating the structures which will insure adequate future opportunities. Pirates act now. They are rude if they must be. But speech is action; and it can be formal creative action, if it is undertaken seriously (*not* impersonally). "Be a pirate," Rosenstock-Huessy might tell my threatened student, "to establish moral authority where there is none. You have nothing to lose but your paralysis of fear."

Rosenstock-Huessy made apparent in his writings the necessity of preserving and creating our families, communities, and planet. He insisted that our fate is not sealed, that courageous women and men can make history. He wanted from all of us who would be, directly or indirectly, his students, the commitment to work to assure that the affiliative opportunities exist on this planet to insure its continued survival. He clarified our choices. Now Rosenstock-Huessy's legacy of thought and example ought to be made the burden of every person who would choose the path of mercenary or pirate.

Labor and the Spirit

Patricia A. North

It is about ordinary things that I wish to speak. Guided by the thought of Eugen Rosenstock-Huessy I wish to speak about a working world I have come to know.

Abstract analysis seems a meaningless enterprise when responding to Rosenstock-Huessy. His vision of a new age–the age of the spirit–takes on meaning for me only concretely–in specific places, at specific times. For this reason I feel compelled to reflect on a new, personal vocation–work in seafood processing plants–in Alaska and now on the Oregon Coast.

My words will not be directed to you as if from one who is a PhD in History, one learned in the study of mysticism and comparative religion. This backdrop of intellectual work cannot help but give form to this essay. But it is as if all this training has been funnelled from above now downward to the very ordinary, work-a-day world of the seafood factory. It is with profound respect that I dare attribute to Rosenstock-Huessy the inspiration for these reflections on factory production processes and the community of man.

When I returned from Alaska in 1979, I described my work in King Crab processing to a fellow PhD in History who was teaching at an exclusive school in La Jolla, California. She said, "My God, Pat, how did you do it? I could never have done that!" In truth I am as pleased with completing a full three-month King Crab season on a remote Aleutian Island as I am with my six-year-to-complete dissertation. How could two such diverse endeavours hold equal value in a heart? Rosenstock-Huessy is one of–perhaps–very few intellectuals who would understand this pride of a factory woman, member now of Seafood Workers Local 554-P.[1]

When I returned from my first King Crab season, I spoke excitedly to several academic friends about the new world of manual labor that I had discovered and both men recommended to me

For E. Fern Puckett, a woman of courage, gifted supervisor, friend.

1. Since this writing Seafood Workers Local 554-P has merged with United Food and Commercial Workers International Union, AFL-CIO-CLC, Local 143-A.

Rosenstock-Huessy's *The Multiformity of Man,* which I ordered and read, but with some disappointment. What I understood from his essay about the mechanization of man, I had encountered in the thought of others, especially the essays of Marx, who also deplored the specialization of production processes and its dulling, dehumanizing effect on man. What I did *not* understand in *The Multiformity of Man,* however, aroused a desire to read his other works. I was led to *I am an Impure Thinker, The Christian Future or the Modern Mind Outrun, The Fruit of Lips or Why Four Gospels, Speech and Reality.* These works and the bit of biographic information I learned, especially Rosenstock-Huessy's applied devotion to communal labor projects, gave renewed hope that indeed he would welcome these, my reflections on factory work, as amendments to *The Multiformity of Man.*

In rereading Rosenstock-Huessy's introductory remarks, my first response to him would be–but man himself makes these machines and when the various processing machines malfunction, as they often do, it is man again who repairs them, or, who creatively utilizes his labor force to compensate for the loss of time. It was astonishing to me and then amusing to see almost every key conveyor belt involved in butchering, gilling, washing and packaging King Crab sections fail to function properly. A multimillion dollar business brought to a halt by an obsolete, faulty conveyor belt system. The butchers, who halve the live King Crab on dull-edged blades adjustable to any belly height, had to expend an enormous amount of added energy to throw the crab sections onto the gillers belt because their conveyor was too narrow and too inconveniently located. Butchering in this manner, twelve hours a day, seven days a week was so arduous a task that after 1 to 2 weeks this particular company could rely on only two men as a steady, dependable unit of labor–the most critical unit in the whole process since their speed set the pace for the rest of us.

I remember well the breakdown of the conveyor belt stretching along overhead the gillers (whose job it was to remove the crab gills by sweeping the sections against a swiftly rotating and groved metal drum). No one dared to stop, neither the butchers nor the gillers–so very shortly the belt was piled with freshly gilled crab sections. One daring worker climbed atop the belt, sat down in his raingear and scooted and pushed with his boots the sections along the belt onto the chain link conveyor that carried the crab under cleansing jet streams and then down to the packaging crew. It was a moment of great fun to have the monotony of work broken by the comic movements of one individual in the midst of an elaborate machinery lay-out.

Another innovation at a moment of malfunction occurred when the gillers simply carried by hand the gilled crab sections and threw them down onto the moving conveyor to be packaged. Such incidents as these were not uncommon, and I came, in this way, to see that man is the most valuable machine in the production process.

Such situations occurred in a remote outpost to be sure. Not so incredible, but similar dilemmas do occur in Mainland factories and they are always solved for the moment by the worker endowed with extra energy and initiative. To a wise supervisor, such human labor is of inestimable value.

This admirable description of long-suffering service to production should be quickly amended by another vivid memory of malfunction. There existed a chain-link floor level conveyor beneath the butchers' stands onto which were thrown the hard back shells of the King Crab. These were then carried directly into a grinder for rapid disposal. When this crucial conveyor stopped, one of the butchers would usually jog and push which sometimes corrected the stoppage. But most often the engineers would have to be called and the butchers would continue their work until steeped so high in crab shells that butchering could be carried on no longer. Sometimes a clever butcher, judging that all had worked beyond measure, would intentionally see to it that the grinder jammed. And sometimes an obvious solution to a malfunction would be intentionally ignored by all workers down the line who simply took a needed break until the supervisor could be found. These moments of communal respite were never prearranged–but agreed to in an unspoken manner, as if all sensed the need for rest at the same time. In this way each day– although monotonous to be sure–held forth the promise of some magic moments when the steady rhythmic movements of the workers would be excited or lulled by the malfunction of machines. An almost uncanny relationship between workers and machines developed over the course of our long hours together. "Oh, there goes that conveyor again–what will happen now?"

One's sense of time in such a setting is quite unique. All were migrant workers transported singly without family to a remote Aleutian port–living only to work from 7 A.M. to 7 P.M. or 7 P.M. TO 7 A.M. The immediate problems of everyday household community life were eliminated. No cooking, no washing clothes, no immediate family crises had to be faced. Only the twelve hours per day, seven days a week. So, although we were paid per hour, the full meaning of the hourly wage was very different from that of a unionized seafood processor in a Mainland factory. For in Alaska we knew that in three months time there would be an end to it all. After the season we would return to our own ordinary worlds.

Nevertheless, when Rosenstock-Huessy says that "Taking an interest in hours makes a man into something new and different from either" (that is, from either a citizen or a Christian),[2] he is right. The isolation of the Alaskan factory worker–paid by the hour– only served to intensify a unique experience of time that is shared by the Mainland seafood worker as well.

This experience of time is multifaceted. There is the objective fact of the disciplined organization of time into a 12 minute break after two hours of work and a 30 minute lunch after four hours of work. If enough raw product is at hand, there will be another 12 minute break two hours after lunch. This structure of time is the basic framework within which we work. But the character of these durations varies according to the type of work one is doing and its specific spatial setting. This could be seen as an objective fact also, for there is a noticeable difference in attitude between, for example, crab banders and shrimp pickers on the one hand, and crab pickers and filleters of fish on the other.

Crab banding and shrimp picking are both carried on at a conveyor belt setting, and so in the workers' awareness of time, something common is shared. Since there are no piece work incentives for either task, the monotonous flow of the conveyor is broken only by the anticipation of the first coffee break, then lunch, then break, then home! For some, swiftness makes time pass quickly but most settle in at a mediocre speed, and a glazed look in their eyes is evident at coffee time. Not so with crab pickers and filleters of fish! These more technically skilled workers are paid per hour, but in accord with their poundage output. Time for them is translated into numbers of crab dumps and baskets of fish. Their breaks are marked by much chatter. Awareness of time then is necessarily bound to our immediate spatial environment and the specific activities we must do within that space.

At the Oregon plant where I now work shrimp pickers would stand on either side of two conveyor belts situated in a small room which housed three "separators," two "shakers" and two "blowers." These various machines served to eliminate much excess shrimp shell and antennae after the cooked shrimp had passed through the peelers (six huge machines located outside our room which "rolled"

2. Eugen Rosenstock-Huessy, *The Multiformity of Man* (Norwich, Vt.: Argo, 1973), p. 20.

and "hammered" off most of the head and shell of the shrimp). These are useful machines and yet the deafening noise from the blowers and the shakers caused our room to be designated a hazardous noise area, and spongy ear plugs were required.[3] The conveyor belts rose slightly from waist to shoulder height, and pickers had to select standing positions on four graduated metal platforms in order to "pick" effectively. There is no choice spot for picking shrimp. It is excruciatingly painful for the backs of all, hence the frequent turnover in the shrimp-picking crew. Still, those who persevere usually select a particular level on a platform as well as a particular side of one of the belts and this becomes "their" favorite place. Any new recruit soon learns where she may or may not stand.

The possessiveness of a particular spot is amusing to one who understands the dynamics of conveyor belt work, but frustrating too. For no two shrimp pickers work alike. Some are speedy but inconsistent. Some meticulous beyond what is necessary. Some simply do not see very well. And many like to hold the shrimp back with one hand while picking with the other. The variations are incalculable! Hence the nature of one's movements are affected immediately by the personalities working at either elbow. Friction is not uncommon.

There is the paradox then, that one's own objective space can become an alien, uncomfortable place if some new picker arrives at your side whose habitual movements conflict with yours. A knowing supervisor will intervene and adjust the human alignments along either belt so that work can continue harmoniously and productively. But there is always to be considered the problem of physical suffering–that some pickers simply cannot bear to stand anywhere but in their own spot. These variables in individual capabilities and communal coordination combine to transform the experience of the shrimp pick room into a lively human organism. To an unaware observer looking into that room, we appear in our aprons and boots to be automatons, motionless in the midst of whirring machines, except for our hands.

Alas, crab banding is not nearly as interesting! Whole cooked Dungeness crab (1 1/2-2 1/2 lbs) are lifted out of their cooking cages and placed by hand upside down on a chain link conveyor which moves them through a metal housing of jet streams and then onto a rubberized conveyor where we banders stand ready with

3. Since this time the entire process has been expanded so that we now have twelve peelers, three separators, three blowers and shakers taking up nearly one-third the available in-plant space. Hence the machine noise is much diffused. Still, all are required to wear ear protection in accord with state safety regulations.

rubber bands and "extra parts." Our job is simply to stretch a rubber band around each end of folded-in crab legs. If a leg or claw is missing, we find a suitable replacement among our extra parts and band it tightly into its rightful place. Banding is necessary because after freezing these crabs can then more easily be slipped into their final plastic-bag package. One must take care to band even the tiny last legs which could otherwise tear the bag, inhibiting the flow of work for those in cold storage, next stage in the production process. One tries to focus on the work at hand–perhaps making the selection of "the perfect" extra part a continuous challenge. Still it is endlessly boring, for there are few variations in technique possible when banding crab legs. And it is painful too because there is no escape from the constant manipulation required at the cold, wet setting of the banding table.

Or, one comes to notice the time it takes to band one cage of crab and so turn the mountains of minutes into intervals equivalent to "a cage of crab." We "play" with the clock. But even this game can become a trap, for inevitably one begins to wonder how many cages are left to be banded. Some eager assistant may look to see the number of cages remaining in the cooling tanks and then the calculations of an end come up. Our private mental tumblings with time are extinguished by a final answer. The assistant hopes that her words will spur us on to finish faster so that the figures–pounds per man hour–will be even more impressive in the front office. But calculated words often do not accomplish this end. Sometimes it is that your supervisor will say playfully that there are 10 cages left when everyone knows that only 3 remain. A shout will go up–everyone is suddenly released from the burden of time–and work proceeds rapidly to its close. It has been a good day.

It came as a great surprise to me that, while banding crab, the power of the spoken word would become so apparent. Since we crab banders stand working in silence for such long periods, a word spoken, a glance given becomes unusually accentuated. Some personalities cannot bear the long silences and seek a spot next to another with whom they can talk–about food, sex, family predicaments. Others find such talk burdensome, preferring the solitude of their own thought. But true friendship shows itself in little ways. That someone, sensing your common despair, utters even one profane word becomes a source of consolation. That someone will offer a glance of knowing renews your strength to continue. That someone– who need not be there–will come and share your place, banding next to you in silence, and then leave to resume her own duties becomes an offering of self and so expands your heart in compassion for our common effort of working together that even banding is a joy, and time almost ceases to be.

Almost everyone agrees that the more highly skilled jobs of picking crab and filleting fish cause time to speed up. In the eyes of management this sensation–of not enough time!–and hence greater speed is created by the institution of incentive rewards. For instance, a crab picker at our plant is offered a set wage per hour if she makes poundage (14 lbs. per hour for fresh crab) plus 18 cents per pound over this minimum requirement. A filleter is paid per hour according to the amount of fish fillets she can produce–each species of bottomfish being given a set hourly production goal. The higher a filleter's percentage of this set amount, the higher her hourly pay. The incentive system serves more as an indicator of one's level of entry into the profession. It is only superficially related to a crab picker or a filleter's experience of time. Managers of manual workers would be well served to recognize that speed, quantities in time (production), is more closely bound to the specific nature of these technical arts.

Much time and thought are required to master the arts of picking crab and filleting fish. They are arts because there is a basic knowledge necessary in the use of mallet and anvil (used to crack crab legs and claws) and the various knives (different knives for different species). But then true mastery comes only after years of concentrated experience. Since no Dover sole is exactly like another, a true filleter adjusts her knife cuts in response to the constitution of the very fish before her. The structure of crab legs and claws is complex. An experienced crab picker is one who has learned to smack just the right spots on the shell of the leg and the claw. These are only two examples. The occasions for artistry are endless. One cannot be a good crab picker or filleter without this very pointed exercise of her mind engaging in the task of her hands. It is her thought and her act united by her desire to excel that causes time to fly.

After working for over a year in a variety of jobs at the same factory and often with the same people in different settings, I have come to understand much more of Rosenstock-Huessy's *The Multiformity of Man*. This is not to say that the truth of his four ecodynamic laws–of the plural, collective, dual and singular of man–has been exhausted for me. By no means! His words are words of exploration, words that can be re-worked, and must be re-worked–and perhaps one good place to do it is in the factory atmos-

phere that he was so concerned with. His words seem to me sometimes like a new light and may suddenly make accessible a pathway,
once worn but hidden for a time. It is encouraging that this kind of
free literary achievement comes, not only after years of studious
application to the subjects of law, history, education, but also after
hours of hard manual labor–as coal miner, lumberman, stone mason.
When Rosenstock-Huessy says:

> It will take a whole new generation to develop fully the power and
> capacity of men to conceive and express the secrets of the world
> into which we are bewitched by the modern form of production.[4]

I have hope.
I have hope.

For who of us is not after some secret? And once uncovered–perhaps
through a glance, a word, a mere profanity at the conveyor belt–the
secret leads always to a greater vision, for the very occurrence of
such a secret shows an insatiable thirst for life's secret. What is
important for us all is that we work with whatever talents we have to
hold forth the possibility of the mystery of man.

4. Rosenstock-Huessy, *The Multiformity of Man*, p. 13.

The Bridge Builder
in Quest for Community

Terry Simmons

Eugen Rosenstock-Huessy's work is ubiquious and influential despite the fact that "no one" seems to have heard of him.[1] Though a life-long and very productive scholar, he found most university life incomplete and dull. His work in the university remained provoca-tively somewhere on the edges too. At the same time, he understood that his apparent lack of disciplinary focus was necessary and part of the process of learning and of understanding itself. His vast writings and innovative community service had pattern and purpose, although that pattern is somewhat obscured by his nineteenth-century style and by the diversity of his work.

Eugen Rosenstock-Huessy was a man with a great breadth of knowledge, wide-ranging interests and varied experiences, as essays in this volume illustrate. A man with many interests is difficult enough to comprehend and certainly impossible to pigeonhole. Rosenstock-Huessy knew this, too. And he probably enjoyed this situ-ation since he understood the hazards of "disciplines" and the barriers created by labels. This "impure thinker" welcomed pluralism in learning.[2]

As a German and American scholar, Rosenstock-Huessy spent the majority of his years as a university professor in Germany and in the United States. However, he had many other public and professional roles as well. Central to Rosenstock-Huessy's individual and social roles were those of a student and of a teacher, on and off the campus, within, without, and sometimes despite the limitations of the university as an institution. He was equally a student in the trenches of Verdun as he was in the University of Berlin library, and equally

1. This essay is a revised version of a paper presented at the First International Conference on Eugen Rosenstock-Huessy, Renison College, Waterloo, Ontario, June 6-9, 1982. I wish to thank Page Smith for his leadership over the years and Darrol Bryant for his cheerful service, patience and tolerance.
2. Eugen Rosenstock-Huessy, "The Homecoming of Society," in *Adult Education Towards Social and Political Responsibility*, ed. F.W. Jessup (Hamburg: UNESCO Institute for Education, 1953), pp. 76-83.

a teacher at youth work camps in Silesia as he was on the Dartmouth College campus.

This essay discusses some of Rosenstock-Huessy's central ideas concerning history and education, with particular reference to adult education and his innovative leadership with youth work camp programs. Although Rosenstock-Huessy's practical leadership in adult education has been largely forgotten today, he remains quietly influential.

Rosenstock-Huessy on History and Education

According to Rosenstock-Huessy, history and education together mediate the paradox of change. The social roles of students and teachers are basic aspects of his autobiographical view of history and of the interaction between society, church and state. "No individual can go very far. Real achievements must be based on the continuity of many generations,"[3] he wrote. History requires generational interrelationships and at least three or four generations of collaboration toward the same goal.

Education is essentially a process for creating contemporaneity between generations and for maintaining the sovereignty of the group as defined by the interaction between society, church and state. By definition, education is far more than institutionalized classroom activities for children or for adults. Anthropologists, for instance, call this transmission of culture from generation to generation, acculturation. Education, therefore, is an intregal process for the maintenance of a sustainable, vital society.

While societies are dynamic, they are also fundamentally conservative. Thus they are never totally static, but are simultaneously striving for change, continuity and stability. Education has a special social function. It is to provide the intellectual context for meeting the political and spiritual challenges for change that are created as we respond as individuals to our many societal roles and duties in everyday life.[4] Education is an intergenerational affair. It stands between the promise of the future and the promise of the past. Education, like history, is the story of crisscrossing backwards and forwards across the present and between generations. As Rosenstock-Huessy observed:

3. Eugen Rosenstock-Huessy, *Out of Revolution: Autobiography of Western Man* (Norwich, Vermont: Argo Books, 1969), p. 8.
4. See, for example, Rosenstock-Huessy, "The Social Function of Adult Education," *Bulletin of the World Association for Adult Education*, OS 44 (1930):10-21 and "The Homecoming of Society."

...the proper sequence of any study in adult groups is first, on changes, the social, including adult education itself; secondly, on stabilities, the political, including the national laws and constitutions; and, thirdly, the spiritual, as the course between the Scylla of mere change and the Charybdis of mere sameness. Education is forever based on man's freedom of deciding between the two....
Adult education would have no business were it not for teaching to change with honour, neither too indifferently nor too reluctantly....To change with honour is impossible to those who have not experienced the life of the spirit, in good fellowship....[5]

The social consequences of change rest with the quality of fellowship or with the vitality of the community and its capacity for change. On the individual level, the essence of the social function of education is characterized by the generational nature of the student-teacher relationship. This is the point where Rosenstock-Huessy's ideas on history and on education coincide most explicitly and distinctly.

The difference in age between co-workers may be accidental; the time difference between teacher and pupil exists by establishment. By definition, a teacher is—in some way or other—ahead of his student. Teacher and student represent past and future, and, also, the bridge of communication between past and present. They are, therefore, distemporaries, not contemporaries. Two times exist of which one is embodied by the teacher, the other by the pupil. In learning, in teaching, in education, the miracle is achieved by bringing both together in a third time.[6]

The relationship between the student and the teacher is fellowship at the most personal level, written both large and small, spanning moments in the classroom and years in the community. Together, two individuals in the present construct a bridge of continuity from the past into the future.

In particular, Rosenstock-Huessy was acutely aware of the special burden of his own generation, which had "...survived social death in all its variations." As a teacher, he was desperately aware of the generational gap between his own generation and those that followed after 1914. And thus he was driven to say that "...the human soul dies from consumption in the hell of social catastrophe, unless it makes common cause with others."[7]

5. Rosenstock-Huessy, "The Homecoming of Society," p. 81.
6. Rosenstock-Huessy, "St. Augustine's De Magistro" (Norwich, Vermont: Argo Books, 1969), p. 2.
7. Rosenstock-Huessy, *Out of Revolution*, p. 758 and Page Smith, *The Historian and*

Bridging this gap was one of his principal missions in life. Although he made many fine efforts to construct the bridge of communication between past and present, many of his attempts were frustrated, at least in the short term. Rosenstock-Huessy was both too archaic and too advanced. Perhaps, it may still be too early for us to comprehend fully the lessons taught by his generation.

Building Bridges, Creating Communities

The challenge for change and the quest for common cause led Rosenstock-Huessy away from the university after World War One. Turning his back on traditional academe and on his obvious career path, he became much more directly involved in the quest for change in German society. In later times, one might say that he left the university in order to be "relevant."

Prominent among Rosenstock-Huessy's post-World War One efforts in this regard were his distinquished roles as a leader in the German adult education movement from 1919 to 1933. He was instrumental in worker education and in the development of youth work camps. And he served as the Vice-Chairman of the World Association for Adult Education from 1929 to 1933. Today, the best remembered aspect of these activities is the establishment of twelve volunteer work camps, beginning in Silesia in 1926. They evolved into the German Volunteer Work Service.[8]

The purpose of these camps was not to house welfare recipients nor were they summer camps for idle youth. To overcome the despair of war and to bridge the schisms created by it, Rosenstock-Huessy's quest was a hopeful one, for he sought the revitalization and reformation of society through the mobilization of the latent energy of the people: students, workers, and peasants, employed and unemployed. He understood the malaise of "underemployment" in society and the unfulfilled promise of noble, purposeful endeavors. Rosenstock-Huessy independently developed and advocated in Germany the fundamental concepts of universal service and of the moral equivalent of war that were proposed in the United States by William James.

History (New York: Alfred Knopf, 1964), pp. 95-97.

8. See, for example, M. Balfour and J. Frisby, *Helmuth von Moltke* (London: Macmillan, 1972), K. Holland, *Youth in European Labor Camps* (Washington, D.C.: American Council on Education, 1939), O. Nichols and C. Glaser, *Work Camps for America* (New York: John Day Pamphlets, 1933), and E. Rosenstock-Huessy, "The Army Enlisted Against Nature," *Journal of Adult Education* 6 (1934):271-274.

If there were, instead of military conscription, a conscription of the whole youthful population to form for a certain number of years a part of the army enlisted against Nature, the injustice would tend to be evened out, and numerous other goods to the commonwealth would follow. The military ideals of hardihood and discipline would be woven into the growing fibre of the people....

Such a conscription with the state of public opinion that would have required it, and the many moral fruits it would bear, would preserve in the midst of a pacific civilization the manly virtues which the military party is so afraid of seeing disappear in peace. We should get toughness without callousness, authority with as little criminal cruelty as possible, and painful work done cheerily because the duty is temporary, and threatens not, as now, to degrade the whole remainder of one's life.

I spoke of the "moral equivalent" of war. So far, war has been the only force that can discipline a whole community, and until an equivalent discipline is organized, I believe that war must have its way. But I have no serious doubt that the ordinary prides and shames of social man, once developed to a certain intensity, are capable of organizing such a moral equivalent....It is but a question of time, of skillful propagandism, and of opinion-making men seizing historic opportunities.[9]

The concept of the moral equivalent of war expresses two of Rosentock-Huessy's essential ideals for community building: the need for vigorous purposeful service and the existence of a latent, untapped reserve of human spirit in society. He used James' concept frequently, implicitly in Germany and explicitly in North America. William James and his essay, "The Moral Equivalent of War," were held in high esteem and cited often in Rosenstock-Huessy's practice and writing.

Ever conscious of the great width of the Atlantic Ocean, and of the unfair, but common, negative association of everything German, including himself, with National Socialism, Rosenstock-Huessy rarely made explicit reference in the United States to his own essay, "Ein Landfrieden" or "A Peace Within," or to his experience in German adult education and with the German Volunteer Work Service.

9. William James, "The Moral Equivalent of War," in *Memories and Studies* (New York: Longmans, Green, 1912), pp. 267-296. See, also, Eugen Rosenstock-Huessy, "Ein Landfrieden," in *Im Kampf um die Erwachsenenbildung 1912 bis 1926*, eds. W. Picht and E. Rosenstock-Huessy (Leipzig: Quelle und Meyer, 1926), "The Army Enlisted Against Nature," "A Peace Within" and "Youth and Authority," in W.T. Winslow & F. Davidson, *American Youth* (Cambridge: Harvard University Press, 1940), pp. 197-206 and 3-25.

These were two separate worlds to be understood singularly within their own contexts. His American role was that of an advisor, not that of a public leader.[10]

Nonetheless, after moving to the United States in 1933, new opportunities to build upon the German experience presented themselves. First, he served as a commentator on the work camp experience in the United States and in Europe. And then, more actively, he became the principal advisor to the Dartmouth and Harvard college students, Vermont farmers and others who established and/or resided at Camp William James in 1940-1942.

Rosenstock-Huessy was fundamentally dissatisfied with and critical of the Civilian Conservation Corps, although he approved of the program's goals in principle. He distrusted governmental motives, military regimentation and make-work schemes. He always stressed the importance of long term personal commitment and of the moral equivalent of war. Camp William James was an attempt to transport the vitality of the German experience to the United States and to revitalize the Civilian Conservation Corps program, which was sometimes little more than a network of relief camps. Thus, Camp William James was a reformer's reaffirmation of principles as well as an application of them within a new political and social context.

The naming of this experimental farm for William James was a direct tribute to the author of "The Moral Equivalent of War," the essay which *inspired* the students and the professor (Rosenstock-Huessy) who founded the camp. Appropriately, Camp William James was dedicated by two of James' sons on 14 December 1940 in Sharon, Vermont.

The camp began as an experimental leadership training program within the Civilian Conservation Corps in an explicit, although somewhat covert, attempt to reform the CCC from within. After loss of government sponsorship, Camp William James relocated to Tunbridge, Vermont with volunteer participants. There, as an independent co-operative and a social experiment in rural living and community development, the camp community initially flourished. Then it floundered due to the typical internal stresses of intentional communities and the external stresses caused by the advent of World War II.[11]

10. See, in particular, Jack Preiss, *Camp William James* (Norwich, Vt.: Argo Books, 1978) and Rosenstock-Huessy's two addresses to the Annual Conference of Civilian Conservation Corps Education Advisors on May 21st and 23rd, 1940, "What They Should Make Us Think" and "What We Should Make Them Do," First Corps Area, Dartmouth, New Hampshire.

11. Jack Preiss, *Camp William James*, Stuart Chase, "Young Men in Tunbridge,"

Both the German work camps and Camp William James achieved some short term, individual successes, but were frustrated by external circumstances. The German experiments suffered from the social and economic pressures of inflation, unemployment, then depression, and finally, the coming to power of Adolf Hitler. Indeed, these were the very elements of political and social disintegration that the work camps were meant to prevent. Camp William James was bogged down by political intrigue and bureaucratic red tape within the Civilian Conservation Corps, the very agency it sought to reform, and within the Government of the United States more generally. Later, the camp was overwhelmed by the growing American preoccupation with the war that led to U.S. participation in World War II.

Ultimately, both enterprises were frustrated by the state during periods of rapid change. They were without time and opportunity to mature or to demonstrate their full potential values. Consequently, the camps influenced individuals more than society as a whole. Good fellowship, principled work, and co-operative living produced meaningful experiences and a small army of camp veterans, who had shared short chapters of their lives together. The camp volunteers' experiences may not have been extraordinary in themselves. But an unusually distinct and well thought-out sense of purpose existed. While they did not achieve Rosenstock-Huessy's goal of reintegration, simpler goals were achieved.[12] Many earnest conversations were begun.[13] In the end, the firm philosophical and moral *raison d'etre*, the moral equivalent of war, prevailed, albeit on an informal basis. Valuable personal experiences could be and were transformed into solid examples. Firm, life-long friendships were established.

Of course, Rosenstock-Huessy saw beyond the official purposes of Camp William James–those of a Civilian Conservation Corps leadership training facility–and beyond the personal rigors of group living.

> I solemnly deny the thesis that Camp William James had the purpose of informing people about social problems, or of any unique and risky situation, mastered from day to day, by a group living on a higher plane than we, as individuals, could live. It had no "purpose," unless it was a purpose to create an experience and a record of what real life is, and what it entails....that which does

Reader's Digest 40, no. 5 (1942):69-72, and Dorothy Thompson, "A Call for Young Workers on the Land," *Reader's Digest* 40, no. 5 (1942):66-68.

12. Eugen Rosenstock-Huessy, *The Christian Future, or the Modern Mind Outrun* (New York: Harper & Row, 1966), p. 26.

13. See, for example, Eugen Rosenstock-Huessy, *Planetary Service* (Norwich, Vt.: Argo Books, 1978), pp. 39-43.

not spread has no life. Growth is not a matter of choice, but of vitality.[14]

Certainly, original vitality was evident. At the same time, however, Camp William James seems, in retrospect, to have moved beyond the original focus of adult education patterned upon the German experience, and, after being freed from government sponsorship, to have acquired the characteristics of a North American intentional community.

Three Legacies

Rosenstock-Huessy served as a personal bridge across three generations of government sponsored, volunteer work camps. At the same time, Camp William James is an obscure juncture in the history of German adult education. The camp represents the direct transfer to and the immediate survival of work camp ideas originating in Germany in an American context.

Nevertheless, after World War II, the German adult education profession rejected its work camp experience and moved from social change programs to an emphasis upon adult vocational training. Today, Rosenstock-Huessy, the German adult educator, is remembered in German adult education circles as a member of a previous generation.

In the United States and to a less extent in Europe, the German camps were used as examples of or models for depression era work camps with only partial success.[15] A generation later, the Civilian Conservation Corps and Camp William James provided part of the inspiration for the establishment of the U.S. Peace Corps and later the Youth Conservation Corps and its counterparts at the state and local levels.[16]

The early models have served their purpose. The Peace Corps and its counterparts in other countries combine governmental makework programs, volunteer social service, and political ideology in useful, albeit sometimes self-serving ways. The Government of Canada's Katimavik program, for example, has been a youthful mirror of Liberal Government goals and a nationalistic recruiting ground for the Liberal Party. Understandably, the new Conservative

14. See Rosenstock-Huessy's letter to Dan Goldsmith, 4 March 1945, cited by Preiss, *Camp William James*, p. 227.

15. See, for example, K. Holland, *Youth in European Labor Camps*, "Work Camps for Youth," in *American Youth*, eds. Winslow & Davidson, and Nichols & Glaser, *Work Camps for America*.

16. See, for example, Page Smith's "Preface–1977," in Preiss, *Camp William James*.

government may change the emphasis of the program or abolish it altogether.[17] Similar government sponsored programs exist in many countries with mixed success. Nonetheless, the genre is established firmly.

It is still possible, but unlikely in the foreseeable future for the United States, for example, to establish a universal conscription program for public service by young men and women in military and/or civilian endeavors. Such a program was proposed in 1940 by Rosenstock-Huessy and others in conjunction with the reforms suggested for the Civilian Conservation Corps and as an alternative to what ultimately became the Selective Service System. At the same time, it is clear that governments find it inherently difficult, if not contradictory, to wage the moral equivalent of war.

A more genuine future for principled volunteerism is in the private sector. Rosenstock-Huessy's extensive international list of volunteer social service organizations in the appendix of *Dienst auf dem Plantem*–but omitted from the English translation, *Planetary Service*–is instructive. The thrust of both editions is clear as Rosenstock-Huessy, the international adult educator, returned to the global concerns of volunteer service, international development and social change for his last book. Here we see individual enterprise applied broadly in international agencies; here we have, literally, *planetary service!*

Waging the moral equivalent of war with volunteer forces is difficult at the best of times. Founding and maintaining a stable volunteer community is even more difficult. Camp William James is a case in point. Such enterprises are quite fragile. The outward differences between Camp William James in Sharon, the government camp, and in Tunbridge, the private camp, were not great, but subtle changes occurred that are difficult to recognize, except in retrospect. But they were significant. The basic motives and daily activities were similar. However, when a camp becomes a community, the entire basis for personal interaction changes. The enterprise turns inward and becomes more comprehensive, more rural and more timeless.

I was surprised by the character or personality of Camp William James in Tunbridge in 1941-1942 as described by Jack Preiss. This was not "Rosenstock-Huessy's" camp. As a long time observer of the back-to-the-land movement, intentional communities, co-operative organizations and rural change, I recognized Preiss' description immediately as a description of an incipient intentional community.

17. See, for example, Jacques Hebert, *Have Them Build a Tower Together* (Toronto: McClelland & Stewart, 1979).

Preiss' book, *Camp William James,* is not unlike accounts written twenty-five or thirty years later by members of the back-to-the-land movement who have repopulated the same New England countryside in the last fifteen years.[18] Clinton Gardner, a Camp William James resident in Tunbridge, confirms this indirectly.[19] The evolution of life at Camp William James followed familiar patterns.

This third legacy is more striking than the other two and somewhat out of character for Rosenstock-Huessy. One understands intuitively the links between the Civilian Conservation Corps, the Peace Corps, the Youth Conservation Corps, the German work camps and international voluntary service. The parallels are clear. Nevertheless, while Rosenstock-Huessy was an important social thinker and teacher, he was not personally a community resident and leader. Camp William James, for example, took on the characteristics of an intentional community only after the original camp purposes were frustrated and had lost their vitality. Rosenstock-Huessy approved of the experiment's end.[20] I doubt that he would have been comfortable with the prospect of being the progenitor of "hippie communes." But this may be his most "American" of legacies.

Oddly, despite his obscure, eclectic, nineteenth-century style, Rosenstock-Huessy remains influential. Certainly, he is an important historian, social philosopher, adult educator, teacher and student of the world. Three of his several legacies have been discussed here. But, at the same time, his influence seems to be inversely proportional to his notoriety. His important contributions to the understanding of how to wage the moral equivalent of war seem to be a case in point.

18. See Hugh Gardner, *Children of Prosperity* (New York: St. Martin's Press, 1978), Sam and Elly Hartman, "Ten Years at Rosenstock-Huessy House," from the Renison Conference, unpublished, Terry Simmons, "But We Must Cultivate Our Garden" (Ph.D. diss., University of Minnesota, 1979), and Benjamin Zablocki, *Alienation and Charisma* (New York: Free Press, 1980).

19. Clinton Gardner, *Letters to the Third Millennium* (Norwich, Vt.: Argo Books, 1981), p. 211.

20. Preiss, *Camp William James,* pp. 202-218.

Eugen Rosenstock-Huessy in
Frankfurt/Main where he established an Academy
for Workers prior to his return to university
teaching at Breslau in 1923.

Eugen and Margrit c. 1916, a year or two following
their marriage in 1915, when Eugen was on leave from the
Western Front near Verdun where he was serving
as an officer in the German army.

Rosenstock-Huessy often rode horseback
during World War II from his home in Norwich,
Vermont, across the river to Dartmouth College.

Rosenstock-Huessy in class
at Dartmouth College where he taught
from 1935 until 1958.
c. 1953.

Margrit Rosenstock-Huessy in Switzerland in 1958,
one year before her death.

Contributions to Psychiatry
from the Writings of
Eugen Rosenstock-Huessy

Hans Huessy

If the Romans had used good "mental health practices," they would have offered Jesus the services of a psychiatrist when he was wrestling with his impending crucifixion. Jesus did not need a psychiatrist. This simple example illustrates the quandary of mental health today. Suffering and sacrifice are considered unnecessary. Our theories assume either a humanistic faith in the essential goodness of man or a deterministic view of man, or they completely ignore consideration of these philosophical questions altogether.

When I first became "intellectually aware," I knew that my father was in serious disagreement with the prevailing ways of thought. I knew that not only was he a Christian personally, but that he firmly believed that an acceptance of Jesus was essential for an understanding of modern man. I also knew that, despite his love of the academic world, he had become aware during the First World War that not only had this academic world failed in playing an active role in the prevention of the disaster of World War I, but that it had actually actively contributed to the occurrence of this disaster and the following disasters of Hitler and World War II. I was also aware of his proposing a new method for studying the social sciences which combined his belief in Jesus Christ with the grammatical method based on his study of language. To me he was a walking encyclopedia whose information frequently differed from that provided by the textbooks and whose opinions on important matters I always accepted.

Whereas my readers have come to my father's ideas through hearing him or reading him after having been thoroughly indoctrinated by the Greek mind of today, I started with his ways of looking at the world and have gradually learned to specify how these disagreed with the prevailing ways of thought today. As I have developed professionally as a psychiatrist, in both adult and child psychiatry, I have become increasingly aware that our modern psychological theories do not allow for man's multiformity, for the fact that we fulfill multiple roles simultaneously. The theories are totally inadequate for dealing with heroism and artistic achievement, explaining them away as neurotic compensations. They do not deal with time, but only with space, and they deny the important role of the future dimension. The mental health movement over the years has tended to insist that it knew how everybody should live, how we should raise our children, how we should educate our children. Every few years the field would be dominated by some new fad: fads based on models which tended to be uni-causal and deterministic. Much misery has been caused in the name of modern mental health practices.

Psychiatry can be neither taught nor practiced without making a serious effort to cope with all these questions. These questions take one into the realm of belief and religion. If there is to be any relationship between psychiatry and religion, the two must be cut from the same piece of cloth. As long as we talk of a psychology of religion, religion remains a creation of man's intellect. If religion has validity, then our final goal should be a religiously-informed psychiatry. The psychiatrists whom I admire are characterized by a faith in their fellow human beings; not a blind faith in man's goodness but an awareness of a greater purpose. They have a sense of mission and humility and can show very human reactions to their patients. They are comfortable with the fact that we know very little. Scientific knowledge is used to implement and supplement these qualities of faith. Methodology does not dominate as it does in so much of psychiatric teaching. They are truly believing psychiatrists. Unfortunately, being believing is not sufficient since the psychoanalyst is also a believer but he is a believer in his psychoanalytic theory. They would be easier to argue with if they admitted their faith instead of insisting that they have a science.

Many years ago, Dr. John Whitehorn of Johns Hopkins tried to discover why some chronic schizophrenic patients in a research project had benefitted from psychotherapy while others had not.[1] He was unable to find the difference in the patients, but found by studying the therapists that there was a difference between those therapists who had success and those who did not. The successful therapists, on the basis of their personal human reactions, had repeatedly broken with the technical rules of treatment whereas the unsuccessful therapists had been excellent technicians. Yet our

1. J.C. Whitehorn and B.J. Betz, "A Study of Psychotherapeutic Relationships Between Physicians and Schizophrenic Patients," *American Journal of Psychiatry*, III, 321, 1954.

training programs stress techniques. The psychiatric literature is dominated by articles and books on therapeutic techniques. The many schools of psychotherapy make the Protestant churches look like a unified body. Yet there is no evidence that the theory to which a particular therapist subscribes makes any difference in the outcome of the treatment.

Professional therapists talk about the importance of the quality of their relationship with their patients, but they have the arrogance of thinking that the one, two or three hours a week of their relationship can override what happens to the patient for the rest of the week, and also that those few hours are a major influence in the patient's life. Particularly when dealing with chronic patients, someone must supply the kind of caring which is commonly supplied by members of the family but which these patients have lost some time ago. Professional relationships are always limited. The professional goes home after office hours to live his own life. He is paid for what he does and this bears little relationship to the kind of caring that occurs within a family. Yet, in our long-term programs for chronic patients, no provision is made for this kind of caring which can be supplied by any motivated human being and professionals are, by definition, almost the only ones who cannot supply this kind of caring. If human relationships of genuine quality are needed by many of our patients, we, the professionals, must learn to admit that we cannot supply these. Psychiatric training teaches us about mental illness; it does not make us into "superfriends." The more professional training we have, the more specific and circumscribed are the aids we can offer. Professionalism implies clear-cut limitations to our patient relationships. We do not include them in our private lives.

While finding my bearings in the field of psychiatry and psychology, I continually found that ways of looking at things which I had absorbed from my father seemed to offer more successful ways of dealing with the issues faced. I will try to share with you some of these insights and point out how they relate to present-day mental health dilemmas. I will in no way try to present a complete theory of psychiatry or psychology and would like to stress that my father always emphasized that he was proposing a method for study and not a final answer.

My father, Eugen Rosenstock-Huessy, is little known in North America, although there are more than a dozen of his books available in English. In the early twenties, he belonged to a group which included Paul Tillich, Martin Buber, Franz Rosenzweig and Victor von Weizsaecker. Tillich and Buber are well known in America. Rosenzweig was the outstanding Jewish theologian in Germany after World War I, while von Weizsaecker was a major pioneer in the field of psychosomatic medicine even though he hated this term because it institutionalized the separation beween mind and body. He preferred to speak of biographical or anthropological medicine. This tradition is carried on today at the University of Heidelberg. Rosenstock-Huessy is perhaps better known in theological circles because of his correspondence in the trenches of World War I with Franz Rosenzweig which led to the latter's famous book *The Star of Redemption*. I shall try to summarize in succession a number of these insights which I have found most helpful in my work. I am sure the list is incomplete. I was never a student of my father, but his speech thoroughly pervades me and has shaped all aspects of my life.

I. *The Pyramid of Knowledge, or Levels of Living*

When modern psychology and psychiatry had their beginnings, they tried to imitate the so-called exact sciences which had made dramatic progress and were greatly admired. The philosophical viewpoint of the exact sciences could be likened to a pyramid. If one collected enough building stones of knowledge, one could build the pyramid higher and higher and finally reach a peak of complete knowledge. Psychology and psychiatry have continued to operate on this basic concept despite the fact that in the exact sciences there has been a philosophical revolution. As new theories, such as relativity and quantum were developed, it became evident that insights at higher levels along the pyramid were not always derived from the building stones below, but that new insights often required a re-explanation of the lower building stones. In other words, the higher level insights changed our view of the fundamental building stones. The simpler did not explain the more complex; rather the opposite was true. Applying this philosophical revolution to the social sciences, my father postulated at least five different levels of human functioning. If we think of a pyramid of five levels, the bottom level of functioning would be physiological and autonomic. The second level would deal with eating, sleeping and playing. The third level would deal with work and other purposeful activity. The fourth level would deal with love and the recreation of values, and the fifth level with heroism and self-sacrifice. Man's highest possible level of functioning would be at level five. This level is seldom achieved and when achieved it is only for short periods of time.

If the important revolution in the philosophy of science is applicable to the science of man, our insights into the functioning of man would come from a study of people functioning at these highest levels. Instead, we have studied the lowest levels of man or even animals and tried to explain the highest levels from information derived from these lower levels. Most psychological and psychiatric theories are comfortable in dealing with the first three levels of man, while they either deny or explain away as pathology any functioning at the highest two levels. Thus psychoanalysis sees all artistic creations as a compensation for neurotic complexes, and heroic deeds are explained as defenses against psychopathology. Goertzel and Goertzel and Illingworth and Illingworth in their extensive studies of the lives of famous individuals are led to the conclusion that the sublimation of conflicts is an inadequate explanation of greatness.[2] Sickness or disturbance in man can occur at any one of the five levels, and a disturbance at one level can affect another level. Treatment, therefore, would have to be varied on the basis of the level at which the primary pathology was thought to be. The formulation of the different levels allows for rational help at any of the levels by means appropriate to that level. Some of my college student patients may need inspiration and commitment to help them reach life at level four. Obviously, a therapist has no inspiration to hand out. All one can do is help them into life situations where there may be a greater chance of inspiration being transmitted to the patient from other inspired individuals. Sometimes patients "find themselves" when placed in the position where others depend on them. Someone may suddenly get over some psychosomatic disorder when he or she finds a true love and literally begins a new life. Psychotherapy cannot provide these kinds of answers.

If there is a chemical abnormality on level one, it makes sense to use drugs or other organic therapies to try and minimize this defect. If there are problems at level two, training programs in a controlled environment may be appropriate. If the difficulty is at level three, training programs and some type of communal living experience may be needed. For many chronic psychiatric patients, level three is the highest level they can achieve. In many of these patients the psychological determinism of our dynamic theories can be useful in dealing with specific symptoms, just as behaviour therapy can be useful with symptoms, particularly at level two. But neither of these will have

2. See V. Goertzel and M.G. Goertzel, *Cradles of Eminence* (Boston: Little, Brown, 1962), and R.S. Illingworth and C.M. Illingworth, *Lessons from Childhood* (New York: William and Wilkens, 1966).

any impact on the patient's ability to occasionally reach levels four or five. The goal is to make possible experiences under the motto "respondeo etsi mutabor" (I respond even though I may be changed).

The major psychoses seem to involve some basic biological problems with genetic contributions. The biochemical pathology at this level would interfere with all other levels, and correcting the biochemical deficit would be a prerequisite for improving the functioning at any of the higher levels. On the other hand, a problem at level four might produce problems at the lower levels, and even though organic and psychological therapies might ameliorate these problems, they obviously will not resolve the problem if something is seriously wrong in our most important love relationship.

In line with the commonly held deterministic theories, many studies have tried to predict psychological behaviour. If only the first three levels of functioning existed, then prediction probably would be possible. But functioning at the top two levels in response to external influences which inspire us and lead us to commitment can overcome many things at the lower levels and explain the consistent failure of all attempts at long-term prediction. The motivation of college students, so important for admission policies, is at this level, and therefore almost impossible to predict. Inspiring encounters are not predictable and not under an individual's or therapist's control. And yet they will dramatically alter an individual's level of performance. For some patients, we may be able to increase the readiness of an individual to respond to an inspirational encounter. However, any therapist who believes that he can supply the needed inspiration for his patients is attempting to play God. The biography of Malcolm X is a dramatic example of new inspiration totally overcoming his past. There was nothing in his past history to explain the change.

II. *The Temporal Anatomy of Experience*

My father's "grammatical method" holds that the grammar of language is a mirror of the laws of human experience. He held that the vocative and imperative are the earliest forms of speech, and all other grammatical forms described the various stages of the experience initiated by the vocative or imperative. He also distinguished between speaking and talking. Talking is what we do most of the time when nothing is at stake and we are being pleasant, passing the time of day, or just transmitting everyday information. Speaking is when the speaker is taking a stand and what he is saying is important to him and could have consequences. In other words, it could alter his future. When my father speaks about grammar, he refers to speaking and not talking. If we follow an experience through the various grammatical forms that describe it, it runs a course through time. This movement through time can be studied and reveals certain basic patterns. We can speak of a phasing of an experience and can describe emotional disturbance as getting stuck in one particular phase of an experience or as being due to an attempt to skip an essential phase of an experience. Illness can also be related to an inability to enter new experiences.

Four basic stages of experience are described. One, inspiration; two, communication; three, institutionalization; and four, history. Some examples will help to clarify this. When a person says that he or she has fallen in love, we are speaking of an experience which could change lives. It is not entered into logically. Genuine love inspires the individual. When the person falls in love, he or she writes love poems hopefully, sings some love songs and, usually, talks about his or her love extensively. Thus the stage of inspiration is followed by a stage of communication. In the stage of institutionalization, we translate this new experience into a social fact. We get married before witnesses, but the experience is not over at this point, since when we walk out of the church we still find it an emotionally charged experience to introduce our new bride as Mrs. Only as we go along, usually after the first child is born, does our marriage become history. That is, it becomes an integral part of us. We are at a stage when we can hardly imagine ourselves as unmarried. This does not mean that the romance or love has gone out of the marriage, but only that the phases of this particular experience have been fulfilled.

Another example would be when we suddenly find ourselves wanting to follow a certain profession. In the past people spoke of "getting the call." Often our reasons for feeling strongly towards a particular profession are rather vague at the beginning. As we discuss it and explore it, we gradually get to the point where we do something about it. We go to a professional school and some years later, after graduation, we are what we set out to become and have achieved the stage of history. Again, we see a point of inspiration followed by communication. Going to professional school represents institutionalization, and finally we reach the point of history when we are whatever it was we chose to become. These experiences absorb much emotional energy, and it is probably crucial that we complete these experiences to free up this energy for new future experiences. Many problems in the modern social sciences are due to a lack of appreciation of the need for these temporal sequences. In attempting to achieve a certain goal, we often aim for the stage of history without helping people go through the previous three states which are necessary to reach the stage of historical fact. If we want our students to have some true appreciation of the American Revolution, we must help them in small ways to go through the experiences our ancestors did. Teaching them the final facts or events will not achieve this.

Another example of this insight would be the development of women's suffrage: first there were only some excited women who were viewed as troublemakers or as slightly crazy. Secondly, there was a great deal of speech making and writing, parades and such. Thirdly, came the passage of a constitutional amendment. Certainly following this, feelings still ran high about the matter, but finally the stage of history had been achieved. Women's suffrage is an accomplished fact, and nobody gets particularly excited about it in this country any more. This contains implications for any type of political reform. A successful political change would have to be carried through these stages of experience before it could work. Any attempt to start with an accomplished fact at stage four would be doomed to failure. In relation to education, this insight forces one not only to teach facts but to help students, in some small way, to go through the same stages of experiences that our ancestors went through if we want them to understand history.

Two separate investigators have developed formulations which come very close to this insight. Gerald Kaplan at the Laboratory of Community psychiatry at Harvard, and James Tyhurst at the University of British Columbia at Vancouver have been studying human crises situations.[3] They were led to formulate three stages of experience which can roughly be called impact, tumult and resolution. Their studies have concentrated on what might be called traumatic or negative experiences. A fourth stage of experience such as in our model would easily fit into their scheme. Tyhurst feels that his findings apply to all meaningful experience and that such experiences invariably involve change and hopefully maturation. In line with our motto of *respondeo etsi mutabor*, he also documented that as an individual goes through these stages, there may be evidence of various psychiatric symptoms which do not necessarily mean there is psychiatric illness. Psychiatric symptomatology must always be evalu-

3. See G. Caplan, et. al., "Four Studies of Crisis in Parents of Prematures," *Community Mental Health Journal*, vol. I, no. 2, pp. 149-161, and J.S. Tyhurst, "Research on Reaction to Catastrophe" in I. Gadston, ed., *Panic and Morals* (New York: International Universities Press, 1958).

ated to see whether it is a sign of illness or a sign of the stress of a positive maturational change that the individual is going through. Dambrowsky, a Polish child psychiatrist now in Canada, arrived at a similar formulation documenting that when children as part of healthy development undergo a major step of maturation, they will often show signs of psychological stress which, if treated as a sign of illness, can lead to disaster. Eighty percent of all the school children he studied in Warsaw showed at different times various psychiatric symptoms. He demonstrated that maturation occurred by steps, and at each step there would be symptoms reflecting the stress of change. These symptoms were similar to those seen with illness. A physician's judgment would be required to decide whether it was illness or the stress of maturational change. His work is available in an English translation called *Positive Disintegration.*[4] Joseph English has described extensive psychiatric symptomatology for as long as two years among returned Peace Corps volunteers.[5] He stresses that these symptoms should not be viewed as psychopathology. They are signs of the stresses of moving from life at a level of intense commitment to more routine living as the Peace Corps volunteer moves from his highly committed and stressful experience to the point when his Peace Corps experience becomes one of the facts of his history.

Change is accompanied by pain which may reveal itself in psychiatric symptoms. Symptoms, therefore, are not valid indicators of pathology. The error of many epidemeological studies like the Midtown Manhattan Study[6] is that they imply that a psychiatric symptom is equal to psychiatric illness, which then leads to rates of psychiatric illness in the general population which should keep thousands of psychiatrists thoroughly occupied forever. Years ago I worked as a college psychiatrist and there, especially, I was struck with the number of students I saw with psychiatric symptoms who needed non-psychiatric help. If treated as ill, they come to view themselves as ill, with negative, long-term consequences. Their need most often was for inspiration or commitment; something therapy could not offer. An exploratory therapy seduces them into blaming all problems on past experiences or especially on their parents, an attitude which can paralyze them for years. Hopefully, as we study experiences with the grammatical method, we will learn more about the timing of the stages of experiences which will allow us to more

    4. D. Dabrowski, *Positive Disintegration* (Boston: Little, Brown, 1964).
    5. Joseph English and Joseph Coleman, "The United States Revisited: The Peace Corps Volunteer Returns," June, 1964, Peace Corps, Washington D.C.
    6. L. Srole, et.al., *Mental Health in the Metropolis - The Midtown Manhattan Study* (New York: McGraw-Hill, 1963).

readily judge whether a symptom of the moment is relevant to a stage of healthy experience or due to a lack of involvement or inspiration, or whether the symptoms should be classified as due to illness.

III. *Secrets, Seeds for the Future*

My father used to get especially upset at the presumption of most psychotherapists that it was their right to ask all types of questions and to explore innermost secrets. He held that secrets are often the seeds of important future life experiences. These seeds may lie dormant and never blossom forth, but that should not obscure the insight that their significance is not known until they do blossom forth. Like seeds, if their protective covering is removed too soon, they cannot grow but die. Most psychotherapies insist that they must be uncovered and that their significance be assessed right now. This robs the patient of his future. It takes away what could have become the first stage of new experiences. In school we must learn many things the significance of which we will not understand until many years later. Students today have been led to believe that they should be able to understand everything immediately, that all learning should have immediate applicability, and in many places they are even encouraged to design their own curricula on the basis of their obviously limited life experience. Past experiences frequently gain significance during later life events which are unexpected and unpredictable and not part of any self-made life plan. The development of these seeds depends on meeting conditions suitable for sprouting. Many never will, but their wanton destruction by many modern forms of therapy has negative consequences.

A successful childhood and education could be studied from the point of view of planting as many potential seeds as possible. Success in this type of venture would, of course, never be testable by our usual means of assessing progress and learning.

IV. *I - Thou*

An understanding of the anatomy of experience and its various stages suggests that Martin Buber's famous book *I and Thou* should be retitled "Thou - I".[7] Psychology, ever since Descartes, has begun with "I" and then worked out from this "I" to include other members of the social group. The assumption is that there could be a single "I" in existence, but one cannot understand man if one

---

7. Martin Buber, *I and Thou* (New York: Scribner's, 1958, 2nd edition).

begins with "I". According to Rosenstock-Huessy, the vocative and imperative are the earliest forms of language, and all other grammatical forms are successive responses through time to these two beginnings. The vocative and the imperative are equivalent to what we now call "Thou", a form of address requiring a response. In response to this Thou, we answer I, We, and then when someone else describes the experience He, She, They or even It is used. As an individual passes through an experience, different pronouns are appropriate for describing the individual at that time. At times we are a subject–at other times an object. Thus, the response "I" can occur only after someone has addressed us as Thou. Support for this formulation is found in the observation that children learn the pronoun "I" last, and some severely autistic children never learn to use the pronoun "I". Yet we continue to believe in the priority of the "I". A one hundred and eighty degree shift in our thinking about man is essential. Infants are literally spoken into membership in the human race. The first human being had to be addressed as a Thou before he could become an "I". According to my father, this is the Spirit part of his conception of God. It is only when the spirit addresses us that we become truly human beings; the Spirit speaks to us through others, through our parents first.

When reading the biography of Helen Keller, I was struck by the extent to which she really behaved more like an animal than a human being until she was given the use of grammatical language, and once she had this available to her, how rapidly she developed psychologically. Most of our psychological theories concentrate either on a purely objective study of man or try to go completely on the subjective side. Both approaches will reveal only part of the story. Buber's "I - Thou" concentrates on one dimension. He begins to conjugate man, but does not conjugate him through all the different roles in the relationships which man must fulfill.

The vocative or imperative Thou calls us to action and response. As we go through this response, we go through the various stages of an experience, and in each stage, we are called by a different name and a different grammatical form is appropriate. An experience literally transforms us as we begin as a Thou, respond as an I, and end up as They or sometimes even It. In working with college students, one often finds individuals whose problem is that they do not feel called; they are uninspired and uncommited. Such a problem is not amenable to the usual forms of psychotherapy, but sometimes one can help these students place themselves in situations where a spark of inspiration may come their way. Many Peace Corps volunteers have described this experience during their voluntary service, finding their future direction and purpose through participation in the intense service experience they had. Senator Tsongas of Massachusetts has repeatedly stated that his Peace Corps experience changed him in a major way. He was not the same individual when he came out of the service as when he went in. He experienced being called by an imperative, and his response changed him. All young people need a chance to respond to such a call. My father's call for a voluntary labour service was his attempt to answer this need.

V. *The Cross of Reality*

This insight of my father's pervades his whole method of studying human affairs. The cross is not a theoretical absolute which can be rigidly applied in a predetermined way to all experiences, but it insists that in studying any meaningful experience, we must always consider two axes, namely, time and space. The simplest example would be that one dimension of the cross would be from past to future–the other dimension from inward to outward–with man nailed to the center of the cross, continually being required to switch directions between those four fronts. In the center, the quality of mental health or emotional maturity is the ability to make these changes as required. This includes the need to alternate between living on different fronts which often are not compatible. Rosenstock-Huessy, in looking at the functioning of a family, said that in general the son lives on the future front; the father on the outward front dealing with the world in terms of providing sustenance and housing; the mother on the front representing the past, maintaining the values and traditions; and the daughter living on the inward front awaiting her future. Again, this is not absolute. Obviously, many families function even though not all these individuals are present as members. But someone must fulfill these various roles. The same insight can be applied to social groups where the same roles must be carried out or the organization will not function. For instance, a mental hospital I know functioned very well until the superintendent retired. The assistant superintendent, who had played the son's role, always ready to try new things and leave behind the old tried traditions, had been counterbalanced by the superintendent, who played the paternal role and kept stability. When the assistant superintendent became superintendent, no one was there to balance his tendency to jump too readily into new directions, and the hospital became quite unstable in its functioning. When thinking of society as a whole, when the younger generation takes control, one has revolution, and if the older generation takes control, one gets rigid ossification. For society to function well, the generations must work to balance each other to prevent absolute rigidity or wanton revolution. How this dialogue between the generations affects society's health is detailed in my father's book *The Origin of Speech.*[8]

When dealing with a particular individual, the direction or front of the cross on which he is living at the moment will be most important to our evaluation. Behaviour appropriate to one direction is often inappropriate to another. And pathology can be found in the inability to move in one of these directions, most often the future, when the person has no inspiration. For instance, in working with chronic patients, success depends on finding some small way of making the individual feel that he or she does have a future to live towards. Often we achieve a certain plateau of functioning with chronic patients and then find ourselves stuck. On closer analysis we find that they see no future for themselves and they will not progress further until we can help them find a future direction for themselves. Pathology can also consist of being stuck in one direction—someone who is totally preoccupied with the past. Since in a social group different people will represent the four directions of the cross, we must know not only the direction the particular individual is representing, but the relationship of his direction to the roles fulfilled by other members of the group before we can understand the functioning of the person we are concerned about. To this extent the family therapists are quite correct that we must have a picture of how the whole family functions before we can understand the functioning of any of its members. The failure of an administrator who is fulfilling the father role may not be a failure strictly in the administrator's functioning, but may be due to the fact that no one in the organization is representing the son's role, which would help the organization to stay alive, to keep trying new things and not get stuck in its past traditions. Any individual can live primarily in one direction as long as the group is balanced by others emphasizing the other three directions. Mental health requires, therefore, to be able to sense in which direction we should be primarily living in regard to any particular situation, and further, it would require our ability to switch direction as needed. Since these roles are not always compatible, man at the center of the cross is always under stress. A common example of incompatible roles being combined in one indi-

8. Eugen Rosenstock-Huessy, *The Origin of Speech* (Norwich, Vermont: Argo Books, 1981).

vidual and leading to problems is the physician-spouse who often tries to combine the role of spouse and that of therapist. These roles are incompatible, and when the physician tries to become therapist to his or her spouse, he may produce serious pathology in the spouse. Many physician's wives have ended up with chronic psychiatric problems, especially drug addiction, which can be traced to the attempt of their spouses to be both husband and therapist. The arguments today in the psychotherapeutic literature in regard to sexual activity between therapist and patient are another example of the attempt to combine two incompatible roles, namely that of lover and therapist. We are a part of multiple groups and experiences, and may represent different directions of the cross in simultaneously running experiences.

When someone under the force of an inspiration is creating a new institution and living on the forward direction of the cross, he or she will behave very differently than once the institution has been created, when he or she is more likely to live on either the outward or the past direction of the cross in the activities of keeping the institution alive and preserving it for the future. Obviously, in order to understand the problems of any one individual, we must at least attempt to learn which directions of the cross he or she is representing at that particular time. Cartesian thinking is neatly applicable to the outward direction when we deal with space and things. It leads us astray when applied to the other three directions. Psychoanalysis and dialectic materialism have impoverished man, insisting that he is always the same and can be studied almost exclusively through his functioning in the outward direction. This leads to the dehumanization so frequently talked about today. When human beings are dealt with as things, we number them. With numbers we can do anything. That is why we use numbers in prisons, in the military, and in concentration camps. I must emphasize again that the cross is a method of studying social situations and the different arms of the cross may be described differently when dealing with different social situations. Using Malcolm X again as an example, he lived almost exclusively on the outward dimension, manipulating the world of things until the spirit called him to a new future, at which point he began living almost exclusively in the future direction of the cross.

VI. *The Trinity*

For a long time I could see the Christian Trinity only as a protection against man thinking he can know all of God. It took me a long time to add to this the biblical statement that man is created in God's image and that therefore the Trinity applies to man, as Rosenstock-Huessy has pointed out. Any human being at any time can be called by a number of different names. A man may be a son, a husband and a father. These three roles are not always compatible, and he may seem like a different individual when fulfilling these different roles. The quality of his performance in his different roles may vary greatly. The ability to shift roles as needed may be one of the basic ingredients of what we call mental health. I have long been convinced that a fundamental deficit in the illness schizophrenia is a comparative inability to move from one role to another. This, in part, accounts for some of our failures in our long-term treatment programs for schizophrenics. The therapist would like the schizophrenic to live life as the therapist, him or herself, would like to live life. And yet, in our modern industrial society, we have developed the division of labour or social roles to the highest degree ever. And, in asking these chronic patients to fulfill a multitude of these roles as we would like to do, we are asking them to do the very thing that they cannot do and which will produce a relapse. This notion is further supported by reports from more primitive societies. The incidence of schizophrenia appears to be amazingly similar all over the world, but the course of the illness is quite different. In societies where the organization is more agricultural or tribal, with comparatively small groups, these groups seem to have learned to assign unitary social roles to the schizophrenic patient. All members of the group know what this role is and no conflicting demands are made on the patient. In this kind of situation, these chronic patients get along well and have very few relapses. Unfortunately, modern industrialized society makes this kind of thing impossible. There is no way that we can put signs on a person's back which says "I am playing this role only—please don't ask me to fulfill any other."[9]

Another example of our misunderstanding of the importance of these social roles can be found in how we handle mourning. In years gone by, a man in mourning wore a black band around his arm. This identified him as being in a specific social role and called forth from all people who met him special consideration and response to help him deal with that role. Because in some conservative societies this practice became abused and became a prison by forbidding all kinds of social interactions, we have abandoned this practice. But now we find that for most people who are in a grief situation, extra social supports disappear about three weeks after the death of the family member. Therefore many of the automatic social supports which were made available to these people when they were clearly identified as in grief are no longer forthcoming, making grieving much more lonely.

Sociology speaks about "role-playing," but this is misleading since we do not play at these roles—we genuinely live these roles under the power of a name which has been given to us for that purpose. It is real life and not play. Two books about mental hospitals—one by Caudill and the other by Stanton and Schwartz[10] are really talking about the application of this concept of social roles and of the cross of reality to the functioning of a social institution. These books give, I think, examples of how, when social roles and the cross of reality are not understood, malfunctioning of a social organism results. Any reorganization of a social institution must provide that the directions of the cross and needed social roles are adequately fulfilled. The grammatical method which encompasses these various insights saves us from the subject/object dilemma as it makes clear that we continually change from one to the other. When psychology speaks of object relationships, it denies this basic truth. The grammatical method shows us how in any one experience we begin as Thou, change to I, and end as a He or It, moving from object to subject to object. Some scientists claim that they are objective, but the physicist Ames showed many years ago that even in that exact science, the preconceptions of the physicist influence what he sees and what he does not see.[11] Recent historians have pretended that they are sitting on the bank of the stream of history, objectively describing it. This is an impossibility, as a historian is right in the middle of the stream, swimming along with everyone else. He cannot objectively study the stream.

In healthy living, human beings respond to one another and to being called by different names. The process is describable, but the events are unpredictable.

10. W. Caudill, *The Psychiatric Hospital as a Small Society* (Cambridge: Harvard University Press, 1958), and A.H. Stanton and M.S. Schwartz, *The Mental Hospital, A Study of Institutional Participation in Psychiatric Illness and Treatment* (New York: Basic Books, 1954).

11. A. Ames, *Personal Communication*, 1940.

VII. *Ontogeny Recapitulates Phylogeny*

The principle that ontogeny recapitulates phylogeny was a major achievement of the study of comparative anatomy. It basically states that at each higher level of development, the embryonic development of the individual will pass through all the previous developmental steps. In Volumes III and IV of his book on human speech, Rosenstock-Huessy develops the same principle in regard to man's psychological and social development.[12] As man's social setting has evolved from its beginnings in the family, each step has required the addition of new psychological and social complexities. The move from family to tribe required social rules of greater complexity. The organization of large numbers of people around a specific territory in the nation/empire, as first seen in Egypt, was a further tremendous development in social complexity, and in these two volumes, all of Egyptology is, for the first time, interpreted from this viewpoint. Later followed the organization of a people around a religion not tied to a specific geographic territory, as seen in the history of Israel, and the organization of man in one world is still before us as the pressing task of the future. Both Chinese Communism and Christianity agree on this necessary next step. The one speaking of the world revolution of the proletariate and the other of the brotherhood of man. Man's conception of time and his relationship to the greater world is very different on each of these four evolutionary levels. Modern man contains pieces of all of these different levels, and in studying man, we must ascertain at which level our subject is functioning, and we must learn how to relate to individuals who are functioning at a different level. In the world today, we still live with representatives of each of these earlier levels.

When Marshall McLuhan spoke about the need for the retribalization of modern society, he was addressing himself partially to this issue. How man moves from one of these levels to the next more complex one must be understood before we can help the "underdeveloped" people of this world move to the higher levels and finally into the one world of the twenty-first century. Solzhenitsyn cannot understand American democracy. The Eastern Orthodox Church never experienced the bloody struggles of the West which established the separation between church and state on which our democracy is based. To Solzhenitsyn, church and state are synonymous. He is not upset because the Communists in Russia have absolute control, but only because they believe in Marxism rather than

---

12. Eugen Rosenstock-Huessy, *Die Sprache des Menschengeschlechts* (Berlin: Lambert Schneider, 1963-1964).

Christianity. He would be quite happy to have a totalitarian regime as long as it was based on the beliefs of the Eastern Orthodox Church. Thus if we are to have any meaningful dialogue with the Communists, we must begin with an understanding of this difference in our traditions. Most Russians cannot understand what we take for granted. For them, democracy is purely an intellectual concept and not part of their heritage.

In dealing with human development, we need to study when a child can move from life revolving only around the family to a tribal form of organization and then to ever more complex forms of organization. Some of our failures in social organization and education may be related to our lack of attention to this dimension of human development. This insight also should lead to a better understanding of anthropology.

VIII. *The Limitations of the Intellect*

This insight concerns the place of abstract reasoning in life. When someone dear to us dies, we cry. Death is reasonable and predictable, yet the essence of life is in the weeping response to death. The intellectual comprehension of the inevitability of death is knowledge, but it is secondary. Intellectual knowledge is the arrangement of weeping and loving responses of our past in an orderly fashion.

It is life at second hand, only past life. Intense life is at the intersection of future and past time, inward and outward space. Intellect cannot live there. Abstract reasoning follows life. Real life is unpredictable and new. We enter new experiences not knowing where they will take us. After we have been through the experience, we can intellectually analyze it and describe it.

"Spirit names, thought comprehends." Life at the crucial intersection is lyrical. As the experience recedes, it is next described in dramatic form; then in prose or historical writing, and finally in scientific terminology. Living speech is lyrical. All other forms are less intense, less passionate, less moving. Scientific description is the end point of this process of emotional cooling off.

The academic world behaves as though thought precedes life, as though we could think ourselves into and out of experiences.

At a recent memorial service for Mrs. Carmelita Hinton, founder of the Putney School in 1935, I described how it was her faith and passion that had made possible the successful founding of the school which, at that time, was quite revolutionary, being both coeducational and built around a work program with many extracurricular activities in the evenings instead of study halls. All reason would

have told one that in 1935, it was not reasonable to try to found a
new school which, because of its radical forms, would tend to make
it especially difficult to obtain students. Yet Mrs. Hinton was a
passionate believer in reason and developed her curriculum with that
faith. Fortunately, in her daily life she was unreasonable enough to
found the school. Without her passion and faith she never would
have succeeded. Now we can write a history of the founding of the
school and objectively identify the various steps she took and judge
their success or failure. Pure reason would never have founded that
school. When she talked of the school at the beginning, it was her
enthusiasm about the school that obviously persuaded others to help
her.

The tools of the intellect are not related to the processes of the
spirit. Spirit can pass from one human being to another and could be
called "superhuman". This superhuman quality is the essence of true
love which has in it the foundations of life, both pain and joy. When
we write the story of a people or a person, it is love which enables us
to choose and select from the endless facts those which we feel will
tell the important aspects of the story. We only know those we love.
When we pretend that we know others without loving them, we
travel toward an intellectual dead end and are likely to collect
endless amounts of data which do not produce understanding. The
dialectical method mixes logical postulates from life already passed
with the complaints of sufferers at the center of the crucial intersection of real life, and from these, formulates truths for all time. But
history must be retold anew for each new time. The methodology of
thesis antithesis and synthesis cannot solve these problems. Only true
speech, in which we fully respond and allow ourselves to become
involved even though we cannot predict where it will take us, leads
us from our dilemmas to our future. With true speech, the future
can overcome the past and negate the determinism of psychology.
Sol Alinsky, without having ever heard of this idea, described the
process very well. Whenever he went into a problem area, he set out
to find ways of bringing the diverse groups into dialogue. He
admitted that he did not know the specific goal he was aiming for,
but he knew that such a goal could only come out of meaningful
dialogue between the participants. He brought great faith to his
work. Reason cannot deal with either faith or passion. Descartes'
"cognito ergo sum" has led us to believe that thought precedes
speech, that intellectualization is more real than experience. It has
led Western man to lose himself in various "isms" to find his salvation. The Platonic method has been seducing man into abstract intel-

lectualizations. The Cartesian method works with things and has taken us to the moon. But to understand man fully, we must operate under multiple ways of thinking.

The Russians are so Cartesian that they put their dissidents in psychiatric hospitals where some of them honestly believe that by reasoning with these people, they can show them the true way and convince them of the correctness of Marxist theory. This is an example of the Cartesian logic leading finally to utter rigidity. In other words, all truth is already known. My father proposes that we can know only the truth of today, that it may be different tomorrow, and that only through ongoing dialogue between individuals and generations can we keep generating the new truth.

IX. *The Corpora Quadrigemina Theory*

Rosenstock-Huessy was always more of a materialist than the Marxists who fought him. He always believed that someday his grammatical method would find its organic substrate in the human nervous system. The Marxists still are caught up in the dualism of mind and body. Richard Koch, a neuropathologist, was part of the group that worked with my father in the early 1920s. He developed the corpora quadrigemina theory. He arrived at this theory by asking himself which parts of the brain we could do without and still remain an individual with an awareness of self and the recognition of our name. Since we began studying the nervous system, we have been preoccupied with the cerbral cortex as the place where reasoning takes place. Only later did we become aware that the older structures at the base of the brain which controlled our emotional state may be more important than the cortex. Through Koch's extensive experience with brain injuries behind the Russian front in World War II, he arrived at the notion that a small structure at the base of the brain called the corpora quadrigemina was the locus of what we would call the soul, and that the essential trait of this structure was its multitude of connections to other parts of the brain and the probability that the kinds of meaningful experiences which change us must be laid down along four different neuronal networks which have their one shared site in the corpora quadrigemina. Thus the corpora quadrigemina would contain the essence of the individual, the basic switching mechanism which determines our very individual responses to new experiences. My father was convinced that these different neuronal networks through which an experience must pass would in the end be found to correspond to the stages of an experience that we pass through according to his grammatical method.

Some recent research about memory seems to corroborate this theory, in that long-term memory may have to be experienced through multiple modes. There are learning studies which also show that we learn more successfully when we take in information through more than one sensory mode, such as hearing and seeing simultaneously. Work with teaching machines has shown that when purely visual learning is not reinforced by some other mode, the learned material disappears from memory very quickly.

In research related to traumatic experiences, there is now evidence that our inclination to explore these experiences in great detail and to, so to speak, desensitize the individual to them, may be doing just the wrong thing. There is evidence now that our natural tendency to suppress painful memories and to deal with them only gradually through time until at some time in the future we can deal with the complete experience, may be much healthier for the individual. This would be in line with our postulate that experiences must go through various stages, and my assumption would be that as we are ready and let the experience go through another stage, the necessary switching apparatus would be in the corpora quadrigemina.[13]

X. *The Stages of Life*

In the past, an individual's relationship to his society went through a series of stages from child to student to worker to administrator to teacher. With the extreme division of labour associated with industrialization and urbanization, this no longer works. Our job is likely to keep us in one stage indefinitely. We must find ways of allowing everyone to experience the other stages despite this intense role division. We must find ways of allowing each individual to sometime in their life experience the intense commitment of the soldier, the exhaustion of the worker, the satisfactions of the craftsman, the challenges of the administrator, and the enthusiasm and inspirational activity of the teacher. The intense commitment of soldiering can be built into a peaceful society through voluntary service like the Peace Corps or VISTA, and would be in line with William James' original call for a "moral equivalent for war." Industrial workers can go to schools through adult education and can find ways of becoming teachers of other workers. The personal caring of family in small communities for its handicapped members, which vanishes with

13. Richard Koch, *Die Corpora Quadrigemina* is a handwritten manuscript, c. 1950, in the author's possession courtesy of Richard Koch's daughter, Mrs. Laqueur.

urbanization, can be experienced by short-term volunteers, working in organizations that take care of chronically ill or handicapped members of our society. The experiences necessary for a full life have not changed, but we must find new ways for allowing everyone to have these different experiences, in concentrated form for short periods of time. My father's effort with work camps in Silesia and later with Camp William James in the United States, plus his role in founding the Academy of Labour after the first World War, were attempts to come to grips with this issue.

XI. *Gender and Sex*

Sociology has often discussed the need for feminine and masculine roles being filled in social organizations independent of the actual anatomical sex of the individuals concerned. Rosenstock-Huessy in his book *The Origins of Speech* distinguishes between sex and gender and stresses especially that calling a third sex neuter is untenable. Neuter is asexual and applies only to things. When used in the study of man, it leads to terrible consequences. When neuter is used with humans, namely by calling them by number or by "it", we dehumanize the individuals; and then we can do with them all the same things that we can do to things that have no feelings. You can experiment with things, but you cannot experiment with human beings. With things it does not matter if the experiment does not come out as planned–you just start over again. But a failed experiment involving human beings will have produced changed human beings which you cannot change back. The change is irreversible.

Gender identifies the minimal social roles needed regardless of anatomical sex. Thus in the military unit, functioning under battle conditions, not only must the masculine role be fulfilled, but someone must also fill the feminine role of supporting, nurturing and caring, despite the fact that all the individuals in the unit are anatomically of the male sex. When two experts in social organization studied a department of psychiatry which was not functioning, they concluded that the feminine role was not being fulfilled by anyone in the administration, and made a suggestion of how this could be done by bringing in a member of the department who had these traits and making him assistant chairman. Most social scientists are aware of the difference between gender and sex, yet in social science studies the two are continually confused. This relates back to the previous discussion about social roles and also some aspects of the cross of reality.

Epilogue

I have tried to describe how during my years as a psychiatrist I have formulated my father's method of studying the social sciences and related it to the practice of psychiatry. Following this approach is a lonely road. My colleagues cannot understand me and, as is documented in a number of other essays in this volume, other social scientists following in my father's footsteps lead a lonely professional existence. I have only encountered one psychiatrist during all these years who fully understood what I was talking about and, unfortunately, he died of cancer two years ago. The introduction of a genuine time dimension, the abolition of the mind/body dichotomy, the limitation of reasoning to dealing with things, make us totally unacceptable to our colleagues who have never questioned the adequacy of space thinking, the supremacy of abstract reason and the mind/body dichotomy. The multiformity of man as expressed through the grammatical method and the cross of reality force us to live with much more uncertainty. They force us to acknowledge that truth changes with time, that the future has as much of an impact on the present as the past, and that the new future must always be created through living speech in which we allow ourselves to become involved despite the fact that we do not know where it will lead us and what the result will be. I am convinced that the insights described can lead to very fruitful research which will greatly increase our understanding of human society and how it functions. They free us from the object/subject, organic/psychological dilemmas. They provide a basis for the use of multiple therapeutic approaches for the treatment of mental disorders, and will lead us away from the present Tower of Babel of the social sciences where every school has its own language so that they cannot understand each other, much less be understood by the nonprofessional.

Through his method we can become citizens of one world with one shared history, the task of the coming Johannine millennium. Responding to his insights changes your life. His whole life was a response to these insights, very full but unpredictable. The sterility of pure academic knowledge produces little change in an individual. You can judge a good teacher by the extent to which his own teachings have altered his life, according to my father. By this criterion, he was a great teacher.

Eugen Rosenstock-Huessy and Fritz Perls: A Study in Complementarity

Cynthia Oudejans Harris, M.D.

Rosenstock-Huessy said:

> Anybody whose eyes have been opened to the fact that life depends on dying, knows that the resurrection has its severe laws.[1]

Fritz Perls said:

> To suffer one's death and to be reborn is not easy.[2]

Alexander Altmann said of Rosenstock-Huessy:

> Rosenstock not only taught but lived his philosophy...in accordance with his faith.[3]

Martin Shepard said of Fritz Perls:

> Perls had a fierce determination..to BE his message–to live what he preached (or preach what he lived).[4]

We are presently entering a planetary society. This development, which is obvious now to many people, was one that Rosenstock-Huessy foresaw long ago.[5]

My purpose in this essay is two-fold: (1) to stimulate the reader's questionings about the knowledge and human behaviours we and our children will need to seek out and cultivate as this new society unfolds; and (2) to share my assessment of what Fritz Perls and

1. Eugen Rosenstock-Huessy, *The Christian Future or the Modern Mind Outrun* (London: S.C.M. Press, 1947), p. 145.

2. Frederick S. Perls, *Gestalt Therapy Verbatim* (Lafayette, California: Real People Press, 1969), title page.

3. Cited in *Judaism Despite Christianity*, edited by Eugen Rosenstock-Huessy (Alabama: University of Alabama Press, 1969), p. 30.

4. Martin Shepard, *Fritz: An Intimate Portrait of Fritz Perls and Gestalt Therapy* (New York: Saturday Review Press, E.P. Dutton & Co., 1975), p. 124.

5. Eugen Rosenstock-Huessy, *Dienst auf dem Planeten* (Stuttgart: Kohlhammer Verlag, 1965). Translated into English by Mark Huessy and Freya von Moltke, *Planetary Man* (Norwich, Vermont: Argo Books, 1978).

Eugen Rosenstock-Huessy have to offer us in our new situation.
  We are entering a time when
–nations are declining as foci of guidance and power
–multinational corporations are increasing in influence
–churches are declining in importance
–cults are increasing in numbers
–the individual, thanks to assorted media, has an immensely
increased influence, if only momentarily
–thought and reason and logic are decreasing in influence
–etc., etc.
Please add to this list. It is meant only as a bare beginning. We are
indeed heirs of an exhausted religious tradition and an exhausted
scientific tradition.

  Rosenstock-Huessy said that the planetary society would require
new argonauts.[6] What will they be like? If we become argonauts,
what will *we* be like? Two things especially stand out. A new kind of
inner freedom will become important, that is the freedom to
abandon past behaviours and beliefs when they no longer serve our
search. And an overarching planetary view as well as a profound
faith will be needed. We will need a tough daily discipline and a high
vision.

  In this situation, both Rosenstock-Huessy and Fritz Perls have
important nutrients to offer us. Perls offers a discipline;
Rosenstock-Huessy offers a vision and a faith. My credentials for
juxtaposing these two men is that I knew both of them well, as their
student and as a long-time friend. I knew Rosenstock-Huessy for
thirty-two years, Fritz Perls for fifteen. I have been taught, influenced, blessed by knowing each of them. Their confluence in my
own life has been of great benefit.

A Brief Introduction to Perls and to Rosenstock-Huessy:
Early Years. Both Perls and Rosenstock-Huessy were born into athe-
istic Jewish families in anti-Semitic Berlin before the turn of the
century. Both were educated in the powerful intellectual/scholastic
ambience of the German Gymnasium and University prior to World
War I. Both struggled with the intellectual leaders of their youth,
Fritz Perls with Freud and Rosenstock-Huessy with all the ghosts of
the University.
Influences. Both were shaped and determined by World War I. Both
were shaped and determined by the existential thrust alive in the

6. Rosenstock-Huessy, *Dienst auf dem Planeten.*

Germany of the 1920s. Both emigrated to the United States and joined the army of refugees from Hitler which has so vastly enriched American life during the past fifty years. Both embraced their own brand of existentialism. For both, significant encounters with women were essential elements in their mental lives and spiritual growth.

Education. Fritz Perls was educated as a physician, was psychoanalyzed and became, at first, a psychoanalyst. He rediscovered (his verb) Gestalt therapy which is currently much in vogue.

Eugen Rosenstock-Huessy was educated as a German scholar in history, law, sociology and theology. He was the writer of a shelf of books, discoverer of multiple marvels in language, history, theology and sociology. He was a convert to Christianity (in his teenage years). He remains virtually unknown.

World War I. Experiences in the trenches of World War I were formative for both. Fritz Perls was a medical student when the war broke out and spent many months on the front as a medic. He was wounded, underwent gas warfare, saw suffering and death and was supposed to alleviate the worst. Later on Perls was to write:

We fools believed we could build a new world without wars.[7]

He also said that he was so hurt by what he had seen and experienced that he didn't care to discuss it. Seeing Mozart's *Figaro* while on leave in Berlin, he ran sobbing into the street, unable to bear the contrast with the front.[8]

Rosenstock-Huessy was in charge of all railroad lines in the battle for Verdun. He wrote, in the preface to his great history of Europe, *Out of Revolution:*

The idea of this book originated in an experience we went through in the trenches: that war was one thing to the soldiers of all nations and another thing to the people at home....Scholars cannot demobilize until the World War has reformed their method and their purpose in writing history.[9]

Adversaries. Perls and Rosenstock-Huessy were each formed by their adversaries. Of his struggle with Freud, Fritz Perls wrote:

---

7. Frederick S. Perls, *In and Out of the Garbage Pail* (Lafayette, California: Real People Press, 1969). Perls existentialism is seen in this book, his autobiography: it is provided neither with chapters nor with page numbers.

8. Shepard, *Fritz.*

9. Eugen Rosenstock-Huessy, *Out of Revolution: Autobiography of Western Man* (New York: William Morrow, 1938), p. 5.

Many friends criticize me for my polemical relationship to Freud. 'You have so much to say; your position is securely grounded in reality. What is this continuous aggressiveness against Freud? Leave him alone and just do your thing.'

I can't do this. Freud, his theories, his influence are much too important for me. My admiration, bewilderment, and vindictiveness are very strong. I am deeply moved by how much, practically all alone, he achieved with the inadequate mental tools of association psychology and mechanistically oriented philosophy. I am deeply grateful for how much I developed through standing up against him.[10]

Rosenstock-Huessy had no single adversary to oppose–there was no fit one. He therefore shot his arrows–scattered throughout his works–at many game unworthy of his marksmanship. His true opponent was the entire platonic/scholastic/objective/scholarly intellectual tradition. In another era he might have been a prophet rather than a professor.

Hitler. Both Perls and Rosenstock-Huessy lost relatives in the concentration camps of Nazi Germany. Perls lost his mother and a sister in the Ravenstadt camp. Eugen's mother, fearing her imminent deportation, took her life.[11]

Existentialism. Both men were existentialists. Describing his youth Perls wrote:

I felt a belonging–not completely, more fringelike–to the existential Gestalt group....Though being preoccupied with psychoanalysis in Frankfurt, I remained uninvolved with the existentialists there: Buber, Tillich, Scheler. This much had penetrated: existential philosophy demands taking responsibility for one's existence.[12]

Indeed the central theme of the Gestalt discipline–a name which I prefer to 'Gestalt therapy' since it is more accurate–is learning how to take as full responsibility as possible for one's existence from moment to moment as one's life unfolds.

When I myself first heard of existentialism in the early forties, I asked Rosenstock-Huessy what it was. He looked rather angry and shocked over my ignorance and then replied slowly: "Well, of course Christianity *is* existential."

The existential mode was reflected in different ways in each of their lives. In a famous passage, Rosenstock-Huessy wrote:

10. Perls, *In and Out of the Garbage Pail.*
11. Eugen Rosenstock-Huessy, *Ja und Nein* (Heidelberg: Verlag Lambert Schneider, 1968), p. 93.
12. Perls, *Garbage Pail.*

I am an impure thinker. I am hurt, swayed, shaken, elated, disillusioned, shocked, comforted, and I have to transmit my *mental experiences* lest I die. And although I may die. To write a book is no luxury. It is a means of survival. By writing a book a man frees his mind from an overwhelming impression.[13]

Thus Rosenstock-Huessy equated the writing down of thoughts with his life itself. His mind as well as his body had been under fire at Verdun. This passage is an expression of Rosenstock-Huessy's existentialism. He is an impure existentialist thinker. His works are paradoxical since he thought profoundly about the evils of thought.

Perls' existentialism found expression in his work as a psychotherapist. He wrote:

My function as a therapist is to help you to the awareness of the here and now; and to frustrate you in any attempt to break out of this. This is my experience as a therapist, in the therapy role. I haven't managed it yet for many segments of my life.[14]

Thus Perls was an existential therapist.

Perls: The Daily Discipline

As pointed out above, the argonauts will need a tough daily discipline. The old ways are no longer available. Fasting and chapel and prayers and the confessional are inappropriate now. In the therapeutic encounter–and perhaps also elsewhere–one can learn an existential discipline. A discipline of daily existence–in between the high holidays–is and will be important in the new society.

Our life, intellectual and otherwise, consists of the series of transformations through which we must pass–or through which at our peril we refuse to pass. Therapists, among others, are skilled in helping people to learn new patterns of thought and behaviour and to give up old patterns which no longer "work."

Rosenstock-Huessy commented on the Christian nature of this process:

At the center of the Christian creed is faith in death and resurrection. Christians believe in an end of the world, not only once but again and again. This and this alone is the power which

13. Eugen Rosenstock-Huessy, *I am an Impure Thinker* (Norwich, Vermont: Argo Books, 1970), p. 2, emphasis added. The German original for "mental experiences" is "geistige Erfahrungen:" See *Das Geheimnis der Universitaet: Wider den Verfall von Zeitsinn und Sprachkraft* (Stuttgart: Kohlhammer Verlag, 1958), p. 97. For me "mental experiences" is an adequate translation, although English lacks a proper equivalent for "geistig" with its layers of mental, intellectual and spiritual meaning.

14. Shepard, *Fritz.* p. 10.

enables us to die to our old habits and ideals, get out of our old ruts, leave our dead selves behind and take the first step into a genuine future.[15]

M. Scott Peck has listed...roughly in the order of their occurrence, some of the major conditions, desires and attitudes that must be given up in the course of a wholly successful evolving lifetime:

The state of infancy, in which no external demands need be responded to

The fantasy of omnipotence

The desire for total (including sexual) possession of one's parent(s)

The dependency of childhood

Distorted images of one's parents

The omnipotentiality of adolescence

The 'freedom' of uncommitment

The agility of youth

The sexual attractiveness and/or potency of youth

The fantasy of immortality

Authority over one's children

Various forms of temporal power

The independence of physical health

And, ultimately, the self and life itself.[16]

Another word for describing the passage through these transformations is maturation. We give up childish things. We grow more mature. Frequently the pain of these transitions leads an individual in our culture to seek out a therapist. But therapy itself is a very frightening and painful process–for in therapy one attempts openly to reveal oneself and one's innermost foibles to the scrutiny of another. Many people are too fearful to risk it. As Peck says:

Entering psychotherapy is an act of the greatest courage. The primary reason people do not undergo psychotherapy is not that they lack the money but that they lack the courage.[17]

Therapy is an educational process. Among other things, a good therapist will help his/her client learn two basic things: how to be aware and how to express him/herself fully.

Awareness is a difficult skill. To see accurately–rather than seeing what we want to see, or not seeing what we fear to see–that is the fine art of using our eyes. Yet such accurate seeing, though a rare achievement, is essential to perceiving the intricate reality about us.

15. Rosenstock-Huessy, *The Christian Future*, pp. 61-62.

16. M. Scott Peck, *The Road Less Travelled* (New York: Simon and Schuster, 1978), pp. 71-72.

17. Peck, *The Road Less Travelled*, p. 54.

Likewise the art of listening, the art of really hearing and perceiving the meaning of the other, is essential to a mature life, as is the ability to experience fully our inner life. The sharpening of all these skills of awareness is a part of the education one can receive in therapy.

To foster such honed attention one needs a degree of inner security and ease as a ground for the figure of one's own awareness. Therapy helps one cultivate this ease, helps one cut down the inner chatter obscuring the clarity of one's perceptions. Such inner ease is essential if we are to take any new and creative step, leaving behind the comfort of our old and proven ways.

We also know that the Spirit bloweth where it listeth. Such inner tranquillity may help make us ready for the Spirit's coming. That we can do. We cannot summon the Spirit. But we can try to be ready, should the Spirit come.

Fritz Perls emphasized growth and health rather than psychopathology and curing. Because of this emphasis he developed the Gestalt discipline, a discipline for the cultivation of awareness and the learning of new ways of speaking and behaving. Like Rosenstock-Huessy he fought the analytic mode of thinking. His therapeutic mode, as mentioned above, was grounded in existentialism.

Rosenstock-Huessy's Faith

Rosenstock-Huessy's life and his life work grew from, were based in, grounded in, his Christian faith. Born into a free-thinking Jewish family in Berlin–one forebear had been a Rabbi–Rosenstock-Huessy converted to Christianity in 1904 when he was sixteen. He married a Swiss Christian and was buried at the Congregational Church in his American home town, Norwich, Vermont.

His life work was an unfolding of his faith as he confronted the events of our century. Of this process he himself wrote (1962) in the preface to *Die Sprache des Menschengeschlechts*:

Because the soul is the heart which beats out beyond the body, the central theme of this book is the life-long unpredictability of ensouled speech....In this process the details of my life need not concern the reader. But the readers of this book must not fail to perceive the long periods in which the truths became clear and evident to me.

I didn't invent these volumes. They do not reflect some momentary insight nor a world view based on a timeless system. They are simply the wonderful gift made by three quarters of a century to a lover of the word.[18]

I want to share some of the facts of this "wonderful gift" and then tell something of how I saw Rosenstock-Huessy's faith during the period of my intimacy with him and his wife, roughly 1941-1959.

By the end of World War I in 1919, Rosenstock-Huessy had gathered and begun exploring virtually all the themes which were to dominate his life's work. All are already present in *Die Hochzeit des Kriegs und der Revolution.*[19] One central and ongoing theme was the story of Europe. Although the central vision of the European development of Christianity was clearly already present, Rosenstock-Huessy spent almost another fifteen years of work, study and reflection before *Die Europaeischen Revolutionen* was written and appeared (1932).[20] In the meantime he had done what he characteristically did: went where his free soul directed (in this case to work in the office of an automobile factory rather than to a professorship or a proper editorship); and worked like a beaver on the issues that current experiences gave him or awakened in him, while new pieces of the "wonderful gift" were given and while his new telling of the European story was taking shape in his mind and heart. During the twenties, growing out of his factory experience, he wrote *Werkstattaussiedlung*, a book dealing with the decentralization of industry.[21] He also helped to found the work camps–later so distorted by Adolf Hitler–which were intended to unite the German classes–working class, middle class, intellectuals and nobility–in a common front against the evils of the surrounding economic and social chaos.

His encounter with Josef Wittig led to their sharing the authorship of *Das Alter der Kirche*, a two-volume study of the medieval church.[22] During all this he continued to write essays dealing with the linguistic and sociological themes already sounding in his life.

In 1933, knowing he did not wish to stay in Germany to see how things might work out under Hitler, he emigrated to the United States. In order to assure his becoming known in the States, his

18. Eugen Rosenstock-Huessy, *Die Sprache des Menschengeschlechts: Eine Leibhaftige Grammatik in Vier Teilen* (Heidelberg: Lambert Schneider, 1963), Vol. I, p. 19, my translation.

19. Eugen Rosenstock-Huessy, *Die Hochzeit des Kriegs und der Revolution* (Wurzburg: Patmos Verlag, 1920).

20. Eugen Rosenstock-Huessy, *Die Europaeischen Revolutionen* (Jena: Eugen Diederichs Verlag, 1931).

21. Eugen Rosenstock-Huessy, *Werkstattaussiedlung* (Berlin: Julius Springer, 1922).

22. Eugen Rosenstock-Huessy and Josef Wittig, *Das Alter der Kirche* (Berlin: Lambert Schneider, 1927-1928).

energies, for the next five years, went toward re-creating the *Europaeischen Revolutionen* in English and for American readers. Meanwhile, he first took over the chair in the Harvard Divinity School which had been established for Paul Tillich (an ironic turn of events) and later he accepted a lifetime appointment at Dartmouth College (1937)–a most welcome change to country life for himself and particularly for his wife. "Four Wells," the home he had built in Norwich, Vermont, became a proper setting for the next years of their lives. *Out of Revolution* appeared in 1938.[23] He continued to work on many themes, both in the context of his college lectures and at the desk in his study. Their home and mailbox were seedbeds of lively activity.

Meanwhile his next major work was taking shape, the *Soziologie* which appeared in 1956.[24] Again he used the outer events of his life to provide sparks for his pursuit of things which attracted him and which ultimately made up the mosaic of his life. For example, his son's need to learn Latin led Rosenstock-Huessy to write a Latin grammar, and also heightened his own awareness of liturgical language. As another example: during World War II most college-aged men were at war; the college needed basic science teachers for the officers' training corps stationed at the college. So Rosenstock-Huessy became a teacher of physics. Out of that encounter with modern science grew his paper on Michael Faraday which in turn was expanded to a discussion of "Zahlensprache der Physik" in his speech book.[25]

During this period Rosenstock-Huessy, in addition to teaching physics, used the relative quietude to immerse himself in the details of the ancient tribes and of Egypt. He thus completed attending to essentially the whole life of mankind from our tribal beginnings up to the present day. While he was delving into these topics he used me as a foil for his writing, knowing that he would have to express things with the greatest simplicity if I were to understand them. He wrote me a series of letters on these topics which subsequently appeared (in somewhat different form) in a couple of his books, namely *Judaism Despite Christianity*[26] and the speech book.[27]

In 1964, when Rosenstock-Huessy was seventy-six, his last large work came out, the "speech book," the two-volume *Sprache des*

23. Rosenstock-Huessy, *Out of Revolution.*
24. Eugen Rosenstock-Huessy, *Soziologie;* Erster Band, *Die Uebermacht der Raeume;* Zweiter Band, *Die Vollzahl der Zeiten* (Stuttgart: Kohlhammer Verlag, 1956).
25. Rosenstock-Huessy, *Die Sprache,* vol. II, pp. 221 ff.
26. Rosenstock-Huessy, *Judaism Despite Christianity,* pp. 178 ff.
27. Rosenstock-Huessy, *Die Sprache,* vol. II, pp. 595 ff.

Menschengeschlechts which is essentially a collection of earlier writings.[28] Then came *Ja und Nein*[29] and lastly *Dienst auf dem Planeten,* translated into English as *Planetary Man,*[30] the book which deals especially with the new society addressed here.

Rosenstock-Huessy's faith in "ensouled speech" is expressed in this lifelong sequence of inspired books. Being present for part of this process of creation, I could see his faith from day to day. It has been a powerful example for me. When I asked him about his praying, he replied that his speaking *was* praying. When I asked him about the Creed (parts of which at the time seemed absurd to me), he replied matter-of-factly that he had never had the slightest doubt as to its full truth.

He prayed and sang hymns and not infrequently attended the Congregational Church in Norwich of which he was a member. But his real faith was present at the core of his own being. He never talked about his faith. What little I know from his own lips I learned only by asking direct questions. He did not volunteer anything. But I certainly saw him living his faith. There was never a mention of the privations he and his wife underwent–he earned in the late thirties and forties very little as a professor, and at that time he had no other income. I learned the uses of all the cheapest cuts of meat at his table. His library was sold to the college so that they could build "Four Wells." As a result, I can remember his former books coming *from* the Darmouth library into the house–in laundry baskets. No mention of what these necessary steps may have meant. Even so, the attic was filled with old clothes and foods which were shipped following 1945 to the hungry and threadbare surviving friends in Germany. It was as if Rosenstock-Huessy followed after his own life as it unfolded.

He always worked immensely hard. But as noted above, he did not dream up his works. He worked them out as they came to him. He speaks of this process himself in *Ja und Nein*, a book of autobiographical fragments which he wrote when he was eighty, looking back over his life.[31] He also followed his speech as it came out of his mouth. He liked the joke: "How do I know what I think 'till I see what I say?" His faith enabled him to follow the red thread of his life through the thickets of his twentieth century experience.

---

28. Rosenstock-Huessy, *Die Sprache,* vol. II, pp. 595 ff.
29. Rosenstock-Huessy, *Ja und Nein.*
30. Rosenstock-Huessy, *Dienst.*
31. Rosenstock-Huessy, *Ja und Nein.*

Thus although Rosenstock-Huessy called himself an impure thinker, he was in fact an impure believer. His impure thinking grew from his faith. His profound belief in God and in Christ informs each part and all of his *oeuvre*. To read him without an awareness of this can only be to misread him. He *believed*, but without obeisance. His faith seemed never to waver, even as it did waver. He drew my attention to Christ's words on the cross: "My God, My God, why hast Thou forsaken me?" Faith was the very fundament of his and his wife's life. For me also, his faith is his single most important characteristic. Any attempt to secularize his thought does him an immense injustice.

Summing Up

As argonauts we will need immense existential strength and flexibility. We will face immense existential changes as we lose our nations, our churches, our families, our jobs, our old ideas and our old identities. Rigid beliefs and strict codes, from whatever source, will not suffice us. Knowledge will not be enough. Even our wisdom will have to be cast aside. Perls' existential discipline will be an important tool.

As argonauts we will need faith.

Rosenstock-Huessy was a man of faith, faith was the cornerstone of his life. His vision of history can undergird out lives, help us to be sustained in difficult days, help us to see the headlines in perspective. His faith can nourish us, enable us.

Even together these two giants of another age can be only partial guides as we enter the third millennium, the new planetary society.

The Grammatical Method in the Light of Research in the Psychology of Learning: A Posthumous Letter

Richard Feringer

If our friend and colleague were still with us, this letter would have been written to him, and hopefully become the subject of a direct conversation. The occasion of this conference can perhaps offer a substitute.

Several years ago I transferred from an administrative appointment dedicated to leading a department for community development into full time teaching for the education department. This meant that I had to contend directly with the research produced by social science in relation to learning and instruction and attempt to interpret this body of knowledge to my students. An additional, almost overwhelming, challenge was to distill meaning from these writings and to re-establish the language of social science in the lives of my students. I found that these students had little faith in social science as a tool for examining human experience because it was confusing to them, and the more they read, the greater this confusion seemed to be. This, then, is the context in which such a letter might have been written.

Dear Professor Rosenstock-Huessy:

As you recall from your visit to our campus, I have been struggling with interpreting learning and instruction theory to prospective adult educators. Although our program as a whole is oriented toward the problems of community building, the problem to which I refer here is how people learn. In the course of preparing curriculum for this course, I found considerable confusion in social science research: this is to say contradiction, fragmentation, irrelevance to living situations and questionable methodology. All of this added up to little meaning for myself and even less for the students who reviewed the literature with me. As you know, I was generally familiar with your writing relating to the status of social science and in particular to your *grammatical method*. My new assignment, however, required me to look at your method with renewed interest. Actually it was more in a spirit of desperation, as the more I read in the social sciences, the less I understood about human nature. My knowledge of social science research studies was informative to students up to a point, but nothing seemed to come together into vital concepts. Data from experimental psychology and especially statistical methods seemed to students no more than dead artifacts. Basic research could not be applied to real classroom situations (as admitted by many of the researchers themselves), instructional theory today is little more than a collection of disjointed aphorisms (as pointed out by Jerome Bruner of Harvard) and statistical treatises written for the social sciences speak of golf score probabilities. There exist enormous amounts of unintegrated data, and the tendencies in the field are to produce more of the same in the hope that eventually some meaning might be gleaned from them. In the light of my new assignment, I was determined not to paint myself into the same corners in which I saw my colleagues; I could neither accept their narrow interpretations of social science methodology, nor move in the opposite direction of ignoring science, passing it off as irrelevant to the solution of real-life problems (and thereby fall prey to seasonal fads with their temporary appearance of success). I felt as though I were adrift in a vast sea, and your *grammatical method* were the only visible navigational aid at hand.

This is, then, an interim report of my attempt to apply your method to solving this dilemma with students trained in traditional social psychology. I may be taking liberties and making interpretations not intended by you; however, I must admit to unashamedly using your ideas in whatever way I could to solve my problems. Let me briefly describe your own criticisms of social science as generally practiced and as I understand you. Then I want to go on to report my experience in applying relevant aspects of the grammatical method to psychological theory with my students.

You assert that social science as presently defined is not complete enough as a method to describe all the different dimensions of human experience, and thus falls far short of its promise. The reasons you cite are briefly as follows:

1. It has virtually factored away *time* as a major dimension of experience in all except actuarial research, which deals with large numbers of people, over extended periods of time and where people are treated as numbers.

2. When time is injected into a situation, it only moves inexorably forward, to be measured incrementally on metric scales.

3. Social scientists' preoccupation with space is also manifested in terms of observation of behaviour (i.e. from the outside), while inferring environmental (outside) or physiological forces as the primary cause for behaviour (or action?). Cause/effect is thus determined by calculating probabilities (i.e. their penchant for numbers), and is therefore largely inferential.

4. As a result of this rather mechanical model of behaviour, intention is not considered important by these scientists.

5. This discounting of intention and the assumption of objectivity blinds the researcher to his own passion for his own method and diminishes the possibility of correcting his own errors. He thus tends not to address problems that are likely to be difficult for this highly-defined method, and his research often comes out as a self-fulfilling prophesy.

I realize that this account is brief and oversimplified, but hopefully it captures the thrust of your argument. Of course there are exceptions. For instance, the existential/phenomenological branch of social psychology (a term this group often uses themselves) attempts to give credence to intent and perception; however even this group is guilty of at least several of your criticisms. They too factor away time. Ironically, this branch of psychology often calls itself the humanist school, but even here the major elements of "accepted" social science methodology are never far below the surface–a methodology almost taken *carte blanche* from that of natural science.

This is the situation, then, that led you to call for a new method, one more attuned to human nature as we experience it rather than one developed for the analysis of sticks and stones.

As my students and I read the literature from social science (as related to learning problems), little convincing was needed for us to accept your conclusion that something was very wrong. It simply made no sense or connection with real life experiences, but nevertheless the narrow ritual of method was demanded of students as a condition of graduation–ritual seemingly for its own sake, just as in churches where the spirit behind it had died and little or no questioning is brooked.

My problem, as I received these students into my classroom with such a grounding, is to unpry them from those attitudes. This is, of course, difficult. Data appears so absolute and compelling, and therefore any method that produces accurate data (never mind its meaning) must not be all wrong. Of course, it is not *all* wrong–but breaking habits of a professional lifetime does not come easily. This is to say, classifying and attempting to use research according to narrow categories of mental functioning such as behaviourism, cognitivism, or humanism, or in terms of the latest classroom gimmick for raising multiple-choice test scores. What I do to widen their perspective is to review the basic research with them, and then begin to redefine it in terms of your "cross of reality" paradigm.

For you to understand specifically how this might work, I will briefly review the major streams of social science research as related to our field of inquiry. The following categories of research broadly reflect the literature as related to mental functioning and omit many details, for example, transfer and memory retention, which are not necessary for making my point here.

1. Although it is clear that sensory experience is the origin of all thought, the nature of this relationship is by no means understood. Molecules affect thought and thought affects molecules, but having said this we can only conclude that the differences in our hereditary sensory organs vary considerably between individuals, as does life experience. Since, to some extent, learning filters what is perceived, individuals end up with very different mental maps of reality. The literature does not point out, as you do, the enormous difficulties this raises in terms of bringing about common understanding and agreement as to acceptable social mores.

2. Research from the behaviourist school is commonly familiar to us. Behaviourists generally assume the mind is a blank slate upon which experience etches its tale. The mind, according to this view, is chiefly influenced by an outside stimulus, and important learning occurs automatically–mechanically–in response to that experience. Major successes of these researchers in teaching the mentally retarded, athletes and, generally, persons with noxious habits related to drugs, smoking or over-eating have clearly been recorded. One must conclude that the blank slate metaphor is a useful representation of one aspect of mental functioning.

3. Cognitive psychologists take the opposite point of view from that of behaviourists: they argue that the way those environmental stimuli are viewed depends upon some inner filters, or hereditary traits of the human mind. In general, the traits are seen to be in the nature of word fluency, number fluency, verbal meaning (that is, meaning in a limited technical sense rather than a broad life-situational sense), reasoning, space perception and perceptual speed. These factors are also broken down into sub-sets by some researchers, but the general idea holds. Problem-solving is seen as

indicative of the combined effect of these traits. Emotion is studied by some in this school, but it is often relegated to the status of a barrier to reason and to the realm of another school within psychology.

4. The three categories of research cited above are generally construed as the schools of "scientific psychology" (the name these psychologists usually accept for themselves). The humanist or existential/phenomenological school is generally looked down upon as non-scientific by this group because, I suppose, methods are primarily directed toward observing real life situations and avoid attempts to control directly. A number of reserachers including Maslow, Robert White, McClelland, Atkinson, Sherif, Frankl and others have identified what they believe to be crucial emotionally-laden attitudinal factors which are necessary conditions for growth. These factors are hope, security, comfort, belonging, usefulness, competence and meaning. Students relate much more easily to this body of research as they can test it in their own experience.

5. Still other attributes of the mind are variously accepted by all of these schools. *First,* the idea of simple structures which suggests that we can deal only with seven or eight variables at a time before a situation becomes so confusing that problems require reclassification to render. them more manageable. That is, after the model of biology, classifying in terms of phylums, classes, species, etc. *Second,* there are claims to evidence that younger minds are more accepting of new ideas, and conversely that more mature persons are more adept at solving problems requiring life experience for solutions. This is to say, younger minds seem accepting more readily of rote memorization and mature minds to resisting such experiences by demanding meaning. *Third,* development tends to be seen as occurring along four lines, physiological, mental (rational), social and ethical, although degeneration and regeneration as an alternating pattern has been little studied except perhaps in medicine.

One could add volumes of detail, but while this summary is rather gross, it represents enough of the flavour of research to give you an idea of how students who come to me are thinking. Research into classroom methods for manipulating students purports to be based on these foundations of theory in the main. Clearly, the mind is dissected as a thinking entity out of the context of real-life problems. Even with social psychologists studying personality theory and other life experiences such as prejudice, greed, etc., the situations studied are short-time spans. That this point of departure has *not* borne the desired fruit is admitted by a few of the giants of social science who have lead this very field of research–then looked back upon their own work with healthy skepticism. I submit the following quotations as examples:

"Model building and hypothesis testing become the ruling ideal, and research problems were increasingly chosen to fit that mode. Taking stock today, I think most of us judge theoretical progress to have been disappointing. Many are uneasy with the intellectual style of psychological research.

In attempting to generalize from the literature, Shaw and I have been thwarted by the inconsistent findings coming from roughly similar inquiries."[1]

"...the induction from experience that a compulsive need for intellectual certainty–abetted, I would suppose, by longings for personal security–is very apt to lead to deadly falsifications and distortions of reality."[2]

"The idea is that we can find one specific indicator for each intervening variable. Everything else being constant, the variations in the indicators correspond to the variations in the intervening variable. We have grave doubts whether such a procedure is feasible even with animal experiments. And we are confident that it is the wrong idea as far as the study of human behaviour is concerned."[3]

"As we will see later, all authorities in this study who work at the levels of epistemic complexity set by the problems of social psychology and personality raise questions concerning the status of their concepts which suggest any 'defining experiment' basis for construct inference to be utterly beside the point."[4]

"The scholastics systematized a world of unripe knowledge and thereby have protected it from its enemies, but at the same time they denied it the chance for progress."[5]

1. L.J. Cronbach, "Beyond the Two Disciplines of Scientific Psychology," *American Psychologist*, February 1975, pp. 116, 119.

2. H.A. Murray, "Preparations for the Scaffold of a Comprehensive System," in *Psychology: A Study of a Science*, ed., S. Koch, vols. I-VI (New York: McGraw-Hill, 1959), III, p. 49.

3. P.F. Lazarsfeld, "Latent Structure Analysis," in *Psychology: A Study of a Science*, ed., S. Koch, vols. I-VI (New York: McGraw-Hill, 1959), III, pp. 482-483.

4. S. Koch, ed., "Epilogue," *Psychology: A Study of a Science* (New York: McGraw-Hill, 1959), III, p. 739.

5. E. Guthrie, "Association by Contiquity," *Psychology: A Study of a Science*, ed., S. Koch (New York: McGraw-Hill, 1959), II, p. 193.

These astonishing admissions have not found their way into popular reading in social science, and no new models have been proposed, other than your own. That the mind is still seen principally as a thinking machine, ever responding helplessly to the forces of life in an ever-present time span is clear. Commitment is only to a method, certainly not for any accountability for the state of the community. One wonders why these critics were not able to break out of their narrow point of view. Although Guthrie penned his statement shortly before his death, his rather cynical view might be closest to the mark. Furthermore, curriculum can become rather capricious–that is, the discipline is what the scholar says it is, unfettered by validity in the community. I am reminded of your perception that the discipline is always between the student and the teacher–needing to be justified to both. Finally, it is understandable that students trained in a scientific method, transferred and little transformed from that of physical science, attempting to make it work for analysis of their own life experience, became confounded.

The most thoughtful of my students appear to have become distrustful, even angry at academe and its social science, highly suspicious of attempts to re-establish respect for a more responsible scientific method. I find them either anti-scientific, or at least a-scientific.

Imposing the paradigm of the grammatical method, at least its skeletal ideas, has been enormously useful in beginning to re-establish order to the thinking of my students. Pointing out the limitations of what they learned, limitations they have felt intuitively, seems to be the first step in establishing confidence within themselves as well as my own credibility with them. The larger, more comprehensive framework of your method also protects them against the easy charisma of the latest fads. For instance, heredity as a major causal force in all things is waxing now, did you know?

My next step is to base their background in psychology on the four primary mental functions you provide which underlie your method: memory, feeling, logic and anticipation as represented at every event they confront. The students are able to see as well the specific division of labour for science and therefore accept a new esteem for logic when it is contained and described in terms of its rightful part in their thinking–rather than the only, or more desirable mode for all thought. The next natural step is a new understanding of the concept of wholeness and order as the primary goal of thought and action. Considering the popular movement of holistic health, holistic environment, holistic community, they can easily take the next step by extending the metaphor to the larger context of curricula. Traditional social science method, by largely ignoring time or defining it only in terms of the stop-watch, imposes a lifeless, mechanical concept on the analysis of human experience. Such imposition contradicts their intuition of time and timing. The time needed for a courtship, to establish a friendship, for a revolution to evolve, for an idea to capture the imagination and backing of citizens, will all vary enormously. And thus, when a method for social science recognizes these natural variations, students find it much more compatible with the reality of their lives.

In terms of epistomology, I have found it useful to suggest that art and science are something like two separate and somewhat pure methodologies; and that social science is an enormously complex mixture of the two methods. In the past they have been willing to accept at some simple level the cliche, "Teaching is half art and half science," but without seeing how they must be amalgamated into a single conception of a functioning human being.

One of the most important notions I wish to leave with my students is that of authority. At this point I introduce the concept of the twelve tones of the spirit, emphasizing again sequence and timing, where they must listen and accept on faith (which they have done before, but having lost that faith, they have fallen into discouragement). Authority then comes with testing and witnessing and re-establishing validity by their own experience. Here they begin to understand that real discipline is no arbitrary manipulation or game playing, but demands an order that must be followed. Eventually, the power they feel when they have a much more balanced and believable set of intellectual tools, as provided by your method, guides them to a sense of self-worth and commitment that we all hope for.

The notion that knowledge is tenuous and frail is frightening to students, and this is perhaps the most difficult barrier to overcome. Absolute knowledge seems like money in the bank: once there, it continues to draw interest. Commitment to a concept of knowledge having value only in solving the problems at hand and when problems arise directly from the state of the community, seems to be a responsibility they are reluctant to take on. It was psychologically safer to deal only with bits and pieces. The concept of relativity would therefore seem to be a price they only reluctantly pay for a sense of power and usefulness to the community. I am reminded of Erich Fromm's theme in *Escape From Freedom* and try not to allow them to escape back into the simple banking concept of knowledge, where the certainty of simple concepts is their refuge.

Finally, the idea that all disciplines are, in themselves, meaningless abstractions when unrelated to use, and that this "use" is the final court of appeal, brings them to the realization that the cross of reality puts flesh and blood on the skeleton of abstract theories which, before, had little meaning.

Perhaps this is all I can report at this time. I plan to continue developing the themes in your method in other aspects. It is difficult to express how exhilarated these students feel when they discover a method of analysis for human experience that frees them from the stultifying assumptions of natural science, has the fullness to accept knowledge from all disciplines in this analysis and still offers an integrating order.

Rosenstock-Huessy:
My Guide on a Lonely Journey

Richard Shaull

Over the last several decades, I have been pushed slowly but inesca-
pably to the conclusion that the economic, political and social order
we have developed in this country–and most of the attempts to copy
it in Third World countries–is in decline. It cannot respond to
present challenges nor open a future of promise. The only hope I
see for us as a nation lies in recognizing this movement toward death
and attempting to overcome it by a tremendous effort to create a
new order. I also happen to believe that Christian faith can
contribute significantly to this end, even though I see little evidence
that it is doing so at the present time.

As I was struggling with this question, I came upon the writings of
Eugen Rosenstock-Huessy. Realizing that my own journey in this
direction had isolated me from most of my own generation, I was
fascinated to find someone who had come to similar conclusions
about Europe a quarter of a century earlier–during and at the end of
World War I–and had used his great intellectual powers over a lifetime to understand and work at this task of creation. I first came to
this conclusion about the American system through my experience in
Latin America and thus gained a perspective from which to understand and interpret developments in this country during the sixties
and seventies. Rosenstock-Huessy was the one who enriched and
deepened my understanding of this whole process, gave me a
language with which to speak about it, helped to sustain my determination to follow this route in difficult and lonely times, and at
certain crucial points has pushed me farther along this road than I
would otherwise have chosen or dared to go.

My experience in Brazil during the decade of the fifties was the
turning point. Living and working in dialogue with a new generation
of socially-conscious students, I gradually came to see that my North
American vision of a liberal democratic capitalist society could not
provide a way ahead for Brazil. To follow it would bring neither
rational development of the country's resources for the good of the

people, nor an approximation to social justice. Rather, as it worked itself out, it would mean a type of economic development integrated into and dependent upon the United States economy. It would give great power and economic benefits to a small dominant elite while the masses could expect neither to improve their lot economically nor participate in the use of public power.

I also realized that the dominant order functioned as a total system. Economic and political structures, social organizations, educational institutions and cultural patterns were all of one piece. Each functioned to legitimize and support the others. Each political party, for example, represented one of the dominant economic groups; it functioned "democratically" through its co-opted clientele, willing to serve its interests in exchange for small favours. Gradually, those who dreamed of a new future for Brazil came to the conclusion that this meant *systemic* change. But this "one thing necessary" was also impossible. Existing social and political institutions were not structured to bring about qualitative change; in fact, as it soon became clear after the military coup of 1964, those in power in these institutions would use them in any way necessary to maintain the status quo.

In this situation, I faced another serious problem: A decade earlier I had turned to Neo-Orthodox theology because it provided me with categories for understanding the human condition and interpreting life which I greatly valued. It gave me a perspective on history which allowed me to look at the present in the light of its future transformation, and thus work politically for radical change. Having gotten my bearings from this theological system, I went about teaching it with great enthusiasm. At first, young people in both Catholic and Protestant movements responded enthusiastically. But soon they confessed to me that they were excited about the stance I took but not by my "explanations". My arrangement of theological concepts did not order their life and thought as I had assumed it would. They were searching for a type of thought that would be more authentic for them—and more historical. They found what I was teaching too abstract and metaphysical.

When I returned to the United States in the early sixties, I began to look at this society somewhat differently than I had before. After coming to see how the United States economic and political system affected Brazil, I was more aware of how it really functioned at home. And having discovered how a total social system worked in Brazil, I had to pay much more attention to the systemic question here. As I related to and became involved with Blacks and university students in their struggles, I eventually came to the conclusion that this country could move toward the future they and I had begun to dream of only as it underwent a radical transformation, only as it was able to die to its own past and once again undertake the creation of a new society.

When the efforts of the New Left collapsed, as had the movements I was associated with in Brazil a decade earlier, this double experience somehow led me to reject options chosen by others: I could not "drop out" nor abandon the political struggle; I also could not return to the liberal perspective and politics I had earlier abandoned nor imagine that I could work effectively for transformation by serving the existing institutions of society. I continued to teach at Princeton and to maintain some contact with the church, in the hope that sooner or later new movements for change might arise *on the fringes* of these institutions.

In the midst of all this, the theology I was teaching was challenged even more sharply than in Brazil. I continued to develop a "theology of revolution," as it was then called, and to publish articles in liberal theological journals, only to realize that traditional theological language about eschatology and the Kingdom no longer had the power to shape people's thought or motivate their actions as agents of change. Princeton students who shared my social and religious concerns, especially women and those from the Third World, were searching for a language of faith which would orient their struggle; they also made it clear that the theological categories I and my colleagues offered them could not perform that function for them. Eventually, they got through to me that the problem was not just *what* I thought but *how* I thought: my type of rationality. My analysis of what was happening in American society led me to conclude that we had reached a dead end, and could move ahead only as we transformed it into a new beginning. Now I was compelled to admit to myself that the same thing applied to everything I was trying to do as a teacher and theologian.

I continued to maintain my basic Christian stance and commitment, but I badly needed help to interpret its meaning in the new situation in which I found myself, and to live it out. A number of my closest companions in the struggle in Brazil and in the United States, facing a similar crisis of orientation, turned to Karl Marx. I too learned much from him, but my earlier discovery of the bankruptcy of grandiose conceptual systems kept me from buying a replacement for the one I had given up. Instead, I stumbled upon Rosenstock-Huessy.

At a time when I was becoming more critical of my former mentors and was trying to unlearn much of what they had taught me, I found myself drawn more and more into Rosenstock-Huessy's realm of thought. And, as this happened, I gradually came to realize that his influence over me was of a quite different nature than that of other thinkers.

I got one clue as to what that meant from an African student at Princeton, who was part of a small group with whom I spent a semester reading and discussing Rosenstock-Huessy's work. From the start, he was very critical of Rosenstock-Huessy's thought; at times, he seemed almost hostile. But at the end of the semester he turned in an excellent paper, in which he spoke in most positive terms about the seminar and its importance to him. When I asked him about this, in light of his reactions in class, he said: "Of course, I disagree with him, often violently. But he is the only Western thinker who has not imposed himself and his conceptual system on me. Rather, he challenged me to be myself and find my own way." At first, I was somewhat taken by surprise with his remark. Now I realize that something similar has been happening to me.

On several occasions, I have attempted to take one or another aspect of Rosenstock-Huessy's thought, analyze and order it in a more or less rational way, and do a critical assessment of it. Somehow, every such attempt, which I seem to have no trouble carrying out with others, fails. In the middle of it, I realize that my analytical statement reduces and violates his thought, rather than capturing and communicating it; that the richness of what he contributes to me comes not so much from my attempt to organize and appropriate his thought as from the process of reflection and interaction set in motion through contact with him.

Moreover, this process of interaction provoked by his thought affects me as a whole person. Recently, a man who graduated from Princeton some twenty years ago returned to the campus and met the professor who had profoundly influenced him when a student. In the course of a conversation with him, he said: "I still remember the impact your lectures made on me. I can recall very little of what you said. Through your struggle to think and speak about certain problems, you communicated who you were as a living human being. Consequently, you changed my life."

I can, of course, identify certain specific things I have learned from Rosenstock-Huessy, but they must be seen within this wider perspective. That makes it extremely difficult for me to write this paper. The best I can hope to do is to point to a few areas in which the process I have described has been going on, indicate something of what has happened to me and where it has led me, and lay out a few of the unanswered questions I am struggling with, realizing that "each generation has to act differently in order to represent the same thing."

Thinking Eschatologically as We Approach the Third Millennium

I first turned to Rosenstock-Huessy for help in the theological crisis I mentioned above. I was delighted to find someone who seemed to share my assessment of the present historical situation; looked at the world from the perspective of Christian faith, defined in eschatological terms; and at the same time encouraged me to think theologically in a new way. He declared that the task of the Third Millennium, the creation of a truly human society, called for a secular language of faith, quite different from the theological formulations of the previous millennia. This meant for him that the Christian witness, in the future, would be largely incognito. And he proceeded to develop his eschatological approach without using the old theological jargon; he talked about bringing death into the midst of life and overcoming it, transforming dead ends into new beginnings, etc. I found this shift in language a helpful one, but I was especially attracted to *Out of Revolution*. In this work, he was, as I perceived it, writing theology as history. His eschatological perspective was presented as he traced the social autobiography of "Western man," told the story of the various dramatic efforts to re-create and re-produce society and its institutions, and spoke of the passions of the human heart that exploded in these events. Several decades earlier, I had turned from philosophy and the social sciences to theology because of its power to illumine our understanding of human life and destiny; now once again I sensed a similar excitement as Rosenstock-Huessy laid out his Christian vision of Western history. To this day, what he has done helps me to keep alive, articulate and living out my response to the American crisis and my own stance of faith as well.

Unfortunately, this contribution of Rosenstock-Huessy to my theological development has also brought with it a number of complicated problems. I have not been able to appropriate his approach as a new paradigm within which I might work, and perhaps develop a bit further. For a very simple reason: When Rosenstock-Huessy speaks in secular terms about a Christian vision and stance, he stands firmly within a tradition which he takes for granted. He lived in and was shaped by the world of the Bible; he has drawn constantly on its thought and imagery. Likewise, he knows and accepts the basic creeds and theological developments in Christian history, and his secular theology spells out their meaning for today.

However, the very process of secularization which he describes makes it difficult if not impossible to repeat what he has done. By and large, those of a new generation who are living fully in the world he describes no longer have this foundation. In the seminars and workshops I have done on Rosenstock-Huessy, using *The Christian Future* and *Out of Revolution,* some students have gone along with his "religious" language but have not experienced its power; others have been interested in his thought but ignored his theology; a few others have been turned off by his approach.

I believe that it is important for a new generation to live in dialogue with our Christian heritage and to discover that it can speak to them. But I doubt if many of them will be inclined to turn directly to it to probe its depths, or to study what Rosenstock-Huessy or others have to say about it. Especially at the present time, I believe the problem is acute because the tradition has been repeated for so long, not re-created in each new situation and generation. What I hope for is the emergence of small communities on the frontiers of social transformation, in which there will be an openness to the heritage of faith and a willingness to explore it as it is mediated, in such groups, by a few women and men who are committed to keeping the dialogue going. I believe that our past will be present not so much through written interpretations of its meaning in contemporary terms, but rather in the flow of vital speech among those engaged in the struggle. Perhaps later on conditions will develop for the flowering of a new age of connectedness with our Christian past, but I suspect that such an event will come, if at all, only as the result of much more humble efforts on the part of a few to keep the dialogue going. And if and when it comes, it may use a new language of faith which we at present cannot imagine.

In the meantime, this conclusion sets the terms for my own theological efforts: to try to be situated at the cutting edge of death and resurrection in our society today, to do this in community, and to do everything possible to live out and speak about a way of life and a social struggle inspired and oriented by faith in Jesus Christ. That will hardly produce impressive lectures or theological tomes. But it might create conditions in which a few of us here and there learn to speak passionately to one another and to empower each other. As I learned from Rosenstock-Huessy years ago, this process of speaking vitally to each other across past to present and oriented toward the future is the very essence of our tradition. A tradition is not a body of knowledge enclosed in conceptual systems.

Thus, Rosenstock-Huessy has brought me, against my will, to what I consider to be a frontier for theological thought–and left me standing there, almost alone. For the main lines of theological thought today are moving in another direction. Those attracted to the security of Neo-Evangelicalism want a tradition expressed in authoritative statements and concepts, repeated from the past. And the last thing the academicians are inclined to do is to admit that their intellectual world is in crisis and that they must begin again as they speak in dialogue with their students. At the same time, Rosenstock-Huessy has given me a clear sense of the "timeliness" of this effort. We can be authentic theologians only as we live out what we teach, that life can indeed emerge out of death.

As someone vocationally committed to studying, thinking and teaching, the question, "Where do I situate myself in relation to my time and space?" has always been an important one. Rosenstock-Huessy has heightened my awareness of this. He has helped me to see the sterility of life and thought in structures locked into repetition, slowly sliding downhill; he has also portrayed what can happen as people who refuse to die are caught up by the fires of revolution and discover their creative powers. And he has confirmed my suspicions that such new life is more likely to emerge on the fringes than in the center.

And yet, it is one thing to perceive all this; it is quite another to discover how to live it out at this point of time, and to function intellectually in the midst of incoherence. Thus, it has taken me quite a while to decide to leave Princeton and follow a path that has led me, at present, to the South Bronx. And along this road, I realize that it is much easier to see and move away from the sterility at the center than to find and participate in the precarious expressions of new life on the fringes.

This problem becomes especially acute when I try to discern where to stand in relation to the Church, and Rosenstock-Huessy does not make it any easier for me to solve that problem. He confirmed my own conclusion that I need not waste my time trying to save Christianity: "Saving Christianity is unnecessary, undesirable, impossible, because it is anti-Christian."[1] He strengthened my conviction that the Church, while it frequently follows the same pattern of sclerosis and decline as other institutions, nevertheless has time and

1. Eugen Rosenstock-Huessy, *The Christian Future or the Modern Mind Outrun* (New York: Harper and Row, 1966), p. 61.

again produced movements which have broken out of this pattern. "Christianity has repeatedly been bankrupt. When it goes bankrupt, it begins over again; therein rests its power."[2]

At the same time, he encouraged me to expect to find, in Christian faith, "the power which enables us to die to our old habits and ideals, get out of our old ruts, leave our dead selves behind and take the first step into a genuine future."[3] As a son of the Protestant Reformation, I know that the Church can be the Church only as it points to and participates in the life of the Coming Kingdom:

> Luther changed the church from a neighbour in space to a prophet in time. The church was to be not a hundred steps from the palace or the town-hall, but a hundred hours or days or months ahead of what was transacted in either of these houses.[4]

That leaves me with the unresolved question: How do I live in the community of faith and serve the cause of Christianity, in the in-between times, when the Church is largely invisible? When I face that issue, taking into account how the invisibility of Christianity has affected my children, I realize that Rosenstock-Huessy and I belong to two different generations, and that, here as elsewhere, we have to act differently to represent the same thing.

Cartesian "Reason" or "Impure" Thinking

Twenty years in Princeton were more than enough to convince me that something was radically wrong in the intellectual world in which I moved, and my women students in particular forced me to see that the basic problem had to do with one way of thinking, assumed to have universal validity. They also reminded me that I was locked into this type of rationality even as I protested against it. This led me to a more critical examination of our Cartesian heritage and convinced me that I would have to begin a search for alternatives.

Here too Rosenstock-Huessy's contribution is not exactly what I would have wished for. I would like to have a new paradigm with which to work, an outline which I and others might slowly fill in. What I get instead is the bare minimum I need to make a new beginning on my own. After I have stepped into the darkness, I find that what Rosenstock-Huessy does is throw light on a spot on which I can stand while I prepare to take a greater leap into the darkness.

2. Rosenstock-Huessy, *The Christian Future,* p. 89.
3. Rosenstock-Huessy, *The Christian Future,* p. 62.
4. Eugen Rosenstock-Huessy, *Out of Revolution: Autobiography of Western Man* (Norwich, Vermont: Argo Books, 1969), p. 412.

From Rosenstock-Huessy I learned the crucial importance of *speaking to* others, and how essential that is to the validity of *speaking about* something. But, he speaks about many things, especially about speech. I am grateful to him for having pointed out to me the four dimensions of vital speech. But the more I listen to what he has to say, the more I am led to conclude that these four languages, some more than others, are largely bankrupt. The problem before us at this juncture is not merely that of listening to and integrating these four languages, but how each can be re-created in response to current reality and in interaction with the others. My conclusion from this is that, if I take Rosenstock-Huessy seriously, I must learn from his speaking about speech how *to speak to others about life.*

In the realm of theology, I experience most acutely both the crisis of thinking and the promise of a possible alternative as offered by Rosenstock-Huessy. In this crisis, the theologians have a certain advantage, if they choose to exploit it. Their language is so sterile and inadequate for speaking vitally of the human condition today that it is hard indeed for the theologian to rest at ease in Zion. In Rosenstock-Huessy's words, "the wearing out of the old names, the old words, the old language, is the most widely and deeply felt fact in the crisis through which Christianity is passing, and that is why we must give them up today."[5] At the same time, the heritage on which our scholarship is concentrated is unusually rich in resources for transformation of our thought and language.

It may well be that Rosenstock-Huessy's greatest contribution to theology will yet be made in this area. His life project, centering on speech, flows out of and is directly related to his Christian faith; and he has made this connectedness explicit especially in what he has written about Pentecost and in his understanding of the Four Gospels, as presented in *Fruit of Lips.* Time and again he provides us with insights which could lead us into relatively unexplored territory:

Speech is the Body of the Spirit.

I could not believe in the Holy Spirit unless He had changed his forms of expression relentlessly.[6]

The Gospel always is the common sense of tomorrow, never the common sense of yesterday.[7]

5. Rosenstock-Huessy, *The Christian Future*, p. 128.

6. Eugen Rosenstock-Huessy, *Fruit of Lips or Why Four Gospels,* ed. Marion Battles (Pittsburg: Pickwick Press, 1978), p. 33.

7. Rosenstock-Huessy, *Fruit of Lips,* p. 134.

The question remains: How do we even begin to live and think this way? Under what conditions can we hope that Christian thought will be re-created and re-articulated in vital speech? How can we approach the Gospels so that they point us toward the common sense of tomorrow rather than yesterday? As I have struggled with these questions, two things have occurred to me:

(a). In Latin America at least, a new language of faith has emerged and begun to speak with power as a result of the struggle for liberation on the part of the poor, and the identification of theologians and biblical scholars with them in their struggle. On that frontier, many are discovering that the biblical story interprets the human struggle for liberation and provides the language for ethical discourse in that situation. This suggests to me that, in North America, we can hope for a revitalization of theology as we move out of the academic milieu onto similar frontiers of struggle with the poor or as we learn to become a Church of the Resistence in the coming time of repression.

(b). Some months ago I was asked to prepare a paper on a Christian ethical approach to homosexuality. As I began to work on it, it soon became clear to me that, if I limited my biblical reflection to the exegesis of biblical texts, there was no way I could go beyond "the common sense of yesterday." Unwilling to settle for that, or to turn away from the Gospels, the thought occurred to me: I can interpret the Gospel story as I pay attention to how the insights contained in it have unfolded over the centuries, and as I assess the influence Jesus Christ has had in our history. In this way, I may be able to focus attention on the dynamic inherent in the Gospel story and the direction in which it points us, and thus find a basis for fruitful ethical dialogue.

The Shape of the Next Revolution

I spoke earlier of the ways in which Rosenstock-Huessy has influenced my theological reflection on revolution. However, to do justice to his influence, I must set it in a somewhat broader context. As a result of my life in Brazil in the fifties and the United Stated in the sixties, I came to the conclusion that revolution is and will be the central reality of our age; that we are living at the end of an era and can move to the future only as our various societies–in the West and in the Third World–undergo radical transformation. To that situation I must respond not just as a theologian but as a living human being.

I came to this position before I ever read anything of Rosenstock-Huessy. But as I tried to sustain it over the years, he is one of a very few who has been a constant help to me. Each year I find it important to immerse myself for a time in *Out of Revolution.* Thanks to him, I have stuck with my earlier perception of the nature of this age and have tried to deepen and broaden my understanding of it as a revolutionary time. Likewise, Rosenstock-Huessy has helped to sharpen my sense that "only volcanic explosions to which people give themselves up heart and soul, can create new human types" and a new world. For this reason, I have never counted on liberal reform movements to open the way to the future; at the same time, I have paid particular attention to those movements capable of stirring the passions of the dispossessed, as well as those more privileged who dare to stand with them.

In the last few years, however, the crucial question has become: What will be the nature of the next revolution? In trying to answer it, I cannot get excited about Rosenstock-Huessy's architectionic scheme, but I do find his interpretation of the revolutionary process in the West merging with my own sense of the direction of Christian history and its influence on the world. Rosenstock-Huessy speaks of the movement from the German Revolution (Every Christian a priest), to the English (Every gentleman a king), to the French (Every man of talent an aristocrat), to the Russian (Every proletarian a capitalist). I would like to carry this one step further, and speak now of *Every oppressed woman or man a Subject.*

This term, Subject, may not communicate much to us at the present time, but it is at the heart of the revolution now taking place in Latin America. In liberation movements and especially in the Basic Christian Communities, the marginalized peasants and the urban poor are gaining a new sense of their own worth and are discovering that they can assume increasing responsibility for shaping their own lives and destinies. For them, this means becoming Subjects. Those who are not poor are discovering that they can find new life as they join with and contribute to the empowerment of the dispossessed, if they are willing to abandon their former ways of having power over them and providing services paternalistically for them. Here, I believe, we can see the new fires of revolution, capable of creating a new era. In his discussion of the German Revolution, Rosenstock-Huessy remarks that Luther got thousands of monks and nuns to return to the world and take up trades, rather than continuing the work of their fathers. The result: a revolution in which the free choice of a profession developed. Today, I sense the beginning of a similar movement as thousands of women and men, religious and secular, abandon their positions and careers in order to live and identify with the poor and take up with them the struggle for justice and human survival. But this time, the initiative of a few thousand can contribute to unleashing the energies of the masses of poor people who until now have been convinced that they were "nobodies" and could do nothing.

Rosenstock-Huessy spoke of the next revolution as tribal, within the context of a conscious economic organization of the whole earth. I am inclined to follow this lead, insisting that the process of which I have just spoken suggests the emergence of a new quality of life and new patterns of social, economic and political organization, as the oppressed create a life of their own through the development of multiple forms of local self-reliance and interdependence with each other. Rosenstock-Huessy provides us with no blueprint for the future. Precisely for this reason, he may contribute more to our movement toward the future than other social thinkers who may have a greater appeal because they offer us too much.

Mission as Dialogue

Dale Irvin

Several years ago I had the opportunity to meet regularly with a group of inmates in a Philadelphia prison. During one of our initial discussions, an inmate articulated what became a theme of our meeting for the next several months.

A member of the Islamic community, this inmate had served six years of a life term. That evening he told me, "Your seminary, along with a lot of other institutions, is responsible for building this jailhouse. Your institution has got the blueprints for putting up places like this, but it doesn't know how to tear them down. If you want to know that, you've got to listen to us. We've got the blueprints for tearing them down."

I had gone to seminary without much doubt about the vitality of the mission and faith of the Christian church. I could recite well-formulated credal statements proclaiming Christ as the way of social and spiritual salvation. I might even have gone so far as to suggest that Christian faith is the only way of salvation and hope.

The experience of that prison group brought home to me a different perspective on the current state of affairs in the institutions of faith. In a concrete way I realized that my church participated in building and maintaining those dehumanizing structures. With some-times vocal, often silent assent, it participated in a social structure of which these twelve or thirteen men were products.

Critical discussion of these structures has recently become more common among those of us in the church–so much so that we may miss the human dimensions in which social bankruptcy is manifest. We often talk as if problems were theoretical only, and not being played out in the lives of women and men.

Even more, we may come to grips with the human dimensions of this bankruptcy and still be unable to act. We may find ourselves unable to face bankruptcy in a manner which would allow us to create the world anew.

It is not a question of having lost the blueprints with which our age was constructed. These we have, and they are lovingly preserved in our textbooks and museums, produced time and again for display and examination. But they do not enable us to tear down the walls in such a way that we can begin again.

That group of prisoners in Philadelphia impressed this point upon me time after time. Ignoring the structural injustice and pain of these men would be ignoring my own participation in a bankrupt system. Ignoring the pain and dislocation caused by our political processes, or the cultural dislocation caused by religious propagation, would be a collective denial bound to perpetuate our decadence.

Tearing down the jailhouse walls would be an admission of decay at the very heart of our collective life, as a church as well as a society. It would indicate an ability to face our own death not as the fading light of an old order but as the dawning light of a new day. In Eugen Rosenstock-Huessy's terms, we would then be more capable of "transforming an end into a beginning."[1]

I believe that this Philadelphia inmate was essentially correct in his assessment of the role of our institutions of both church and society in creating structures that dehumanize. I further believe he was essentially correct in his assessment of our need for a kind of transforming death which would enable us to participate in new institutional structures. I suggest that Rosenstock-Huessy can be of assistance to us in this endeavour, helping us learn to listen to those who know best how to tear down the jailhouse walls. He can be of assistance not only in teaching us again that death precedes life and that birth is the fruit of death, but in opening up to us a way to go about this dying and resurrecting.

Rosenstock-Huessy on occasion insisted that his students not tell him facts, but tell him of their experiences.[2] He understood history as our collective biography and asked it be related as such. With his encouragement, therefore, I wish to proceed from my own theological journey in order to discover what the thinking of Rosenstock-Huessy has to offer the church.

I was intellectually nurtured in a thoroughly Christian world, my family belonging to a denomination whose heart was American fundamentalism. Many of my earliest memories are of the stories of missionary endeavours, in far-off countries or near-by cities. I vividly recall these stories being linked to the imminent return of Christ which would usher in the end of the age. I grew up not only with this sense of an impending end, but of the worldwide transformation

1. Eugen Rosenstock-Huessy, *The Christian Future, or the Modern Mind Outrun* (New York: Scribners, 1946), p. 10.

2. This sentiment is heard in various tapes of the Dartmouth lectures, available through Argo Books. Rosenstock-Huessy's major work of history is subtitled *Autobiography of Western Man.*

which was to follow. Individual conversions to Christianity were but a foretaste of the cosmic conversion yet to come.

This urgent sense of transformation was an impetus for the church's concern with missions beyond national or cultural borders. It was a mission of one-way movement, however, allowing itself to be imperialistic in the name of salvation. I grew up hearing of vast and unruly regions known as "mission lands." Great revivals of Christian fundamentalism seemed to be bringing hoards of unbelievers from these places not only into our Christian camp but into our particular cultural expression as well.

There were no resources here which would enable me to listen to voices from outside the tight circle of faith. No resources existed for speaking to and engaging those whose transformation we sought. The term imperialistic is not too harsh: our faith was biblical, our cause was God's and our call was to be warriors out to conquer the whole of the earth.

Political and social cohorts of this faith, in the form of American military might and American cultural superiority, were justified as components of God's overall plan. Overseas, this translated into support for military intervention and policies of colonialism. At home it meant justification of racism, discrimination, and social oppression.

The time eventually came when I formulated more critical questions about faith. I came to realize that I was living in the midst of a cultural and historical upheaval which on the surface corresponded with my apocalyptic religious heritage but on a deeper level contradicted it. The conscious sense of impending disaster then took on less of a religious tone and more of an historical one. Civil rights and militarization were events taking place in time and with identifiable characters and consequences.

The religious response with which I was most familiar sought either to ignore contemporary issues or regard them as fulfillments of an eternal scheme recorded ages past. But events themselves seemed to me to command an awesome sense of time, of history.

It is this sense of time that I found lacking in my own religious tradition, a sense of the future taking shape within real dimensions of life. Recognizing limitation and incompletion, I discovered that the end was not yet written and faith not yet complete.

The world of American fundamentalism, on the other hand, was one of historical denial. Faith was complete in the sense that nothing beyond biblical revelation could affect it. It laid claim to being a-historical and a-political, untouched by events of a worldly nature.

Such a faith simply assumed stages of history to be passages of God's preordained plan and empty of significant human participation. Both future and past collapsed into the present of God's time, closing off the possibility of a real end and a real beginning. Humanity, the world, the divine nature itself, all took on a static nature. While the apocalyptic stories of the Bible should have belied it, the nature of the faith was non-transforming and non-transformable.

Timeless and immovable, the new historical imperatives of a changing world were unheeded. Those who bore this faith were often deaf to the call for transformation being raised by those whose conversion they sought. In various manifestations this faith continues today to ignore the challenge to face the world in such a way that it may die and be reborn.

Particular cultural and social expressions continue to be sanctified by this timeless theology. Revelation is identified with one age and its transmission through one people.[3] Rather than casting the mission of the church in terms of significant groupings of people seeking their own transformation through faith, this theological expression perceives the struggle as that of orthodoxy versus unbelief or heterodoxy. Success comes when there is movement one-way, contamination of the gospel when there is interaction.

At times even Eugen Rosenstock-Huessy appeared to use the language of this imperialism. He spoke of pagans and Christians, for instance. Many of his writings seem to affirm that salvation comes only through one particular story, one particular history. He differs significantly from the evangelical missionary tradition, however, for he never sought to reduce the unfolding reality of a particular human community to a set of preordained principles. He was not prone to foreclose the possibility of a people for a new story, a new future.

Rosenstock-Huessy sought to bring each particular human story into a growing dialogue with other stories. In doing so he was reaching toward a commonality not of dogmatic agreement but of a living future. With his emphasis upon timeliness, Rosenstock-Huessy was capable of taking seriously any people's story. He would not have made a very good missionary of the kind with which I was familiar.

---

3. K. Koyama has pursued this theme from the point of view of being Christian and Japanese. See "Ritual of Limping Dance: A Botanical Observation," *Union Seminary Quarterly Review*, Vol. 36, 1981.

In my own theological journey I found myself leaving behind the timeless faith and seeking a more adequate expression. I wound up studying not only the classic writings of the Reformation, but Protestant theology of the last century in general. In an attempt to capture some notion of timeliness for faith, I found myself studying others for whom the upheavals of time were great.

What I soon discovered was that other expressions of Protestantism, while sharply divergent on issues such as the location of authority or the debt to pietism, nevertheless were in agreement concerning the question of time or human experience.

I remember reading Karl Barth's insistent passage about the Word of God being clouded by the fog of human experience,[4] and realizing that my experience of God had been just the opposite. Whatever sense of grace I had was profoundly cast in time and space. Barth's orthodoxy did no more to equip me for the struggle for transformation than did the brand of evangelicalism I had earlier known. I continued to feel theologically deaf to the imperatives which seemed to be calling me out of one age and into another.

Neither theology allowed me to listen, neither allowed me to affirm that my seminary or my church were responsible for sustaining structures once redemptive but now oppressive. Both were formulated in such a way that human experience paled before God's reality, making consideration of the arena of human activity immaterial.

My sense of the importance of the arena of human activity, on the other hand, brought a crucial awareness that time itself was issuing an imperative for the church. Structures which had once opened up creative opportunities were being called into account by the changing historical reality, and it seemed to me that the mission of the church was to respond. Instead my church seemed deaf to the call.

And it was at this point that I discovered that Rosenstock-Huessy had much to say concerning the bankruptcy not only of the mission of the church but of our society in general. In him I found ears that listened.

What I discovered was his conversation with Barth in 1923, recorded in *Ja und Nein*.[5] Rosenstock-Huessy had come to the realization that tremendous upheavals of history are themselves forms of

4. See K. Barth, *Church Dogmatics*, Vol. I/2, trans. Thompson and Knight (Edinburgh: T & T Clark, 1956), p. 716 f.

5. Eugen Rosenstock-Huessy, *Ja und Nein: Autobiographische Fragmente* Heidelberg: Verlag Lambert Schneider, 1968), p. 81 f.

revelation in that they demand from us new ways of living and speaking (as does any encounter with the divine). Barth and the course of theology for much of the twentieth century carried on as if the horrors of the War had never happened.

For Rosenstock-Huessy, and others with whom he sought to address this experience–Martin Buber and especially Franz Rosenzweig–the War became the imperative which marked the beginning of a new age, a new time. Rosenstock-Huessy pointed me toward the realization that this appraisal of time precedes an ability to listen. To be addressed by the imperatives of our age, to speak a new name in response and to be transformed in the process means to listen with new ears. As he stated, *"Audi, ne moriamur."*[6]

The method of transforming listening, Rosenstock-Huessy and Franz Rosenzweig discovered in the course of their correspondence during World War I, is dialogue.[7] Their interaction has become a challenging example of dialogue, be it religious or not. Passion, intensive responses and new ways of thinking were discovered in the life-blood of speech. Abandoned were neat distinctions between Christian and Jew, as were distinctions between spiritual, historical and personal dimensions.[8] In the course of their dialogue, clear distinctions between where one person's thought ended and the other's began disappeared.

Rosenzweig caught the flavor of this interaction when he wrote:

In the course of a dialogue he who happens to be listening also speaks, and he does not speak merely when he is actually uttering words, not even mainly when he is uttering words, but just as much when through his eager attention, through the assent or dissent expressed in his glances, he conjures words to the lips of the current speaker.[9]

The two participants risked all that was precious to them, intellectually and spiritually, in the course of their dialogue. Rosenstock-Huessy later made his motto the phrase, *Respondeo etsi mutabor!* (I respond although I will be changed.)[10] They were changed, and discovered it as a renewal of both faith and world.

6. Eugen Rosenstock-Huessy, *Speech and Reality* (Norwich, Vt.: Argo Books, 1970), p. 24.

7. Their correspondence is published as *Judaism Despite Christianity*, E. Rosenstock-Huessy, ed. (University, Alabama: University of Alabama Press, 1969).

8. H. Stahmer, in his Introduction to *Judaism Despite Christianity*, p. 4.

9. Quoted by Stahmer, Introduction, p. 4. Quote taken from Nahum N. Glatzer, *Franz Rosenzweig: His Life and Thought* (New York, 1972), p. 308.

10. Eugen Rosenstock-Huessy, *Out of Revolution: The Autobiography of Western Man* (Norwich, Vt.: Ago Books, 1969), p. 741.

Rosenstock-Huessy came to see this renewal as the very essence of what he called Christian faith. Yet, while he regarded Christianity as a source of renewal for the whole world, in its power to create new spans of time through renewal of speech, he was well aware that there are times when Christians experience an absence of power. Then it seems that the word has run dry, the faith bankrupt.[11] At such times renewal takes its first breath from the world, and its second from Christian faith. Renewal of faith depends upon as well as implies renewal of the world, and likewise the world depends on faith. The transforming power of the word, of speech, is drawn from and leads back to history.

Oriented in this way toward the world, he could regard profoundly anti-Christian moments of our autobiography, like the French and Russian revolutions, as Christian events. They are the results of the Christian era, he wrote. "They depend upon it, they complete it."[12]

> Christianity is not a mutual admiration society. It may allot to a certain form of life the necessary area in which to establish its own realm. The chief duty of any member of the Corpus Christi is to strengthen the other forces of humanity and thereby to assure the later co-ordination of the Russian antitheistic form with the rest of the Christian community...the un-Christian forces play their part in the process of reimplantation of every branch of humankind into the one tree, which is the perpetual effort of our era.[13]

It was this unifying force of Christianity that Rosenstock-Huessy saw at work in the history of the West. What was Christian in this history was not the presence of orthodoxy or apostolic succession. What was Christian was "contemporaneity between antagonists,"[14] or an ability to coexist. The sustaining presence of older forms of humanity, creating ever more complex realities, and not the linear unfolding of human events alone, made this history progressive.

"The whole question of progress depends on the possibility of coexistence of all rungs of the ladder," he wrote in *Out of Revolution.*[15] History was neither linear nor cyclical alone, but a kind

---

11. The notion of a bankrupt faith looking toward the world for inspiration Rosenstock-Huessy shared with D. Bonhoffer. See S. Leibholz, "Eugen Rosenstock-Huessy and Dietrich Bonhoffer–Two Witnesses to the Change in our Time," *Universitas,* Vol. 8, 1966, p. 276 f.

12. Rosenstock-Huessy, *Out of Revolution,* p. 716.

13. Rosenstock-Huessy, *Out of Revolution,* pp. 716-717.

14. Rosenstock-Huessy, *Out of Revolution,* p. 459.

15. Rosenstock-Huessy, *Out of Revolution,* p. 465.

of spiraling of creation–or better, re-creation. History was "a new form of recurrent, repetitive life."[16] Or, "In history creation itself is going on all the time, and eternal recurrence of the created kinds is also going on all the time."[17] This complex experience of time was a product of Christianity, and perhaps even depended upon the ongoing existence of a Christian community in the world.

Few of the missionaries I have known would consider coexistence as a particularly valued aspect of faith. Most would tend to endorse the spread of Western Christianity as a necessary component of the salvation of the world, eliminating other rungs from the ladder as far as non-Christian history is concerned. There is no doubt that Rosenstock-Huessy considered the possibility of coexistence to be distinctively Christian; but he was not imperialistic in his attitude toward other histories, other traditions, other stories.

One who so passionately entered into dialogue and risked everything in his endeavour to respond to Franz Rosenzweig, a Jew, would not have been capable of the exclusivism implicit in the notion that Western Christian faith carries the banner of universal truth. Instead, Rosenstock-Huessy recognized in the notion of universal an invitation to an ever-enlarging dialogue. For him, the possibility of coexistence of all rungs of the ladder was itself the universalizing force at work in history. The particular forms of that universalizing element could themselves be (and had been) transformed as far as he was concerned.

Where this element had once been closely identified with the Church in European history, its identity was transformed as Christianity moved out beyond the borders of Europe. He saw the universalizing force of the future to be economics, closely akin but nevertheless distinctive from those forces which are consciously Christian. While Europe of 1000 A.D. was of one Church and many economies, the world of 1986 is of one economy and many churches.[18] In either case, not one story but the coexistence of many is what he meant by universal.

Economic unity offers us today not only an opportunity for co-operation between "forces of life which are consciously Christian and others which suppress their Christian inheritance for the sake of restoring one vital phase."[19] It offers an opportunity for co-operation between forces which are Christian (consciously or

16. Rosenstock-Huessy, *Out of Revolution*, p. 466.
17. Rosenstock-Huessy, *Out of Revolution*, p. 466.
18. Rosenstock-Huessy, *Out of Revolution*, p. 43 and 594 f.
19. Rosenstock-Huessy, *Out of Revolution*, p. 716-717.

unconsciously) and forces which are non-Christian (pagan in Rosenstock-Huessy's vocabulary). We can enter a dialogue that he noted as having occurred at the beginning of this long and twisted journey through the Judeo-Christian heritage, a dialogue between the Jews and their neighbours.[20]

He called this a dialogue between Omega and Alpha. The notion of universality as the totality of the end he called the Omega. Being rooted in the past, in the beginning or in tribalism he called Alpha. Omega and Alpha once existed side by side, in a relationship or tension which opens the door for dialogue.[21]

With Rosenstock-Huessy I find myself affirming the Omega character of Christian faith without conceiving of eschatology as a completed scenario. Other recent forms of eschatological thinking, as the new apocalypticism popularized by Hal Lindsay, or even Moltmann's theology of hope would not qualify as being either Christian or universal for Rosenstock-Huessy. Their timelessness demands flight from the earth, either in the form of other-worldly transformation or "transcendent eschatology."[22] "The truth of eschatology," wrote Rosenstock-Huessy, "is not a theoretical proposition to be rediscovered scientifically and put on our desks in the form of a book. It is an ever-threatening event to be reconquered on and by faith."[23]

With this emphasis upon the reality of a lived eschatology, the danger of total revolution is recognized repeatedly in his work. He rightly identified it as being as destructive as total war or total anarchy. Revolutions were characterized as universal events, but they are so because they are moments in which the end is lived at the beginning, encompassing totality.[24]

The outcome of true revolutions, he believed, is not a permanent state of upheaval but rather the creation of a new type of humanity to be brought into the commonality of the race through dialogue. This process requires that we look toward our commonality in the future even as we experience the incompletion and limitations of our present.

---

20. Rosenstock-Huessy, *Out of Revolution*, pp. 219-229.

21. Rosenstock-Huessy, *Out of Revolution*, p. 229. See letter 16, *Judaism Despite Christianity*, p. 139 f.

22. See J. Moltmann, *Theology of Hope* (New York: Harper & Row, 1967). R. Alves, in *A Theology of Human Hope* (Washington: Corpus Books, 1969), directly addresses this issue, p. 99 f.

23. Rosenstock-Huessy, *The Christian Future*, p. 70.

24. See Rosenstock-Huessy, *Out of Revolution*, p. 457.

Dependent upon a method of dialogue, then, his notion of universality implies an openness to new thoughts and responses. Those who participate in the universalizing task must be open to their own transformation, as well as that of others. It is an historical dialogue, occurring on the axes of time and space. It is not a godless event, for it encompasses the transforming power of faith through speech. As he wrote to Rosenzweig, "Only the man who entrusts himself to language as God has allowed it to become can be carried along by it so that it 'transforms' him and others."[25]

My own sense of mission has been decisively challenged by the possibility of being carried along by language as God has allowed it to become, and of being open to my own transformation through dialogue. I find our most common notions of mission stood on their head. No longer does evangelical faith set the agenda for the world in which it exists, but the world sets the agenda for the church. Language, as it exists in the world, is the means of transforming faith rather than faith a means of transforming language. It is not the church's message which is universal, but rather the church's listening which opens the door to universality.

In *The Christian Future,* Rosenstock-Huessy wrote that he had no doubt about the necessity for a listening church now. He saw that we must renounce our self-centeredness and enter into the predicament of the whole.[26] Without this listening ability, without the ability to be transformed, there could have been no past. And "without the Christian spirit there is no real future...."[27] That there is both a past and a future is the basis for hope.

I share the hope for the church. I have doubts about its ability to achieve its own transformation apart from dialogue with those who have been the objects of its mission in the past. But then Rosenstock-Huessy would have shared these doubts. It is up to us to be willing to risk even our dearest theological notions and historical idols, which may be products of our self-centeredness, in order to discover our life anew.

I have glimpsed ever so slightly what transforming dialogue can mean to those of us who are located within the Western Christian tradition. I have been forced to rethink what the notion of Jesus Christ for the world means and what the vocation of Western Christendom is through encounters with people who locate themselves outside the Christian tradition, or outside the Western cultural

25. Rosenstock-Huessy, *Judaism Despite Christianity*, p. 144.
26. Rosenstock-Huessy, *The Christian Future*, pp. 127-128.
27. Rosenstock-Huessy, *The Christian Future*, p. 61.

tradition. Taking Rosenstock-Huessy's suggestion that we allow speech to work its transforming power, I have found myself changed because of these experiences.

One experience I have previously referred to is that with a group of inmates in the Philadelphia prison system. Another more recent experience involved not only a Christian-Muslim dialogue, but a dialogue between North Americans and Asians. It was a dialogue project taking place in the Philippines between Christians and Muslims. It has consequently meant for me exposure to the attempts by a significant number of people in that country to create their national history anew, in the spirit of their indigenous Asian heritage.

Under the official title of "Seminarians for Peace," this project was established in 1979 as a summer session for students and pastors from several Protestant denominations. It has expanded to include a number of villages and resource centers on the island of Mindanao, and functions as a work/study experience similar to that in which Rosenstock-Huessy was involved at Camp William James.[28]

This is not coincidence. The primary organizer of the project draws upon the pedagogical work of Paulo Freire, the historical experiences of Asian peasant movements and various Filipino traditions–both Christian and Muslim–relating to peace. But the program also draws upon the work of Rosenstock-Huessy in several direct and indirect ways.

Rosenstock-Huessy himself would have been annoyed if such a program of ecumenical dialogue, located so far from the national and cultural borders of European civilization as southwest Mindanao, simply reproduced his thinking. This program has gone quite a distance beyond him in consciously seeking not only the coexistence of various rungs of the Christian ladder, but the coexistence of Christian and Muslim as well.

Given the long involvement of Protestant and Catholic missionaries in the colonial domination of the Philippines, such a program would have been improbable under white missionary auspices. The Muslim people in particular continue to suffer under the policies of the national government which they perceive as being the "Christian government": their distrust of Christian missionaries is linked to their political distrust of the present state.

For the sake of cultural and religious survival, a significant resistance movement emerged in the 1960s from among the Muslim people. Known as the Moro National Liberation Front (MNLF), it

28. See J. Preiss, *Camp William James* (Norwich, Vt.: Argo Books, 1978).

has the support of enough Muslims to put a number of provinces into a civil war.

North American missionary activity continues among Muslims in Mindanao, with representation across a broad denominational range. The most open missions, however, remain largely deaf to the call to dialogue issuing from Filipinos involved in their national transformation. Instead, the dominant missionary method of evangelization seeks to convert Muslims to Christianity, by-passing questions of national importance and excluding dialogue.[29]

Distrust is so great that even Filipino Christians who took part in the early summer programs discovered themselves suspected as being missionaries, spies, or representatives of either the government or white people. Within Filipino Christian communities themselves, issues of national importance are being addressed through a dialogue between church and social movements. The primary relationship of Christians to Muslims, however, remains that of evangelization.

Evangelization is the antithesis of a listening church. It is a relationship which denies Filipinos a significant history of their own, seeking to impose upon them a religion which cuts them off from their own story. On the other hand, mission conceived as dialogue invites participants to engage in each other's historical activity and engage in a common task of transformation.

Even in the face of continuous violence, the Seminarians for Peace program is exploring just this new form of mission. Concrete linkages are being established between Muslim and Christian villages, linkages which lead to peace. Villagers are brought together across religious boundaries for the first time through joint construction projects resulting in economic improvement. For their part, the Christian seminarians and pastors participate in these projects, both in the labour and the religious interaction.

One year witnessed the construction of a landing ramp for Muslim fishing people and a water project for both Christians and Muslims. Another year's project involved a co-operative goat farm located in an uncontrolled zone between government soldiers and MNLF rebels. The farm brought together villagers who lived less than six kilometers apart, but had never had contact before.

---

29. Peter Gowing and the work of the Dan Salan Research Center and Dan Salan Jr. College, in Mindanao, are perhaps the major exceptions to the dominant form of missions in areas of Muslim Filipinos. But here missions takes the form of education and economic development, with the traditional notion of evangelization lurking in the background. Greater knowledge of Muslim culture is brought into service of the extension of Christianity.

At the center of such projects is an ongoing religious dialogue: a challenging, sometimes frustrating, and always intense interaction between Muslims and Christians. I experienced the reality of worshipping with Muslim Filipinos, of seeing their victimization by government and church, of hearing their desire for peace even as they armed for battle. Other Filipino participants experienced the reality of living with Muslim villagers and being themselves victimized by government incursions, and of discovering the richness of the Muslim heritage. Whether the dialogue took the form of actual conversation and exchange of ideas, stories and aspirations; or participation in labour projects; it was the basis for a new form of relationship between Christians and Muslims, more adequate than the relationship of evangelization.

This new form of mission I heard described by Muslims as well as Christians as coexistence. I was amazed to hear nearly illiterate villagers articulate their own transforming experiences which allowed for an enrichment of their story. This coexistence is a more concrete form of historical interaction than the missionaries had thought possible or permissible, for it is one which entails both political and religious interaction.

For many of the Christian participants in the Seminarians for Peace program, it was clear that the categories of Western Christian thought are in their last hours. I was fascinated that this was a similar observation to the one made by the prison inmate I quoted at the beginning of this essay. Filipino Christians and Philadelphia Muslims would not necessarily agree about the nature of the new categories emerging from their historical projects. They should not agree, for they are involved in different efforts of coexistence. But they both are discovering hopeful dimensions in the last hour of Western Christendom.

In *Out of Revolution* Rosenstock-Huessy wrote, "The life of civilization is eternally recurrent, it is immortal, whenever the fear of its last hours is kept present by frank criticism...."[30] Finding that the last hour of the dominant form of Western Christianity was at hand, participants in Seminarians for Peace discovered the impetus for their own historical re-creation.

This is also true for those of us who are from the dominant Western Christian tradition. Hearing the frank criticism being raised

---

30. Rosenstock-Huessy, *Out of Revolution*, p. 561. He goes on to write, "The famous critical power of the Western world is one of its most important Christian qualities. This inner criticism of institutions from the point of view of their death has made them eternal."

around the world, entering into dialogue with those whom we have so thoroughly sought to evangelize in the past, are the first steps into our own re-creation.

We are as close to the last hour as we have ever been, and if there is any hint of transforming faith in our midst, then we will be compelled to find life on the other side of the last hour. In doing so, we must be aware that the very heart of our Christian faith stands to be transformed by this new way of speaking.

We cannot yet tell what form our faith will take on the other side of the last hour, other than it will make as much sense of the past as it will offer hope for the future. We must not skip too easily to this future, for we must first listen and be addressed. Our work must first be a creative dying in order to find our re-created life.

Rosenstock-Huessy called this event the creation of a new form of humanity. I have heard talk in the prisons of Philadelphia and in the villages of the Philippines of such a new humanity. For those of us who yet struggle with the older forms, we must find ways to tear down walls and hear the voice of those who know. Then will our contribution to the coexistence of many forms become integrated into the common life of humanity. Then will we begin to live again the reality of resurrection. Then will we not only listen, but respond and be changed.

To Hear Again
the One Voice of the Gospel

W.C. Strickland

The purpose of this paper is to examine Eugen Rosenstock-Huessy's *The Fruit of Lips or Why Four Gospels*[1] in order to determine his understanding of the nature and character of the four Gospels. *The Fruit of Lips* was written in English in 1954, but the author refused to publish it because he thought that he would not be heard in view of the firm grip liberal critics had upon the Gospels.[2] By 1964 he sensed a shift in the tide and published his work in German under the title *Die Frucht der Lippen* (a section of *Die Sprache des Menschengeschlechts*, 2:796-903). In 1968 he re-issued *Die Frucht* with a new title: *Die Umwandlung des Wortes Gottes*. Finally, the Pickwick Press published the original English version in 1978.

What was the situation in 1954 which led Rosenstock-Huessy to withhold publication of his book? To answer this question we must analyze the main developments in the criticism of the New Testament beginning in 1778. Before 1778 "no one had attempted to form a historical conception of the life of Jesus."[3] In 1774, G.E. Lessing began to publish, under the title *Fragmente eines Ungenannten*, essays still in manuscript form written by Hermann Samuel Reimarus (1694-1768). There were seven of these fragments, the last of which was entitled *Von dem Zwecke Jesu und seiner Junger* (The Aims of Jesus and His Disciples, 1778). Reimarus here attempted to separate the historical Jesus who lived and taught in Palestine from about 4 B.C. until his death in about A.D. 29 from the Son of God presented in the Gospels. He would strip Jesus of what he thought were accretions added by the church. As shown by his essay on *The Impossibility of a Revelation Which All Men Should Have Grounds for Believing*, Reimarus grounded his belief on natural reason and denied any such

1. Eugen Rosenstock-Huessy, *The Fruit of Lips or Why Four Gospels*, ed. Marion Davis Battles (Pittsburgh: Pickwick Press, 1978).

2. Rosenstock-Huessy, *Fruit of Lips*, p. xv.

3. Albert Schweitzer, *The Quest of the Historical Jesus: A Critical Study of Its Progress from Reimarus to Wrede* (New York: Macmillan Co., 1948), p. 13.

thing as revelation. Thus, Reimarus "drove a wedge between the apostles and Jesus. The latter was a man of integrity. His disciples, motivated by greed and their frustration at his death, perpetuated the hoax of a resurrection."[4]

This rationalistic view persisted. Rationalism demanded that the New Testament present a unified witness. Miracles were denied as mere mythology; the supernatural was declared impossible. The remainder was interpreted rationalistically. It was believed that all that was needed "was to remove a few 'ecclesiastical' embellishments to explain away a few obviously 'impossible' miracles, and the historical Jesus would stand revealed in all His impressive simplicity, a fully human, magnificently rational figure."[5]

David Friedrich Strauss (1808-1974) held that the whole of the Gospel is mythological.[6] Jesus is, therefore, only the symbol of an ultimate ideal.

Following Strauss there were three paths opened to the criticism of the Gospels: 1) "Myth" was taken to its logical conclusions (Jesus never existed); 2) Literary and historical criticism could be pursued (done by F.C. Bauer and the Tübingen School) on the basis of the Hegelian dialectic; 3) Literary and historical criticism could follow the methods developed by the "liberal" historians (such as L. Ranke and J. Burckhardt).

Such scholars as C.G. Wilke (1786-1854), C.H. Weisse (1801-1866), K. Lachmann, and H.J. Holtzmann (1832-1910) devoted their efforts to "source-criticism"; that is, to the literary relationships of the Gospels. The Gospel of John was declared to be quite late and distinct from the other three, which were called "synoptics." The Gospel of Mark was judged to have been the first written Gospel and a source for Matthew and Luke. A document called Q (from the German Quelle: spring, source) was postulated to account for the approximately 250 verses common to Matthew and Luke but absent from Mark. Then it was seen that Matthew and Luke each possessed sections found in no other writing. The priority of Mark was accepted as proved.

The Gospel of Mark was not only first, but it also was credited with providing accurately reported history which was interpreted as being a series of objective events related as cause and effect. Therefore, anything found in Mark for which no rationally

---

4. Charles Thomas Davis, *Speaking of Jesus: Toward a Theology of the Periphery* (Lakemont, Georgia: CSA Press, 1978), p. 45.

5. H.E.W. Turner, *Jesus: Master and Lord*, 2d ed. (London: A.R. Mowbray, 1954), p. 64.

6. Davis, *Speaking of Jesus*, p. 45.

conceived cause could be discovered could be excised without damage to this Gospel.[7]

Albrecht Ritschl (1822-1889) taught that "the truth of history consists in the moral truths revealed through the teachings and examples of great men. Thus, Jesus' teachings are of higher value than his action."[8] Jesus, now, became a Jewish rabbi teaching the moralisms of the nineteenth century. This view was reflected in the many lives of Jesus written in the nineteenth and twentieth centuries. Adolf Harnack in 1900 published his *Das Wesen des Christentums* (English translation, *What is Christianity?*), a work in which the essence of Christianity is thought to be 1) the Kingdom of God conceived of as merely a growing spiritual insight within a human heart; 2) God as father of the infinitely valuable human soul; and 3) the commandment that we love one another. All eschatology and miracle are removed. It may be said that these "liberal" lives of Jesus were hardly more than attempts to present the Jesus of the first century as a teacher of nineteenth-century ethics.

Early in the twentieth century, William Wrede concluded that Mark's Gospel is not historical but a dogmatic statement. Julius Wellhausen pointed out that Mark's oldest material consisted almost exclusively of small fragments (for example, fragments of sayings of Jesus). This theory led scholars to attempt to distinguish between the tradition and the editorial work performed by the Synoptists. Work on this aspect of the Synoptic Gospels led to what is called form criticism, as undertaken by M. Dibelius, R. Bultmann, E. Fascher, and others. The form critic presupposes that 1) all literary works assume relatively fixed forms;[9] 2) the Synoptics are made up of individual pericopae (independent, complete-in-themselves, free-floating stories); and 3) these pericopae were connected editorially by the Synoptists so that the whole would tell a story to enshrine the didactic, liturgical, preaching, or apologetic purposes of the church. The synoptic "material" is then to be identified by its "formal" types (such as miracle stories, controversial utterances, parables, etc.).[10] The results reached by form critical analysis are, in summary: Jesus' personal life, both internal and external, cannot be known; Jesus, it is claimed, was a lawgiver and prophet who announced the coming of the Kingdom of God and the ethical demands which his proclama-

7. See James M. Robinson, *The Problem of History in Mark* (Napierville, Ill.: Alec R. Allenson), *Studies in Biblical Theology*, 21 (1954):8.

8. Rosenstock-Huessy, *Fruit of Lips.*

9. Schubert M. Ogden, ed., *Existence and Faith: Shorter Writings of Rudolf Bultmann* (New York: Meridian Books, 1960), p. 40.

10. Ogden, *Existence and Faith*, pp. 42 ff.

tion imposed on those who respond to his message. The Synoptists were collectors or compilers of traditional pericopae to which they gave an ordered arrangement; they were theologians writing from a theological stance. The meaning given each pericope will be discovered from an analysis of the pericope itself as well as from an examination of the context in which it is placed by the Evangelist. In this way, the theological perspective of the Evangelist will become visible.[11]

Reimarus held that the early apostles had perpetuated a hoax, a lie: they said that Jesus had been raised from the dead. Reimarus' view has persisted and been expanded to include the whole church, now portrayed as the great deceiver of men. Yet, enough of Christian truth has permeated the life of the West to make it impossible for Western man to rid himself of some kind of historical Jesus. Thus, the Jesus Christ of the New Testament becomes the "hero," the humble, blue-eyed Galilean, the expression of the finest achievement of man. For this secular thought, Jesus is not the Incarnate One, the Word which transforms the world; rather, he is an example of what man can himself achieve.

These scholars who examined the apocalyptic literature of Jesus' time failed to see that Jesus, in announcing the in-break of the Kingdom of God, was not merely a product and continuator of his cultural milieu, but rather was saying something radically new with a demand for the transformation of vision, life, commitment.

Great liberal scholars such as Conzelmann, Bultmann, Marxsen, and others who are professional theologians could not understand that men like Simon Peter, James the brother of Jesus, James and John sons of Zebedee, the martyr Stephen, peasants all, could bear powerful witness to their experience of the sublime, the holy, the tremendous mystery, the invisible, the ineffable. These scholars were highly competent technicians of words and ideas, but were blind to the Spirit and spirit. They, by their historicist attitudes and antiquarianism, could not interpret the Gospels as four movements of one symphony of the Spirit. They created an inverted Tower of Babel: language was a tool, an instrument of man to express his rational, timeless notions, not a multi-dimensional field of force creating us as human beings; the Gospels were first-century religious "documents" to be interpreted "scientifically."

But listen to Eugen Rosenstock-Huessy:

---

11. Walter Grundmann, *Die Geschichte Jesu Christi* (Berlin: Evangelische Verlagsanstalt, 1961), p. 15.

Poor mortal,
I am stung with a constant sense
Of time. But I can cover time-spans
From one day to a year
To a generation to a century,
With my intent and my understanding.
And I am asked to believe
That neither my creator
Nor the man who revealed him to us
Enters upon the measures of time
Which alone I can understand?

I know they do.
For I have lived through epoch-making events
Which have changed the lives
Of all men on this globe.
And in the light
Of the Lord of the Eons,
I have found my path
Through these ends of my world
And the beginnings of the next eon.

To tell me, 'Oh, the Christian era
Has been a helpful myth
In the past, but now
We don't need it any longer'–
This is like telling me:
'The raft on which you passed over
The abyss must be condemned.'

I have found there is a way
Of living through the end
And the beginning of an era
In perfect freedom,
Neither as the slave of capitalism
    nor as the slave of communism,
Neither as merely a German
    nor as merely an American,
Neither as a soldier
    nor as a scholar,
And I should now go and destroy
The raft, my raft, simply because
People who never passed over
An abyss say:
'There is no abyss:

Therefore the Lord of continuity
Through all the abysses between eras
Can be put up
At our rummage sale
Of old wear.'[12]

Rosenstock-Huessy, himself an incredible master of nineteenth-century learning, repudiated this rigid scholarship and advanced on a track parallel to the customary, professional track of his time. He believed (was committed to) in the Spirit, in time, in history, in the creating power of language which changes mankind. He rejected his "own historicist attitude" of his early period; he broke away from his antiquarianism; he refused the "paramount worship of the Italian Renaissance."[13] During World War One Rosenstock-Huessy was converted, as he says, "to the full life of the spirit."[14] His personal confession was based on his personal experience, and therefore he could let the Spirit speak. He opened himself to the divine, transcendent Spirit and could discern the spirits.

I stated earlier that the purpose of this paper is to examine Rosenstock-Huessy's *The Fruit of Lips or Why Four Gospels* to determine his understanding of the nature and character of the four Gospels. I have traced briefly some of the lines of research on the Gospels since Reimarus. What was Rosenstock-Huessy's opinion of this research? He begins his book by indicating his purpose for writing it: to call clear attention to the reality of the Christian Era, for he thinks that "the Christian Era is no longer recognized as making epoch among all previous eras. And the year Zero is not treated as the turning point and the gateway into a new, the final, and last not least, our own era."[15] As reasons for this failure to recognize the Christian Era, he lists two:

1. The concentrated efforts on the part of liberal scholars to write lives of Jesus by putting him in his own times. They "have tried to change him, the Lord of the Eons of Eons, the Second Adam, the Son of Man, the Judge of this World, into a contemporary of Caiaphas, Judas, Tiberias, and Pilate. They have searched his vocabulary for colloquialisms of his own place and time. Now, as a child of his time, he lost all power over the times....This zeal for the transient environment of Palestine in Jesus' days, then, is one step away

12. Rosenstock-Huessy, *Fruit of Lips,* p. xx. The author wrote these lines as prose (p. xix), but Battles has had them printed on p. xx as the poetry they are.
13. Rosenstock-Huessy, *Bibliography/Biography* (New York: Four Wells, 1959), p. 16.
14. Rosenstock-Huessy, *Fruit of Lips.*
15. Rosenstock-Huessy, *Fruit of Lips,* p. xvii.

from understanding his right to give our era his name."[16] 2. The constant mistranslation of the Biblical term for era (cf. Ephesians 3:21...tou aiōnos tōn aiōnōn; Matthew 28:30...eōs tes sunteleias tou aiōnou). This word does not mean "the universe expanded in space" as we think, but means aeon; that is, age, era, and refers to time. Thus "the Bible knew that man had to live in the perpetual expectation of an end of his little world."[17] The translation of aiōnios by "eternal" is wrong and has poisoned theology. It has led to the belief that there can be made no distinction between B.C. and A.D.

The writers of the last 150 years have turned the Gospels into "material" which can be systematically reduced from four Gospels to one. John was held to be late legend, "while the three synoptic Gospels were made one by reducing them to a written source. Consequently, they could not be called unified as they could not be better than their 'source.'"[18]

Rosenstock-Huessy continues: "Once the three synoptic Gospels were reduced to one source, they became simply material for our reconstruction of the life of Jesus from all the material. Reitzenstein used Oriental mystery-religions, Dibelious used artistic models, Scholem Asch used Jewish Rabbinic traditions to explain 'Jesus.' Jesus became alternately the expression of one of the styles or modes of life preceding him."[19] (In *Die Umwandlung* the author adds to the sentence just quoted: "He belonged now just to the same antiquity from which he was to have redeemed us.") And again: "...according to the critics Jesus became a souvenir of antiquity."[20]

In their work the critics have turned every single stone of our tradition upside down and have made each one say the opposite of what it said.[21]

Let me now list what Rosenstock-Huessy considers to be facts which counteract the whole critical movement from Reimarus to Wrede.[22]

1. John writes as an eyewitness who knows the minutest details when he cares to mention them. The apostle is the author of the Gospel. Therefore, it carries authority (that is, for any who reverence the Spirit or respect historical precedent).

2. All four Gospels are apostolic. Matthew was the converted

16. Rosenstock-Huessy, *Fruit of Lips*, p. xviii.
17. Rosenstock-Huessy, *Fruit of Lips*, p. xviii.
18. Rosenstock-Huessy, *Fruit of Lips*, p. 10.
19. Rosenstock-Huessy, *Fruit of Lips*, p. 10.
20. Rosenstock-Huessy, *Fruit of Lips*, p. 11.
21. Rosenstock-Huessy, *Fruit of Lips*, p. 11.
22. Rosenstock-Huessy, *Fruit of Lips*, p. 11.

publican, and he wrote under James' (John's brother's) eyes in Jerusalem before A.D. 42. *[Die Frucht der Lippen* reads: Matthew was the converted tax collector among the Apostles, and he wrote under the eyes of Peter and the sons of Zebedee and of the brother of Jesus in Jerusalem before the year 42]. Mark obeyed Peter. Luke lived with Paul. John dictated to a Greek secretary.

3. Matthew wrote in Aramaic *[Die Frucht,* p. 809, reads: in Hebrew, not in Aramaic] and he wrote first (that is, as tradition unanimously maintains).

4. Mark states bluntly that he is quoting from Matthew.

On the basis of these "facts," Rosenstock-Huessy refutes the critics who attack "the quadrilateral of four authoritative Gospels." I must now quote him at length because the following presentation is crucial:

> To contradict is one thing. Everybody is free to do so. But he is not free to pretend that his contradiction ever can pull a positive solution out of the mind's magic hat. Applied to the Bible, this means: It is not everybody's business to read the Bible as the lips of which the reader is to be the fruit. It is anybody's privilege to say: I don't believe that John wrote his Gospel, or, we cannot know when it was written. Man can affix his "no" to any statement coming to him from any other man as much as he may attach his "Yes" to it. Never, on the other hand, can he replace the repudiated statement by speculation. This, however, is exactly what critics of Biblical texts have done. They have not acquiesced in disbelieving tradition. They have positively told us who wrote the real story, and how it looked and when our Gospels were written and for which partisan purposes.
>
> It is not given to the mind to know reality by negation. Our tradition may be wrong and untrustworthy. But then we simply do not have the right tradition. No logical somersaults can produce the positive story. When the mind tries to act as the creator of real facts, we have the story of Gnosis all over again. Gnosis in education involves telling people how education should be and then thinking, "Now they are educated." Gnosis in history involves telling people how history might have been and then thinking, "Now, it has been this way."[23]

How did Rosenstock-Huessy arrive at his understanding of the Gospels? By being open in his soul to the action of the Spirit, by realizing that the Spirit changes his expressions time after time, by

23. Rosenstock-Huessy, *Fruit of Lips,* p. 12.

seeing that a change of mind produces a change in literary style. He asks: of whom then did the four Evangelists write? They wrote of Jesus Christ. Who was this Jesus Christ? He was the fruit of all the lips that preceded him. He unified the preceding phases of speech and overcame them: the listeners of the spirits of the dead, the listeners to the sky-world, the listeners to laws and cities, the listeners to the future.[24] Jesus Christ himself was the end of the first aeon. And as the end point of the four modes of ancient speech, he became the starting point of the new aeon.

The four Gospels are the lips of the historically effective Jesus. He made four lips to speak so as to become "the lips of the risen Christ."[25] How were these lips formed? Rosenstock-Huessy puts it this way: "It is our hypothesis that the four Gospels are the lips whose fruits we are expected to be, and that they are His lips. It follows that since the four Gospels are one organ, his lips, the secret of their unity is the secret we have to understand."[26] What is the secret of the unity of the four Gospels? They sing one song; they are four movements in one symphony. How do we know that they sing one song? We know this unity from two sources: 1) the Anti-Marcionite Gospel Prologues written about A.D. 160, and 2) an analysis of the Gospels themselves.

The Anti-Marcionite Prologues are the "first authentic statement of the slow, sober, realistic and reluctant birth of the 'Four Gospels,' the statement of Anno Domini 160."[27] The prologue to Matthew has been lost, but Rosenstock-Huessy appears to believe that it would have most probably read: "Matthew wrote his Gospel among the Jews in their language, and he was the first Gospel writer."[28]

On Mark:

Mark followed in the series [*adseruit*–he formed a series], he was called the stump-fingered, simply because in relation to the big size of his whole body, his fingers were extravagantly short. He was interpreter to Peter. After the passing away of Peter himself he wrote down this very Gospel of his in the province of Italy.[29]

On Luke:

---

24. Rosenstock-Huessy, *Fruit of Lips*, pp. 2-3.
25. Rosenstock-Huessy, *Fruit of Lips*, p. 9.
26. Rosenstock-Huessy, *Fruit of Lips*, p. 10.
27. Rosenstock-Huessy, *Fruit of Lips*, p. 111.
28. Rosenstock-Huessy, *Fruit of Lips*, p. 111.
29. Rosenstock-Huessy, *Fruit of Lips*, p. 111.

The facts about Luke are these: He was from Antioch and a Syrian, a physician in his profession. He had become a student of the apostles and later accompanied Paul, until Paul was martyred, a servant of the Lord with singleness of purpose, unmarried, without offspring in his eighty-fourth year falling asleep in the province of Boeotia, full of holy inspiration.

This man Luke found Gospels already in existence, one which Matthew had written in Palestine, the other by Mark in Italy; moved by the Holy Spirit, he was living in Achaia when he composed this whole Gospel. And he himself made this clear in his own prologue that before him others had been writing and that it was necessary for the faithful of Gentile descent to put forth the precise narrative of the economy of salvation, for their protection, lest they be led astray by the mythological tales of the Jews or, deceived by arbitrarily selected and baseless speculations, miss the truth.

And so later on the same Luke wrote the Acts of the Apostles.
Later John, the apostle, one of the original twelve, wrote "Revelation" on the island of Patmos and, after that, his Gospel.
On John:
The Gospel of John was published and given to the churches by John still in his lifetime, as Papias, a beloved disciple of John reported. And the Gospel was written down under the dictation of John, and it was written down correctly.[30]

Rosenstock-Huessy is convinced that this evidence is trustworthy and indicates specifically that the four Gospels were written in the order of Matthew, Mark, Luke, and John; that Mark was Peter's disciple and Luke was Paul's disciple; and that the four Gospels were intended to form a series. These four Gospels were not rivals but were the links in one connected chain–Mark forged the second link.

We now turn to an examination of Rosenstock-Huessy's analysis of the nature and character of the four Gospels, which analysis confirms the evidence given by the Anti-Marcionite Prologues.

What impelled the first Evangelist, Matthew, to write since Jesus his Master did not write a book but died on a cross to express "his sheer incredible and certainly super-human faith?"[31] Matthew wrote "under the impact of the stoning of Stephen,"[32] for the shedding of the first Christian blood "cleansed the first ink employed in the new

---

30. Rosenstock-Huessy, *Fruit of Lips*, pp. 111-112.
31. Rosenstock-Huessy, *Fruit of Lips*, p. 29.
32. Rosenstock-Huessy, *Fruit of Lips*, p. 29.

dispensation."[33] Why, then, did he write? To save his identity in a crisis. "Matthew gained the right to use the pen as his sword when the blood of martyrs reddened the soil of Palestine. Similarly, Mark wrote with the arena and the cross waiting for Peter in Rome."[34] Luke wrote to teach that the spirits of the times had become subservient to the Spirit of all spirits.[35] John wrote because he was Jesus' friend, and although he (John) was a kindred spirit with Jesus and understood Jesus as God's Word, he came to love the earth as the site of God's redemptive action as the Word had instructed him.

Thus, "speech is a continuum."[36] And "the four Evangelists insist that something happened to this very continuum in their days."[37] What did happen? "All the four Evangelists say unanimously: speech and writing must be changed, in fact they *are* changed, by the Word. If they four do not lie, their own speech and writings must bear evidence of this alleged change."[38]

Matthew wrote facing great personal danger with the echelon of Zion standing proudly.[39] His Gospel "is a farewell plea, a last attempt to convince Jerusalem that they had slain the Just because they had not expected any longer a radical change in the methods of God's government of the world."[40] Thus, he spoke to enemies, and in writing, Matthew progressed from speaking as a Jew to speaking as a non-Jew (compare Chapter 1 with Chapter 28). By professing Jesus Christ, Matthew wrote himself out of Israel.[41] "Christianity is the world as it has always been plus the death of Jesus. Matthew's Gospel was the first proof that this one addition to the world would make a difference to the world of speech, that everything in the world would have to be rewritten in the light of this event."[42] "Standing upright and pleading in danger of his own life, and then abandoning his Jewish allegiance, Matthew wrote his Gospel."[43]

Mark wrote under Peter's control; thus, he was not facing danger as was Matthew; rather, he wrote protected by a faithful congregation. Mark's Gospel begins with Jesus as Son of God and ends with a mission carried out by subservients who obey the Lord and no one

33. Rosenstock-Huessy, *Fruit of Lips*, p. 29.
34. Rosenstock-Huessy, *Fruit of Lips*, p. 30.
35. Rosenstock-Huessy, *Fruit of Lips*, p. 30.
36. Rosenstock-Huessy, *Fruit of Lips*, p. 16.
37. Rosenstock-Huessy, *Fruit of Lips*, p. 16.
38. Rosenstock-Huessy, *Fruit of Lips*, p. 16.
39. Rosenstock-Huessy, *Fruit of Lips*, p. 22.
40. Rosenstock-Huessy, *Fruit of Lips*, p. 22.
41. Rosenstock-Huessy, *Fruit of Lips*, p. 23.
42. Rosenstock-Huessy, *Fruit of Lips*, p. 24.
43. Rosenstock-Huessy, *Fruit of Lips*, p. 24.

else. Mark was not permitted to make Peter an equal to Jesus. Peter was only an apostle like others; Jesus was the Lord. Mark's Gospel is, therefore, a victory over the dangers of time;[44] that is, Jesus is protected against the future. Mark's Gospel "had to establish, once and forever, Christ's uniqueness as the 'Son of God.'"[45] Peter is no more than a sinful man.

Luke, under Paul's influence, wrote two books which are one drama. And together the Gospel of Luke and The Acts of the Apostles reveal the identity of Christ.[46] Luke *must* teach Theophilus who could therefore identify himself in a stream of revelation and be responsible for instructing his own children. "...Theophilus had to be changed from a hereditary or traditional Christian into a primary and immediate listener of the Spirit."[47] Under what pressure did Luke write? Under the pressure to show the intertemporal character of the Spirit. "Luke became the first human being who was able to see the spirits of two periods together and to envisage them as subservient...to one spirit, the Spirit of all spirits."[48] He saw that "the Holy Ghost opens the spirits of the different times to each other."[49] Each generation of human kind must be seen as a body of time and the Spirit as one, connecting all these bodies.[50]

John was removed from any earthly pressure.[51] John as a kindred spirit of Jesus "understands that which nobody else will understand at first: the genius of a living person."[52] Let me continue this quotation:

> Members of one physical family understand each other's background and motive; the origin of each other's reactions and gestures lies open to them. It is not different with kindred spirits. For, the spirit precedes the incarnation; a spirit is the original thought of the Creator of which the living man is the execution. A kindred spirit, then, understands by sympathy and "congeniality," its genuine [original] sense, where Jesus came from, out of which necessity, out of which pre-legal, pre-national, pre-religious, original matrix. John begins, as a kindred spirit, with the real, the original place of his divine friend in God's mind. But the

44. Rosenstock-Huessy, *Fruit of Lips*, p. 33.
45. Rosenstock-Huessy, *Fruit of Lips*, p. 33.
46. Rosenstock-Huessy, *Fruit of Lips*, p. 25.
47. Rosenstock-Huessy, *Fruit of Lips*, p. 26.
48. Rosenstock-Huessy, *Fruit of Lips*, p. 30.
49. Rosenstock-Huessy, *Fruit of Lips*, p. 31.
50. Rosenstock-Huessy, *Fruit of Lips*, p. 33.
51. Rosenstock-Huessy, *Fruit of Lips*, p. 21.
52. Rosenstock-Huessy, *Fruit of Lips*, p. 35.

progress of his Gospel leads him from this heaven to earth. The miraculous process in John is the road from the Word in God to the man in the flesh Jesus.

But that he should identify his brother Jesus in the small events of everyday life, together with the Word's cosmic office as Christ–this is John's victory. John saw the Lord as his alter ego. John's soul was "naturaliter Christiana." Therefore, he did not need signs or happenings to know and understand. He knew him by heart, 'mente cordis.'

John proceeds from the innermost heart to the outer paraphernalia of social office and position, and thereby forbids all hearts who are Christian by nature to flee the world of history and realization.[53]

Consequently: *"All four Gospels then, are processes by which four apostles could deposit their human limitations at the foot of the cross and make their individual experience into a contribution"* (italics in the original).[54]

What was the contribution each of the four Evangelists made? Rosenstock-Huessy succinctly states their "acknowledgements" as follows:

Matthew acknowledged that he was no longer a Jew; Mark, Peter's disciple, acknowledged that Peter had lost his own name; Luke, the companion of Paul, acknowledged that Paul did among the Gentiles that which Jesus had done among the Jews. John acknowledged that although a kindred spirit may understand the eternal meaning without argument, it is equally necessary that the faithful soul be obedient in the division of labour in this visible world with its very slow progress.[55]

The Anti-Marcionite Prologues state that "Mark formed a series." Therefore, there was a necessary sequence in the writing of the four Gospels. Taking the clue from these Prologues, Rosenstock-Huessy finds the sequence conforming to what he calls "the law of speech which always contradicts nature and the mere evaluation of time." This law is: "That which is most central or primary in an event shall become articulated last."[56] Applied to the Gospels this law indicates that Matthew wrote first, followed in order by Mark, Luke, and finally John. The natural order would have called for the sequence to be John, Luke, Mark, and Matthew because John gives Jesus' innermost thoughts, Luke presents Jesus as the Christ, Mark writes

53. Rosenstock-Huessy, *Fruit of Lips*, pp. 35-36.
54. Rosenstock-Huessy, *Fruit of Lips*, p. 39.
55. Rosenstock-Huessy, *Fruit of Lips*, p. 39.
56. Rosenstock-Huessy, *Fruit of Lips*, p. 41.

of Him as Son of God, and Matthew gives the eternal credentials of Jesus as Saviour.[57]

Nevertheless, this natural order had to be reversed by the law of speech since "the world sees not us but our worldly function first...."[58]

In the early Church, the "name" of Jesus was Jesus, Christ, God's Son, Saviour. In Greek the first letter of these four names were IXTHUS (= fish). The four Gospels reproduced this name.[59]

Let me show this reproduction by using a diagram and quoting Rosenstock-Huessy's remarks.[60]

I = Jesus (John's Gospel: John understood Jesus as an older brother and thought of him as "Jesus" personally.)

X = Christ (Luke's Gospel: Luke saw in Jesus the "Christ" who converted Paul to whom Jesus had never spoken).

Th = Son of God (Mark's Gospel: Mark knew Jesus from the
U = first as Son of God).

S = Saviour (Matthew's Gospel: Matthew knew Jesus as his personal saviour).

The linguistic order demands the reverse of the natural order outlined above. The sequence Matthew, Mark, Luke, and John is also compellingly shown when it is observed that the four Gospels form a ring; that is, when it is seen that the end of the first Gospel (Matthew) forms the beginning of the second Gospel, with this "begetting" continuing through the fourth Gospel (John). With the end of John's Gospel we are back to the beginning of Matthew's. This structure is best shown by reproducing the "survey" Rosenstock-Huessy has made on page 51:

1.	Matthew	Beginning:	Son of David and Abraham.
2.	Matthew	End:	The Son of God (baptize in the name of the Father and the Son and the Spirit).
	Mark	Beginning:	Son of God.
3.	Mark	End:	The Ministers of the Word.
	Luke	Beginning:	The Ministers of the Word.

57. Rosenstock-Huessy, *Fruit of Lips*, p. 41.
58. Rosenstock-Huessy, *Fruit of Lips*, p. 41.
59. Rosenstock-Huessy, *Fruit of Lips*, p. 41.
60. Rosenstock-Huessy, *Fruit of Lips*, p. 41.

4.a	Luke	End:	Gospel: Fullness of praise. Acts: Fullness of speech.
	John	Beginning:	In the beginning was the Word.
4.b	Luke	End (Acts):	The Jews have no eyes and no ears. The Gentiles shall hear.
	John	Beginning:	The World has not seen the light. His own people gave him no welcome. We have beheld his glory.
5.	John	End:	This man Jesus in the space of the universe, now redeemed as God's world.
	Matthew	Beginning:	Jesus (Christ, Son of David, son of Matthew).

In *Die Frucht der Lippen*[61] Rosenstock-Huessy writes after finishing the survey: Der Ring ist Geschlossen. Die 'Vier Evangelien' sind nun Eines." (The ring is closed. The Four Gospels are now one.)

If we listen, we will hear again the one voice of the Gospel and become the fruit of His lips in our turn.

I close this examination of Rosenstock-Huessy's *The Fruit of Lips* by quoting the final words of this magnificent little book:

There is only one Gospel
At all times.
If you travel
Through the four decades
Of the four Gospels
You have identified
The unity of the Gospel.
And when after that you meet
The people who live and die
Solely to their own times,
You may not convince them
That there is a Christian Era.
But you yourself may know

61. Eugen Rosenstock-Huessy, *Die Sprache des Menschengeschlechts* (Heidelberg: Verlag Lambert Schneider, 1965), Zweiter Band, s. 847.

That there can be.[62]

62. Rosenstock-Huessy, *Fruit of Lips*, p. 134.

The Grammar of the Spirit:
Time, Speech, and Society

M. Darrol Bryant

Today we are living through the agonies of transition to the third epoch. We have yet to establish Man, the great singular of humanity, in one household, over the plurality of races, classes and age groups. This will be the center of struggle in the future....The theme of future history will be not territorial or political but social: it will be the story of man's creation. The next thousand years may be expected, consequently, to concentrate on the third article, namely to wrestle with the task of revealing God in society.[1]

What time is it? This question hangs over our age and haunts our lives. Ours is a century devastated by two World Wars and still rife with armed conflicts and civil wars, a century still struggling to come to grips with the effects of industrial and technological changes that have profoundly altered the human and social landscape, an age when the patterns of family and social life are in danger of being swamped, a time that has witnessed the emergence of formerly colonized peoples onto the stage of world history, a time haunted by Auschwitz and Hiroshima and dubious about the prospects of human survival.[2] It is in the midst of such a time that a remarkable voice has emerged which has sought to engage the crucible of our times and to wrest from the darkness a vision that could inspire and sustain a new generation to take up anew its tasks in the flow of generations which stretch from the beginning to the end of time. In book after book he engaged the agonies of our era and articulated–

1. Eugen Rosenstock-Huessy, *The Christian Future, Or the Modern Mind Outrun* (New York: Harper and Row, 1966), pp. 115-116. See also Rosenstock-Huessy's description of "metanomics" as "the search for the omnipresence of God in the most contradictory patterns of human society," in *Speech and Reality* (Norwich, Vermont: Argo Books, 1970), p. 42.

2. See the remarkable essays by Jonathan Schell on our nuclear age and predicament in *The New Yorker*, February 1, 8, 15, 1982.

sometimes with more, sometimes less, success–his vision. In all his efforts, he reminded his readers that "a man writes a book, even as he stretches out his hand, so that he may find that he is not alone in the survival of humankind."[3]

This voice belonged to Eugen Rosenstock-Huessy (1888-1973).[4] Born into a German Jewish banking family, he was trained as a jurist and legal historian. While still a young man he entered the Christian church. He taught law at Leipzig University before serving in the German army during World War I. The war meant the end of an era for Rosenstock-Huessy as it did for many other Europeans.

After the war he did not return to the University but went to work for Daimler-Benz in their automobile factory. These were crucial years for Rosenstock-Huessy, and we shall return to them later. When Hitler came to power in 1933, he emigrated to the United States. After teaching at Harvard, he moved to Dartmouth where he taught until his retirement in 1957. As a historian, philosopher, speech and social thinker, he ranged across the landscape of our time igniting fires of insight that continue to stun, perplex, and infuriate the reader of his many volumes. He was, as one of the last volumes of his essays reveals, an "impure thinker."[5]

Here in this essay I want to explore some of the sources of Rosenstock-Huessy's insights and to examine several of his contributions to a coming grammar of the spirit. At the heart of my investigation stands his remarkable, yet still too little known, volume, *The Christian Future, Or the Modern Mind Outrun.*[6] As a way into my interpretation of Rosenstock-Huessy as a Christian social thinker, I want to examine the interpretations of this man and his work offered by Harold Stahmer, Bruce Boston, and Clinton Gardner. This review, then, will generate a context for my reading of the central dynamics which inform the thought of Rosenstock-Huessy and an analysis of several themes central to his writings.

---

3. Eugen Rosenstock-Huessy, *Out of Revolution, Autobiography of Western Man* (1938; reprint ed., Norwich, Vermont: Argo Books, 1969), p. 758.

4. See the *Introduction,* vii-lv to *The Christian Future* by Harold Stahmer for a good introduction to Rosenstock-Huessy. This introduction combines biographical information and an exposition of major themes in Rosenstock-Huessy's work.

5. Eugen Rosenstock-Huessy, *I am an Impure Thinker* (Norwich, Vermont: Argo Books, 1969).

6. While *The Christian Future* plays a central role in this essay, I have also ranged rather broadly in the Rosenstock corpus in order to make my case. The reason, in my view, why *The Christian Future* is so little known is that it does not fall into a recognized genre. What is it? Theology? Confession? Religious speculation? I think it should be recognized as a form of Christian social grammar.

I. Understanding Rosenstock-Huessy: Three Interpretations

Despite the felt conviction among the small circle of his readers of the significance of Rosenstock-Huessy, it has remained difficult to articulate the nature of that significance. In large measure this difficulty is rooted in the work of the man himself: its range, richness and internal character. Nevertheless, there has emerged among his English-speaking readers three major interpretations of Rosenstock-Huessy. In Professor Harold Stahmer's important study, *Speak That I May See Thee*, Rosenstock-Huessy is placed in the tradition of "speech-thinkers" that goes back to Johann Georg Hamann (1730-1788).[7] In this tradition, speech is recognized as fundamental to human existence, it is the "lifeblood of existence."[8] Here Rosenstock-Huessy is seen as part of a tradition of thinkers who recognize the "sacramental" rather than instrumental character of speech. Central to recognition of the sacramental quality of speech is an understanding of human life as unfolding in time such that sacramental speech is, in Stahmer's words, "speech uttered at the right time."[9] Thus speech is not a mere instrument of thought as has been held in the dominant philosophical traditions of the West. Rather it is *in* the dynamic of speaking-listening-speaking that "civilization comes into being, history becomes a fact, and men become conscious of time."[10]

The consequences of the recognition of the primacy of speech within the ecology of humankind are manifold, and Stahmer attempts to explicate some of those consequences through his examination of Hamann, Rosenstock-Huessy, Franz Rosensweig, Martin Buber and Ferdinand Ebner. In this perspective, the understandings of speech found in Rosenstock-Huessy occupies a central place. Stahmer explains his own "preference for Rosenstock-Huessy" as due, in part, to his comprehensiveness, his recognition of the "multiform" relationships of humankind to reality and the multiform modes of speech.[11] Thus a primary emphasis is placed, in Stahmer's analysis, on the similarities and differences between Rosenstock-Huessy's view of speech and those of others in this tradi-

7. Harold Stahmer, *"Speak That I May See Thee!"* *The Religious Significance of Language* (New York: MacMillan, 1968). Here, it should be noted, I am focusing only on those interpretations of Rosenstock-Huessy that are available in English. There are other European interpretations, most notably, those of Georg Miller in Germany and Ko Vos in Holland.

8. Stahmer, p. 2.

9. Stahmer, p. 58.

10. Stahmer, p. 5.

11. Stahmer, p. 278.

tion.

A second major interpretation of Rosenstock-Huessy is found in Bruce Boston's doctoral dissertation, *"I Respond Although I Will Be Changed": The Life and Historical Thought of Eugen Rosenstock-Huessy.*[12] In his study, Boston offers "a systematic exploration, construction and interpretation of the historical thought" of Rosenstock-Huessy. Central to Boston's study is the issue of revolution and its pivotal significance in the unfolding of western history. For Boston, it is Rosenstock-Huessy's historical thought that constitutes "the melody" of his work, its inner core.[13] His approach to Rosenstock-Huessy is justified, he argues, since it is this method that Rosenstock-Huessy himself employs in *Out of Revolution: Autobiography of Western Man.* Rosenstock-Huessy's narrative of western history, is, according to Boston, a work that "makes an interpretative principle of mankind's revolutionary experience."[14] Indeed, in Boston's view, revolution is "the linchpin of our historical existence."[15] Thus we need to see, Boston contends, "how each revolution becomes a new paragraph in man's self-articulation."[16] Thus in Boston's approach to Rosenstock-Huessy, it is his historical thought that constitutes the central thread, the key that unlocks the secrets of his work. In his impressive exposition and interpretation of Rosenstock-Huessy's thought, Boston explores the archetectonic and universal sweep of Rosenstock-Huessy's vision. Central to the interpretation of Rosenstock-Huessy that emerges in Boston's study is the principle of unity that binds together all into one. However, this unity is not uniformity, but it is, in Boston's words, "a presupposition...in the sense of a task which addresses us from the end."[17] In the seeming varied and separate histories of peoples, a common task is being fulfilled, namely, the task of making the one human family. As Boston writes, in stating the central thesis of his study, "the historical thought of Eugen Rosenstock-Huessy can only be understood if we posit the creation of future as the central agenda of history itself, and thus our own: history must be understood eschatologically or not at all."[18]

12. Bruce Boston, *"I Respond Although I Will Be Changed": The Life and Historical Thought of Eugen Rosenstock-Huessy* (Ph.D. diss., Princeton University, 1973).

13. Boston, p. 73.

14. Boston, p. 77.

15. Boston, p. 77.

16. Boston, p. 78.

17. Boston, p. 314.

18. Boston, p. 333.

Unlike other historians, Rosenstock-Huessy reverses the order of time for the historian from future to past. As Boston makes clear, Rosenstock-Huessy's account of the unfolding creation of humankind–an unfolding in which revolution as the movement into open time and space beyond the public order is central to the process of making humankind–is not a simple reading of the "facts" of history. Rather, it is an account, a historical narrative, that is governed by a "sense of the ending," a sense of the common horizon towards which the whole of humankind moves. In this way, then, the past can be appropriated as our collective autobiography. It thus serves to undergird a common future as well. This rich account of history in Rosenstock-Huessy is, as Boston makes clear, grounded in Christianity "which embodies and provides this eschatological perspective."[19] However, Boston remains reserved about the centrality of "the cross of reality" to Rosenstock-Huessy's perspective on time and history, and suspects that history may be precut by Rosenstock-Huessy's categories, rather than their arising from history.[20] Despite this "serious flaw," Rosenstock-Huessy becomes a historical thinker of greatest importance.[21]

Clinton C. Gardner offers a third major interpretation of Rosenstock-Huessy beginning with his introduction to *Speech and Reality*, a collection of Rosenstock-Huessy's essays, and continuing into his recently published volume *Letters to the Third Millennium*.[22] According to Gardner, the essays in *Speech and Reality* seek "to dethrone the Cartesian method as the basis of all science."[23] Against the reign of Descartes emerges the methodological insights of Rosenstock-Huessy which offer a "method for the social sciences" rooted in "the patterns of human speech."[24] The advantage of this new method is, according to Gardner, that it is truly "universal" and "pertains to all of reality."[25] In this view, Rosenstock-Huessy under-

19. Boston, p. 343.

20. Boston, pp. 248ff. For Boston, what he calls the "Law of Four" is "too pat, too contrived, too systematized" (248). But one must ask: is the cross of reality a scheme to which reality must be fitted? Or, is it a way into the analysis of human life that attends to the multiformity of experience? Boston notes that he still cannot "predict where a particular insight belongs in terms of the Cross of Reality," (247) but isn't this to misunderstand the cross? It *does not* lead to prediction, but to understanding and orientation.

21. Boston, p. 256.

22. See Clinton C. Gardner's "Introduction" to *Speech and Reality*, pp. 1-8, and his *Letters to the Third Millennium* (Norwich, Vermont: Argo Books, 1981).

23. Gardner, "Introduction" to *Speech and Reality*, p. 3.

24. Gardner, "Introduction," p. 3.

25. Gardner, "Introduction," p. 3.

took "between 1920 and 1963, to apply his speech method to history, to sociology and psychology, and to theology."[26] The results of his efforts are of epochal proportions since they point the way to a "universal hermeneutic" which profoundly alters "man's knowledge about himself and the world."[27] Thus, in Gardner's view, Rosenstock-Huessy appears as the discoverer of a *new* method that will overcome the partial insights of Descartes in favour of an approach to and interpretation of social reality, a new interpretation of humankind.

Central to this new interpretation of humankind is, in Gardner's view, the grammatical method. This method is founded on the recognition of the centrality of speech to the life of humanity in time and on the corresponding recognition of four orientations to reality, "to future and past in time, to inward and outward in space."[28] These four orientations constitute what Rosenstock-Huessy calls the "cross of reality." Corresponding to this four-fold understanding of reality is a four-fold understanding of speech. As Gardner writes, "it is speech which creates inward and outward space (I and He) as well as backward and forward time (We and Thou).[29] With the method available through the work of Rosenstock-Huessy, Gardner believes we will see a major reorientation of the intellectual task on the basis of Rosenstock-Huessy's discoveries of speech as "man's matrix" and "a new method for the social sciences."[30]

In his *Letters to the Third Millennium*, Gardner extends his interpretation of Rosenstock-Huessy by offering an informal exposition of his ideas together with his own–Rosenstockian inspired–reflections upon the events of our time. He sees his work as an attempt to join Rosenstock-Huessy in the "search for a new, non-ideological language to describe who we are and where we are going."[31] In this way Gardner seeks to make good his earlier claims for Rosenstock-Huessy as the articulator of a new method that can overcome the onesidedness of the scientific era and restore a sense of balance and orientation adequate to the challenges of the coming millennium.

Each of these readings, then, serve to place Rosenstock-Huessy in a context where we might see the significance of the man and his work. Stahmer's view of Rosenstock-Huessy as a "speech-thinker,"

26. Gardner, "Introduction," pp. 4-5.
27. Gardner, "Introduction," p. 5.
28. Gardner, "Introduction," p. 7.
29. Gardner, "Introduction," p. 7.
30. Gardner, "Introduction," p. 8.
31. Gardner, *Letters to the Third Millennium*, p. xii.

Boston's interpretation of Rosenstock-Huessy as a historical thinker whose vision of the past is grounded eschatologically, and Gardner's reading of Rosenstock-Huessy as the formulator of a new method of social research, each illuminate central themes in Rosenstock-Huessy's corpus. But do they illuminate the heart of Rosenstock-Huessy's inspiration? In my view, they do not, though they each allude to many of the same factors that I will be exploring below. Here I want to offer another reading of Rosenstock-Huessy that places the inspiring centre of his work in his *Christian faith.* In the view I will outline here, the Christian faith is neither accidental nor peripheral to the vision we find in Rosenstock-Huessy, rather it is *integral* and *necessary.* The reason, in my view, that we have such difficulty in explicating Rosenstock-Huessy's significance is that we are reluctant—and, ironically, this is in part due to Rosenstock-Huessy himself—to acknowledge the centrality of his Christianity to his project. I will make this case on two grounds: one historical, the other in terms of the inner logic of Rosenstock-Huessy's vision.

However, before turning to the historical and internal grounds for my argument for the centrality of the Christian faith to Rosenstock-Huessy's work, it is important to underscore two things that I am *not* claiming. First, I am not arguing that Rosenstock-Huessy should be viewed as a "theologian." As his own work makes abundantly clear, Rosenstock-Huessy was not interested in offering a science of God (theology) as that was understood in the Middle Ages or even in the Protestant era. While Rosenstock-Huessy's work may well be—and in my view, should be—of import for theologians, he is himself not essentially a theologian. Second, I am not arguing that Christian faith is a prerequisite for our hearing what Rosenstock-Huessy has said. Rather, I am arguing for the centrality of Christian faith—as the inspiring heart—to his own vision and work, and that once articulated, his insights are to be tested by reference to experience and not by measuring them against any doctrinal standard. In a word, then, I will argue that Rosenstock-Huessy is a Christian social thinker in the sense that the heart of his inspiration was the Christian faith which compelled him to begin the articulation of a grammar of the spirit that could open the way to the third millennium of the Christian era. The task which he believed to be that of the coming millennium, namely, "the task of revealing God in society," was the task he set for himself. He is, then, the forerunner of a new intellectual type, one that emerges within the cradle of Christian faith but for the sake of humankind.[32]

32. Here I am groping for a way to *name* what Rosenstock-Huessy did. What

II. The Crucible: The Origins of the Project

Everyone who has written on Rosenstock-Huessy has pointed to the decisive significance of World War I in his life. During the war he had served in the German army. It was, he wrote in the preface to *Out of Revolution: Autobiography of Western Man*, on the "Battlefield of Verdun" that he conceived the plan for this startling retelling of the history of Europe.[33] In the light of these events, wrote Rosenstock-Huessy, our understanding of the past is altered "because it initiates a new future."[34] In his conviction that the War marked a decisive turning point in the history of humankind, Rosenstock-Huessy was not alone. But his response was distinctive. As he said, "a great new event is more than an additional paragraph to be inserted in the next edition of a book. It rewrites history, it simplifies history, it changes the past because it initiates a new future."[35] This "new future" was to become the distinctive theme of Rosenstock-Huessy's life and work. But that "new future" was not a call for adaptation to the changes that were sweeping the world, nor was it a new ideology. Rather, it led Rosenstock-Huessy to ask again about the foundations of human society, the ligaments of civilization. As he ironically notes about himself, "I am so slow at grasping the simplest rules of the game of human society that I have had to turn the subject over and over again."[36] For Rosenstock-Huessy, the way into a genuinely "new future" involved a relearning of the "rules of the game of human society;" it involved a grammar of the human spirit, one that would allow him to "demobilize" because he would, then, have made his "contribution to the common enterprise of humanity."[37] But Rosenstock-Huessy did not demobilize, but instead gave his entire life to find a way of speaking truthfully of that creature who "belongs to the three realms of Earth, Heaven, and Society."[38]

strikes every reader as a problem is how to locate Rosenstock-Huessy. He doesn't seem to fit anywhere. I think that perception is right, and thus we need to find a new name for what he does. This essay is my attempt. I suppose it might be described as another route of access to Rosenstock-Huessy's thought alongside those of Stahmer, Boston, and Gardner.

33. Rosenstock-Huessy, *Out of Revolution*, p. 5. See also my interpretation of *Out of Revolution*, unfortunately entitled "Revolution and World Pluralism," *The Ecumenist*, vol. 10, no. 3, 1972.

34. Rosenstock-Huessy, *Out of Revolution*, pp. 5-6.

35. Rosenstock-Huessy, *Out of Revolution*, pp. 5-6.

36. Rosenstock-Huessy, *Out of Revolution*, p. 13.

37. Rosenstock-Huessy, *Out of Revolution*, p. 5.

38. Rosenstock-Huessy, *Out of Revolution*, p. 7.

However, the project of coming to speak truthfully about human-kind required, in Rosenstock-Huessy's view, that one enter a more open situation beyond "the prevalent departments or divisions of existing social order and thought."[39] World War I signaled for Rosenstock-Huessy the end of an era; it also signaled a new beginning personally and collectively. As he wrote later in a letter to a friend,

> ...it was evident that the spiritual powers by which God's Spirit was represented in the German nation as in any other of the West, that is to say the Church, the Government, the institutions of higher learning, all three had piteously failed. They had not been anointed with one drop of the oil of prophecy which God requires from our governors, from our teachers, and from our churches. Not one of them had had any inkling of the doom or any vision for any future beyond mere national sovereignty.
> However, God had spoken by events which to be sure went far beyond any one man's arbitrary making, and in these mighty judgements, the three representatives of His Word on earth, the law of nations, the sacramental church, the universities, all three had been obtuse. They had lost their *scent.* And Luke 12:54 ff. was read with pertinent application to our days. *For we do not live by sight but by scent, of which faith is the sublimation.*[40]

What is striking here is that Rosenstock-Huessy's response to the War was not a crisis of faith nor despair or nihilism but a historical crisis, a recognition of the spiritual emptiness that pervaded three fundamental social institutions. This recognition lead Rosenstock-Huessy to turn down offers that came to him from the church, the university and the state. As he explained,

> This then was the turning point of my life. I learned what "Hebrews" meant by metanoia from dead works. If the vehicles of the Spirit are sullied, it's no use disobeying the verdict of history over them. I did probably not advance much in personal virtue by this about face towards the future, away from any visible institution. I did not become a saint. All I received was life.[41]

However, the years after the war were not easy ones, since "this recognition of the breakdown of the old standard was communicable to a few friends only. From 1915 to 1923 this group of friends felt

39. *Biography-Bibliography* (New York: private printing, 1959), contains "Biblionomics" by Rosenstock-Huessy, p. 17.
40. Rosenstock-Huessy, "Metanoia: To Think Anew," *I Am An Impure Thinker*, p. 185.
41. Rosenstock-Huessy, *I Am An Impure Thinker*, p. 188.

as though living on Patmos."[42] But they were crucial years. So crucial in fact that Rosenstock-Huessy acknowledged that "...all the seed of my later work, and if I may say so, of my peculiar contribution, stems from this period of total renewal and overhauling."[43]

In the crucible of the War and his response to it, then, lie the clues to Rosenstock-Huessy's work. Rather than continuing on as if things had returned to normal, Rosenstock-Huessy sought to recover the authentic scent of faith. Among other things, this meant that he sought a mode of understanding that went beneath and beyond the then current intellectual options. As he said, "the niceties of the antitheses faith and science, capital and labour, object and subject, Protestant and Catholic, lost their validity."[44] But for most of his generation and since, these antitheses have remained the verities that undergird their intellectual, personal and social lives. The consequence is that Rosenstock-Huessy has always spoken in terms that are outside the dominant assumptions and the reigning intellectual styles and conceits of the time. While this has, in part, led to his being ignored, it also clarifies the nature of the project he undertook. It was a project fraught with peril since, as he wrote, "it takes a lifetime and longer to extricate oneself from the established institutions and to find new ways of establishing some less corrupt forms of expression for the living faith."[45]

Here, then, we encounter a major difficulty in understanding Rosenstock-Huessy: the fact that he consistently and radically speaks beyond the reigning antitheses–idealist *or* materialist, determinist *or* indeterminist, liberal *or* conservative, Protestant *or* Catholic–that have characterized most thinking in the modern era. Rather, Rosenstock-Huessy strove to articulate a *multiform* social perspective and analysis that was adequate to the multiform character of social reality itself. Even the attempt to draw him into the circle of the so-called "secular" religious thinkers is misguided since it is not this frame of reference that is adequate to understanding this impure thinker. For Rosentock-Huessy, the attempt to come to grips with the life of humankind in time required that one abandon altogether the reigning disciplinary and even interdisciplinary debates. Beyond the arguments over the primacy of the economic over the cultural, the spiritual over the material, the progressive over the reactionary stands the fullness of our reality as creatures in and of time.

42. Rosenstock-Huessy, "Biblionomics," p. 17.
43. Rosenstock-Huessy, "Biblionomics," p. 17.
44. Rosenstock-Huessy, "Biblionomics," p. 17.
45. Rosenstock-Huessy, *I Am An Impure Thinker*, p. 189.

Consequently, Rosenstock-Huessy sought to marshall the resources of all forms of speech into a new grammar adequate to the future which places an imperative horizon over the present that we avoid to our peril. Hence, it is crucial that we see the radical–in its proper and not in its parochial ideological sense–character of the project he sets for himself.

But where was Rosenstock-Huessy to turn to find a way beyond the reigning antitheses, a way that could lead to an encounter with the fullness of humanity's life in time? For Rosenstock-Huessy the way was the Christian faith.[46]

III. Faith as Orientation: "Foundations for a History of the Human Spirit"

Already in the wartime exchange between Rosenstock-Huessy and Franz Rosenzweig, earlier a student on whom Rosenstock-Huessy had a profound impact and later a leading Jewish theologian, Rosenstock-Huessy made clear his dissent from the Enlightenment doctrine of the autonomy of reason. For Rosenstock-Huessy this was a modern conceit, a form of idolatry that obscured the "revelational" matrix of human reflection. Later, in *The Christian Future, Or Modern Mind Outrun*, Rosenstock-Huessy confessed that he never had diffi-culty with the Christian creeds, he simply acknowledged them to be true. "God," wrote Rosenstock-Huessy, "becomes known to us in all the powers which triumph over death."[47] The Christian Creeds are, in his view, the elaboration of this truth. As he continues,

> Its three articles guarantee our trust in the unity of creation from the beginning (God the Father made *all* things in heaven and on earth), our liberty to die to our old selves (given us by God's Son, who implanted the Divine itself in human life by living as a man, and dying, yet rising again), and the inspiration of the Holy Spirit which enables us to commune with posterity and start fellowship here and now.[48]

Hence, in Rosenstock-Huessy's view, "the Christian Dogma is not an intellectual formula but a record and promise of life."[49] It is, in my view, this conviction and understanding that is the foundation of all of Rosenstock-Huessy's work.

46. See the "Biography" by Kurt Ballerstedt in *Biography-Bibliography*, pp. 29-38. Ballerstedt concludes that the source of Rosenstock-Huessy's insights "is the Word of God become flesh in Christ," (p. 38).
47. Rosenstock-Huessy, *The Christian Future*, p. 92.
48. Rosenstock-Huessy, *The Christian Future*, p. 98.
49. Rosenstock-Huessy, *The Christian Future*, p. 98.

However, it should be noted that when Rosenstock-Huessy articulates his understanding of the Creeds, he does so in terms that are *not* conventional. Rather, he argues that the heart of the Creeds is the process of *anthropurgy*, the making of humankind. Moreover, Rosenstock-Huessy argues that it is

> ...the third article of the Creed [that] is the specifically Christian one: from now on the Holy Spirit makes man a partner in his own creation. In the beginning God had said, "Let us make man in our image" (Gen. 1:26). In this light, the Church Fathers interpreted human history as a process of making Man like God. They called it "anthropurgy": as metallurgy refines metal from its ore, anthropurgy wins the true stuff of Man out of his coarse physical substance. Christ, in the center of history, enables us to participate consciously in this man-making process and to study its laws."[50]

While Rosenstock-Huessy's life and work is grounded in Christian faith, his project is not that of the classical theological tradition. For him the fundamental issue is not the knowing of God in Himself, nor the systematic elaboration of the Christian faith, but rather it is the life of humanity in time, the making and remaking of the human race. At the same time, Rosenstock-Huessy stands in direct continuity with classical Christianity–the faith of the Early Fathers–in believing that the truth of Christianity is the truth about reality and not the limited perspective of a sociologically circumscribed group in history. Hence, the Christian faith opens out into the truth of God and humanity in time and society. It is, in Rosenstock-Huessy's perspective, the way into the world in which we find ourselves.

While this correlation of faith and the world of humankind has been glimpsed by some commentators, the attempt to link Rosenstock-Huessy to the later Dietrich Bonhoeffer and the theology of secularity is, in my view, unfortunate.[51] It is unfortunate since for Rosenstock-Huessy, the presuppositions are entirely different than those that inform the later Bonhoeffer. For Bonhoeffer, the notion of "man come of age" is grounded in an Enlightenment view of human autonomy, which thereby places the human enterprise in a context that is foreign to the work of Rosenstock-Huessy. Indeed, it is precisely this view that Rosenstock-Huessy argues against in the *Christian Faith*, as its subtitle "The Modern Mind Outrun" underscores. For Rosenstock-Huessy, humanity finds itself within an imperative that is grounded in God, not called upon to find itself in rela-

50. Rosenstock-Huessy, *The Christian Future*, p. 108.

51. See S. Leibholz, "Eugen Rosenstock-Huessy and Dietrich Bonhoeffer–Two Witnesses to the Change in our Time," *Universitas*, vol. 8 (1966), pp. 3ff.

tion to itself as the Enlightenment assumes. Consequently, for Rosenstock-Huessy, humanity is defined by *response*, not by autonomy.

Moreover, the particular direction that Rosenstock-Huessy's thinking develops, while inspired by and grounded in the Christian faith, takes a distinctive turn, namely, to show the truth of that faith in social/historical and temporal terms. Thus for Rosenstock-Huessy the Cross of Calvary is opened out to become the central truth of the life of humanity in time: it is the cross of reality on which the whole of humanity in every generation lives and dies and is resurrected.[52] Rosenstock-Huessy persistently denies the autonomy of the modern disciplines which would ground themselves in themselves. It is this view that he consistently fights against. The starting point of the life of the mind is not, as the discussions between Rosenstock-Huessy and Rosenzweig make clear, in nature and autonomous reason but in time and revelation. Sometimes it is difficult to see this point in Rosenstock-Huessy since it does not result in an ecclesiastical nor doctrinal outlook, but instead in the starting point for understanding the life of humankind in time. This assumption is so problematic in our era. But Rosenstock-Huessy has shown that it is a necessary starting point, since it is in time and in the given context of our lives that we are called to discern the powers that shape our age and name what makes for life and death.

Unlike many of his contemporaries, Rosenstock-Huessy rejected the doctrine of the autonomy of reason as a modern conceit; he also rejected the Nietzchean view of the "death of God" as an untruth and the ecclesiasticism that finally captured contemporaries like Karl Barth. For Rosenstock-Huessy, the truth of the Christian faith is fundamentally to be shown in its capacity to teach us about the life of humanity in time. Thus in his sociology as well as his history, Rosenstock-Huessy's work is permeated by an orientation that arises from his faith. Indeed, faith is orientation, a way of being disposed towards the whole of reality and human life in time. Consequently, his work is pervaded by terms that social thinkers captive to the

---

52. See, for example, H. Stahmer's introduction to E. Rosenstock-Huessy, *The Origin of Speech* (Norwich, Vermont: Argo, 1981), where Stahmer writes "Rosenstock-Huessy's 'Cross of Reality,' which should not be confused with the Christian symbol..." (xiii). I find such comments confusing. While it is true that Rosenstock-Huessy's Cross is not the Cross of Calvary in some literal sense, it is certainly the case that Rosenstock-Huessy's understanding of reality is intimately linked to–no, grows directly out of the Cross–these Christian sources. Wouldn't one better point out to the reader that reading Rosenstock-Huessy may change or enlarge one's understanding of the Christian faith?

modern *intellectus* and its cult of objectivism eschew: inspiration, the life of the spirit, the reversal of times, the cross of reality, the imperative of the future. These are words that grow out of and resonate in a Christian mileau and point to an orientation towards life that has, in the academies of the Western world, come under severe attack. For Rosenstock-Huessy, however, the Christian faith remained a "record and promise of life," a "scent" that could orient one beyond the tragedies of a world always on the edge of madness.

In the midst of the disorientation created by the World Wars, Rosenstock-Huessy insisted that "faith, properly speaking, is always belief in some future, a world to come."[53] Faith, thus, stands on the frontline of the future. It is the guardian of the future, the antidote to decadence, the forward counterpart to thankfulness for the past. Yet faith is continually reborn as it passes through the crucible of life suffered. Faith resides not in some pastoral wayside nor in private subjectivity but at the heart of time as the power of the human soul to undergo "death and resurrection" in time. It is such faith, Rosenstock-Huessy argues, that is not for its own sake but for the making and remaking of humankind (anthropurgy), in order that God might be known as the Living God of the beginning, end and crucial present.[54]

When this burning center of Rosenstock-Huessy's project is recognized, then we can better understand the dynamics that lie at the heart of his writings and why I here argue that the Christian faith is integral and necessary to that project.[55] It is faith in a world to come coupled with the rhythm of death and resurrection that is, in Rosenstock-Huessy's view, the secret of the world-transforming power of Christianity in the successive ages of the Christian era. Thus, for Rosenstock-Huessy, the life of humankind and faith are inextricably linked. This is especially clear later in *The Christian Future* where Rosenstock-Huessy sets the future of Christianity neither over-against nor alongside the future of humankind. Rather, the Christian future is one with the future of humankind, since this

---

53. Rosenstock-Huessy, *The Christian Future*, p. 173.

54. Rosenstock-Huessy, *The Christian Future*, pp. 92-131.

55. See also Eugen Rosenstock-Huessy, *The Fruit of Lips Or Why Four Gospels*, edited by Marion Davis Battles (Pittsburgh: The Pickwick Press, 1978), where his faith is most explicit: "The word of mankind will remain a helpless stammering and a vile repetition of dead words if we...decline to respond to our sponsor, to understand his stand, and to dare the world by the disreputable Words, Christ, Christians. If Jesus is the "Logos", the Word, we must become as the Greeks called it, "homo-logos," which means of the same Word. We must revamp our words by making him explicitly the keyword of all our own words and everybody must do this, in person," (p. 122).

faith is the internal, spiritual dynamic of the making and remaking of humankind. "Christianity and future," Rosenstock-Huessy asserts, "are synonymous."[56] But the making good of this claim requires the articulation of a grammar of the spirit which can show the linkage between faith and the life of humankind to be necessary. Was Rosenstock-Huessy able to perform this task? What are his contributions to this project?

IV. "Making Man"–Foundations for a Grammar of the Spirit

After the First World War, Rosenstock-Huessy entered a period that would be decisive for all his later work. The Patmos circle together with his work in industry provided the intellectual and vocational context to begin the attempt to articulate a grammar of the spirit adequate to the life of humankind in time. For Rosenstock-Huessy, this grammar involved a way of speaking about the human situation that would avoid the temptations of abstraction and reductionism. Later, in *The Multiformity of Man*, Rosenstock-Huessy clarified his task when he wrote,

> I am attacking the thesis of the uniformity of man. I am attacking the premise that the rule "A equals A," can be applied to man. I am attacking the dogmatic self-complacency through which we are treating mankind like everything else.[57]

At the same time, he continued, "I am more than ever convinced of the unity of mankind, of a common goal and destiny for all men."[58] It was in the light of these twin–and to many, seemingly contradictory–claims that Rosenstock-Huessy's explorations proceeded. In his view, humanity revealed itself in its multiformity, but this never resulted in a sheer multiplicity. Rather, there exists a basic and fundamental connection between a common future and the multiform nature of our life together in time. How to grasp this connection was a central problem, since Rosenstock-Huessy was seeking to avoid both the materialist reductionism of Marxism and the abstractions of German idealism.

The way beyond these false antitheses was what he later called the "grammatical method," a method of social research that could accomplish what Rosenstock-Huessy understood to be a central requirement of an adequate understanding of human life in time: it could grasp "a multiformity within unity."[59] Unless the multiformity

56. Rosenstock-Huessy, *The Christian Future*, p. 62.
57. Eugen Rosenstock-Huessy, *The Multiformity of Man* (Norwich, Vermont: Argo Books, 1973), p. iv.
58. Rosenstock-Huessy, *Multiformity of Man*, p. iv.

of human life could be respected, a destructive dynamic was unleashed; unless the unity of human life could be affirmed, disintegration was promoted.

As we noted above, Rosenstock-Huessy understands the life of humanity in time as a process of "anthropurgy" or "man-making." This conviction stands behind his attempts to articulate a grammar of the spirit, a way of understanding the life of humanity in time. Unlike social thinkers who see their task as *explaining* social life and processes, Rosenstock-Huessy saw the goal of social reflection as understanding the "laws" of humankind's being made so that we might "consciously participate in them."[60] Thus the social thinker takes up his task not from an ideal vantage point outside the social process but from within the life he is both sustained by and suffers with others. Social thinking, then, is thinking that arises within society in the unfolding of generations from the end of time back to its beginning and has as its goal understanding (in the sense of standing under and within) social processes. This incarnational approach to social thinking is decisive and is continuous with Rosenstock-Huessy's conviction that the Christian faith grounds one in time and history as the context of our living and dying. To discern the rhythms and patterns of our life in time is to discern the powers of God in the making and remaking of human life. Moreover, unlike the social thinking inspired by Marx and Freud in the modern world, Rosenstock-Huessy's orientation is focused on what makes for life rather than the pathological formations that make for death.

Rosenstock-Huessy's procedure is analogous to what we find in Augustine's *Confessions* where Augustine's review of his own life leads him to an awareness of God's gracious presence long before he, Augustine, responded to it. The awareness of that presence did not give Augustine any control over life nor any enhanced capacity for prediction, but rather it led him to say yes to those things that made for life. The audacity of Rosenstock-Huessy's work is that he sought to discern those life-giving powers present not only in his personal autobiography, but in the autobiography of humankind. For Rosenstock-Huessy, attention to the dynamics of our life in time leads not to control or predictability, but rather to a heightened awareness of what makes for social life in the overcoming of the manifold forms of "death."

59. Rosenstock-Huessy, *Speech and Reality,* p. 9.
60. Rosenstock-Huessy, *The Christian Future,* p. 108.

In the First World War, Rosenstock-Huessy had discerned a fundamental spiritual condition that led to social death, namely, an absence of a living conviction of the unity of the human race. His great work, *Out of Revolution: Autobiography of Western Man*, which arose from this period of his life, was an attempt to retell the story of western man as a single but internally differentiated story so that it might form the common autobiographical background to our common future. For Rosenstock-Huessy, "peoples co-operate and co-exist, not merely geographically and mechanically, but morally, as one collective system of interplay and mutual dependence."[61] This conviction of the spiritual and moral unity of humankind undergirds his entire project and serves as the foundation of his social teaching. Not competing interests (whether benign or malignant), nor modes of production (whether feudal, capitalistic or socialist), nor separate national sovereignties, nor sheer diversity, nor any other discrete factor governed the life of humankind as fundamentally, in Rosenstock-Huessy's view, as does our spiritual and moral interplay and dependence. While we often cannot see–because we have not gone deep enough or attained the right perspective–or hear–because we have not listened hard enough–this ground and imperative, it is, nonetheless, present as the ground tone and goal of humanity's life in time.

This conviction of unity does not lead Rosenstock-Huessy to a mystical monism, nor to a sentimental humanism, but to a distinctive orientation towards the life of humanity. That orientation is one of looking back to discern the emerging patterns of our unity and looking ahead to discern the imperatives that require our common–but different–efforts. The shape our future takes is not written in the stars, but in the responses of human lives to the imperatives that stand over us all.

Thus for Rosenstock-Huessy, understanding the processes fundamental to the making of humankind rests in the conviction of the unity in diversity of the different peoples. In *Out of Revolution*, the story of humankind's "interplay and mutual dependence" is told in relation to western man; in *The Christian Future* Rosenstock-Huessy suggests that we now find ourselves in a situation where we will have to tell this story in relation to all the peoples of a planet. However, Rosenstock-Huessy's vision of a coming unity of humankind is rooted in Christian faith as it provides an understanding of the life of the spirit true to our historical experience. As he affirms in *The Christian Future,*

---

61. Rosenstock-Huessy, *Out of Revolution*, p. 455.

Today Orient and Occident are shaken by a cataclysm which shows the insufficiency of both in isolation. A new penetration of the Cross is required which shall draw together the hearts of men in East and West by showing that each has some essential ingredient of life which the other needs.[62]

Here he refers to the notion of the Cross as the context of humankind's unity. What Rosenstock-Huessy calls the Cross of Reality is fundamental to his social thought. While the life of humankind in time unfolds in response to a common destiny, that future is won—or lost—on the Cross of Reality.

V. Cruciform Reality and the Creature

Rosenstock-Huessy's work assumes, as we have seen, that the life of humanity is internally linked as it unfolds in response to a common destiny. At the same time, he was fully aware of the differentiated and multiform character of personal and social life in time. In his view, societies serve as "nurseries" to nurture certain types of human beings within the family of humankind.[63] And the course of historical experience has shown man, as Rosenstock-Huessy observed, "...to be a beginner and a continuator, a creator and a creature, a product of environment and its producer, a grandson or an ancestor, a revolutionary or evolutionist."[64] These different national types and these different capacities of humankind were called forth by varying imperatives that emerged in different historical eras and situations. Rosenstock-Huessy respects the record of human life in time and it is in the light of that record that he spoke of the creature. This served to position Rosenstock-Huessy overagainst those who sought to reduce humanity to a function of the economic order or environment or ego or biological nature. Instead, Rosenstock-Huessy sought to maintain the multiformity of our creaturehood.

We are—in one of Rosenstock-Huessy's more striking formulations—creatures who have a "triple citizenship" in the earth, society, and the heavens.[65] But the boundaries between these different realms are not fixed once and for all. Instead, it has been the experience of humankind to fix and refix these boundaries from age to age and in

---

62. Rosenstock-Huessy, *The Christian Future*, p. 174.
63. See Rosenstock-Huessy, *Out of Revolution*, pp. 467ff.
64. Rosenstock-Huessy, *Out of Revolution*, p. 747.
65. One sees this tendency in C. Gardner, *Letters to the Third Millennium*, where Gardner wants to see Rosenstock-Huessy in relation to Bonhoeffer, H. Cox, and the theologians of secularity. While I certainly agree with Gardner that Rosenstock-Huessy is a deeper and more important figure than any of those mentioned, I still think he is placed in a context that is misleading.

different societies. This variety was not to be opposed but embraced, since "they are sown in one common field of man's experience and hope" and "like separate branches they are all grafted on the common tree of humanity."[66] It was against the background of his studying the history of western man that Rosenstock-Huessy came to the insights that grounded his grammar of the spirit. The recognition of the multiple dimensions of human life as well as the multiple forms society took in history led Rosenstock-Huessy to see that,

> Reality itself–not the abstract reality of physics, but the full-bodied reality of human life–is cruciform. Our existence is a perpetual suffering and wrestling with conflicting forces, paradoxes, contradictions within and without. By them we are stretched and torn in opposite directions, but through them comes renewal. And these opposing directions are summed up by four which define the great space and time axes of all men's life on earth, forming a Cross of Reality.[67]

Here Rosenstock-Huessy came to a basic insight: the life of the creature is faced simultaneously inward and outward in space, forward and backward in time. And it is in the intersection of these four fronts of reality that the creature lives and dies. And is also renewed.

The Cross of Reality, as the *name* of our condition in time and space as creatures, is fundamental to Rosenstock-Huessy's social thinking. It is his denial of both reductionism and abstractions. It serves to bring into focus those manifold forces which everyday assail our life and, at the same time, to clarify the imperatives inherent in our situation. Moreover, wrote Rosenstock-Huessy, "since the four fronts differ in quality and direction they are *ultimate and irreducible dimensions of human existence,* but the mind with its imperious urge to relate and unify eveything is tempted to over-simplify life and deny the Cross of Reality by reducing the four to one."[68] But it was this temptation that Rosenstock-Huessy resisted and the consequence is a grammar of the spirit infinitely richer than those that have dominated contemporary discussions. In the light of the Cross of Reality, a major revolution in our social thinking is required.

This cruciform understanding of reality reveals, upon analysis, the spatial "conflict of inner and outer processes" and the temporal "conflict between responsibilities toward the past and the future."[69] However, these axes are not extrinsic to the creature, but pass

66. Rosenstock-Huessy, *Out of Revolution,* p. 465.
67. Rosenstock-Huessy, *The Christian Future,* p. 166.
68. Rosenstock-Huessy, *The Christian Future,* p. 169.
69. Rosenstock-Huessy, *Speech and Reality,* p. 54.

through the very heart of our being. We are creatures of the cross. "Therefore," wrote Rosenstock-Huessy, "life is perpetual decision: when to continue the past and when to change, and where to draw the line between the inner circle we speak to and the outer objects we merely speak of and try to manipulate."[70] In the absence of a cruciform understanding of the reality of creaturely life, we tend to see only one or another front, one or another dimension of life. The consequence is a distortion of the situation of the creature which then skews our thinking and our responses.

In our social life, the cruciform character of life results in a certain division of social labour. As Rosenstock-Huessy notes, "society compensates for our individual inadequacies by division of labour."[71] And he continued,

> ...teaching, ceremony and ritual preserve our continuity with the past, and teachers, priests and lawyers serve on this front for all of us. We build up social unanimity by playing, singing, talking together, sharing our moods and aspirations and on this inner front poets, artists, and musicians are typical representatives. We win our living and protect our lives by learning to control natural forces and manipulating them for our ends in farming, industry and war; scientists, engineers and soldiers typify the millions who fight for us on the outer front. Lastly, religious and political leaders, prophets and statesmen are responsible for initiating change and drawing society into its future.[72]

Thus society itself takes on a certain cruciform reality in order to respond to the multiple claims upon its life. The virtue of Rosenstock-Huessy's insight here is that the division of labour is not just an economic phenomenon, but touches the very fabric of our life together in a society: the functions of different groups within society contribute to the welfare of the whole society. This perspective also contains a way of analyzing social distortion and social breakdown. For example, without the presence in society of those whose lives are given over to the fulfillment of the social task of nourishing social unanimity, the evil of inner disunity emerges. Contemporary society, "dominated for several centuries by natural science and its applications, suffers most of all from obsession with the outward front," and this obsession has led to a distortion that threatens our future.[73] Hence, in Rosenstock-Huessy's view, "social

70. Rosenstock-Huessy, *The Christian Future*, p. 168.
71. Rosenstock-Huessy, *The Christian Future*, p. 169.
72. Rosenstock-Huessy, *The Christian Future*, p. 169.
73. Rosenstock-Huessy, *The Christian Future*, p. 170.

health depends on preserving a delicate mobile balance between forward and backward, inward and outward."[74]

When the Cross of Reality is placed at the heart of one's social grammar, the result is a multiform understanding of social life and the multiform character of speech. Against one-dimensional understandings of society and speaking, Rosenstock-Huessy asserts that "whenever we speak, we assert our being alive because we occupy a center from which the eye looks backward, forward, inward and outward. To speak, means to be placed in the center of the cross of reality."[75] However, we do not speak in a single mode but rather in the mode appropriate to the front to which we are most attentive at a given moment. This results, in Rosenstock-Huessy, in a four-fold understanding of speech: prejective (forward), subjective (inward), trajective (backward), and objective (outward).[76] Here again the creature finds himself called upon to differentiate his speaking so that it is appropriate to the dimension of our cruciform reality addressed. Moreover, the maintenance of these different modes of speech is at the heart of social well-being. In Rosenstock-Huessy's words,

> Men reason, men pass laws, men tell stories, men sing. The external world is reasoned out, the future is ruled, the past is told, the unanimity of the inner circle is expressed in song...The energies of social life are compressed into words. The circulation of articulated speech is the lifeblood of society. *Through speech, society sustains its time and space axes.* These time and space axes give direction and orientation to all members of society. Without articulated speech, man has neither direction nor orientation in time or space.[77]

Thus the Cross of Reality when correlated with a four-fold understanding of speech gives rise to a grammar of social analysis and points the way to social renewal. We are, in this sense, creatures of speech.

In making the point about the centrality of speech to social life, Rosenstock-Huessy turns to our actual life in time and space rather than to philosophical reflection upon speech, as has become common in the contemporary interest in the philosopy of language. Contra the search of the early Wittgenstein for an ideal language, or the later Wittgenstein for the disease of ordinary speech, or Cassier's

74. Rosenstock-Huessy, *The Christian Future*, p. 168.
75. Rosenstock-Huessy, *Speech and Reality*, p. 52.
76. Rosenstock-Huessy, *Speech and Reality*, p. 189.
77. Rosenstock-Huessy, *Speech and Reality*, p. 16.

"symbol-making," or Heidegger's view of language as the "house of being," Rosenstock-Huessy turns his attention to speaking and listening as the key to social living and dying. Speech is the matrix of our life together.

Rosenstock-Huessy believed that the cruciform method he developed allowed for "the diagnosis of the complete soul" as well as the "healthy society."[78] Unlike the social thinkers who followed the lead of the natural sciences into a preoccupation with external space, Rosenstock-Huessy sought to turn our attention to the reality of human life on the cruciform of space and time. Here, in the responses of human beings and societies to the imperatives that arise in the unfolding of events, the fate of humankind is lost and won. Rather than searching for timeless abstractions, Rosenstock-Huessy sought to teach us the value of timing and timeliness. Rather than a philosophy of language, Rosenstock-Huessy sought to sharpen our ability to hear the spoken word since "all we can learn is to listen better and better."[79] Here again the "scent" of faith in the living God led the way to his cruciform perspective of the creature's life in time and his incarnational grasp of the multiform powers of speech. The life-creating Word of creation, redemption and consummation pointed the way to life sustaining, renewing and inspiring words we speak on the cross of reality. These faith convictions issued, in Rosenstock-Huessy's work, in a grammar of social life. The issue that confronts society at every moment is the same that confronted the children of Abraham through Moses: "I call heaven and earth to witness against you this day, that I have set before you life and death, blessing and curse; therefore choose life, that you and your descendents may live," (Deut. 30:19).

VI. The Intergenerational Context and the Tones of the Spirit

In his writings, Rosenstock-Huessy articulated a social grammar that affirmed in an unprecedented way the centrality of time to the unfolding of human and social life. But this did not, in Rosenstock-Huessy's case, lead to a form of historicism, nor was it a gloss on Hegel. Against all forms of historicism, Rosenstock-Huessy affirmed the reality of the living God as the ground of the making of humankind. Against Hegel who saw time as the inexorable unfolding of the absolute, such that humanity became a pawn in the dialectics of history, Rosenstock-Huessy affirmed the centrality of human responses to the making of humankind. Thus for

78. Rosenstock-Huessy, *The Christian Future*, p. 172.
79. Rosenstock-Huessy, *Out of Revolution*, p. 710.

Rosenstock-Huessy, the past, present, and future are not abstract categories but are the embodied life of generations that stretch from the end of time back to Adam and Eve.

In his analysis of our cruciform reality, Rosenstock-Huessy observed "the disconcerting truth...that at any hour of our lives we are both older and younger than others in the community."[80] Why disconcerting? The reason lies in the fact that it makes us aware of time and difference. Where many have become preoccupied with a statistical and numerical approach to social life, Rosenstock-Huessy sought to underline the temporal reality of social life. The life of society is intergenerational, and it is fundamentally defined by what Rosenstock-Huessy called "distemporaniety."[81] Grandfathers and grandmothers, mothers and fathers, brothers and sisters–three generations–constitute the smallest social unit. And to speak of all people of the same generation living in the same calendar year as "contemporaries" obscures the reality of our social life. Instead, we find ourselves not only struggling with the realities of intergenerational life in the family and society, but also with distemporaniety among people of the same generation. Thus, Rosenstock-Huessy always viewed society itself, as well as social peace, as a creative achievement. The task of every society at every moment is to harmonize distemporaries into a living unity in order to create "the rhythm of a community."[82]

The remarkable power of speech lies in its ability to make us contemporaries. "That man," wrote Rosenstock-Huessy, "must make contemporaries by conversing, by speech, by teaching, that we read Homer and Shakespeare today, that we sing songs, in a chorus, and pass laws for the future, is the odd situation of society and man in society."[83] What is of central importance here is that contemporaneity does not mean uniformity or everyone saying the same thing–this is the ideological plague that is destroying us. Rather, Rosenstock-Huessy focused on the active power of speech to build bridges, to create relationships. Through speaking to one another we create bonds of communion across the distances of space and the intervals of time that separate us. Society–and social peace–is thereby called into being: community emerges.

However, Rosenstock-Huessy understood that the life of society is not only the linking together of the lives of persons in a given era,

80. Rosenstock-Huessy, *The Christian Future*, p. 172.
81. Rosenstock-Huessy, *The Christian Future*, p. 172.
82. Rosenstock-Huessy, *The Christian Future*, p. 243.
83. Rosenstock-Huessy, *Speech and Reality*, p. 28.

but it is also the weaving of the lives of the present generation into the lives of the dead and the yet unborn. The life of the present generation only attains to its fulness as it is sustained by a respect and thankfulness for the past *and* faith in the future. In the absense of this vital sense of living "between the times," the present generation falls in upon itself. Respect for the past lifts the present generation beyond itself. Thus Rosenstock-Huessy saw that "the decadence of an older generation condemns the younger generation to barbarism. Decadence of parents leaves children without heritage."[84] The antidote to "this evil is faith" which is not "a belief in things of the past, but in the future."[85] In underscoring the temporal situation of every generation between the past and future, Rosenstock-Huessy sought to recover our crucial role in the creation of humankind.

At the same time, Rosenstock-Huessy was fully aware of the deep crisis of our time. As we have seen, it was precisely awareness of crisis that led Rosenstock-Huessy to seek to articulate a grammar of the spirit that could lead beyond our predicament. It was Christianity that provided the clues to a way out, since "Christianity is the embodiment of one single truth through the ages: that death precedes birth, that birth is the fruit of death, and that the soul is precisely this power of transforming an end into a bginning by obeying a new name. Without the soul, the times remain out of joint."[86] For Rosenstock-Huessy the impass of our moment was the end that could become a new beginning. But we needed to learn anew the powers of speech, to be engrafted into the succession of generations, and to recover the "twelve tones of the spirit."[87] For Rosenstock-Huessy the life of society depended upon the "spirit and love" since these are "stronger than death."[88]

For Rosenstock-Huessy, the great secret of Christianity that is crucial to our survival is the reversal of the relationship of death and life. In personal life as well as social life, he argued, "the first spiritual command is: leave a will, endow, bequest." This command gains its priority "because it gives direction and meaning to all our previous steps."[89] Unlike Heidegger who argued that human life is "being unto death," Rosenstock-Huessy argued that "the spiritual life of all of us should be traced from our dying hour backward."[90]

84. Rosenstock-Huessy, *Speech and Reality,* p. 12.
85. Rosenstock-Huessy, *Speech and Reality,* pp. 12-13.
86. Rosenstock-Huessy, *The Christian Future,* p. 10.
87. Rosenstock-Huessy, *I Am An Impure Thinker,* p. 69.
88. Rosenstock-Huessy, *I Am An Impure Thinker,* p. 69.
89. Rosenstock-Huessy, *I Am An Impure Thinker,* p. 72.
90. Rosenstock-Huessy, *I Am An Impure Thinker,* p. 72.

Similarly in our social life, we live off the bequests of the past and replenish this spiritual treasury by lives that endow future generations. When we become–to use Vonnegut's phrase–"unstuck in time," and when the relationship between word and act is broken, then our spiritual life becomes disordered as well.

Rosenstock-Huessy sought to recall us to acknowledge those processes "by which we are threaded into God's creation, day after day."[91]

> I may perhaps have to remind you that in society, in our historical community, we move as men born through the living Word into our times and places, into our future destiny. We have the singular privilege of contributing to the everlasting survival of acquired faculties which we embrace and to contribute to the everlasting relegation to hell of those acquired faculties which we wish to see extirpated. Thus, Creation is taking place under our very noses. And nobody can stay neutral in this spiritual war between bequeathing the good qualities to the future through faith or giving up from despair the task of weeding out the diabolical qualities.[92]

From childhood, through adulthood, to elderhood, each generation carries forward the life of the spirit or squanders that life because it has lost the scent. In childhood, argues Rosenstock-Huessy, we "obey, read, learn and sing" so that as adults we may "doubt and withhold, analyze and synthesize, speak up and insist, wait and persevere."[93] As these faculties are acquired, then we are enabled, as elders, to "lead and legislate, teach and instruct, prophesy and warn, endow and bestow." But the depth of our societal disorientation is evident in the cult of youth, the loss of intergenerational rhythm, and the disregard of the elderly. Instead of initiation of the new generation into the full life of the spirit, we count the growing numbers of old people and calculate the burden they represent for the future. But this order from elder who bequeaths to the child who listens and obeys "has been forgotten in secularism,"[94] and the consequence is that our social teaching further deepens the crisis rather than teaching us the way to social renewal.

The correlation, then, of the "tones of the spirit" with the stages of human development is of vital importance to the process of social renewal. The grammar of the spirit that Rosenstock-Huessy articu-

---

91. Rosenstock-Huessy, *I Am An Impure Thinker*, pp. 71.
92. Rosenstock-Huessy, *I Am An Impure Thinker*, pp. 70-71.
93. Rosenstock-Huessy, *I Am An Impure Thinker*, p. 74.
94. Rosenstock-Huessy, *I Am An Impure Thinker*, p. 73.

lates is not only for the sake of understanding but for the sake of "creating future communities."[95] However, the creation of future communities is not a matter of social engineering, nor is it a matter of allegiance to a particular ideology. Rather, for Rosenstock-Huessy, it is a matter of faithful response to those "eternal conditions under which alone life can go forward among men."[96] In the project of articulating those conditions, Rosenstock-Huessy was a pioneer.

VII. Rosenstock-Huessy as a Christian Social Thinker

To recognize that the inspiration at the heart of Rosenstock-Huessy is the Christian faith is not to appeal to a preemptive authority. The truth of Rosenstock-Huessy's thinking about society is to be judged on the basis of its truthfulness in our experience and in the fruitfulness of the analyses that emerge from his work. The truth of his thinking about society is its capacity to illumine our experience and to inspire our social activity. This distinction between the *sources* of Rosenstock-Huessy's thinking and the *grounds* for judging its truthfulness is critical. A failure to understand this distinction will also lead to a misunderstanding of what it is that I am claiming here. Rather than attempting to obscure Rosenstock-Huessy, or to shroud his work in the much-diminished mantle of Christianity, I am attempting to clarify the basis of his work and why it is that, in part, his work has been so little examined.

When we read Rosenstock-Huessy, there is a well-spring of inspiration and faith that stands behind his work, permeates his vision, and informs his analyses. Consequently, the results of his efforts are often so unusual that the more conventional academic, trained as a technician in the application of a method, must resist them. Failure to resist Rosenstock-Huessy is to call into question that most sacred of all modern academic idols: methodological objectivism. In the modern world, objectivity does not mean, as it properly does, that the results of an investigation are publically open to be arrived at by others, but rather that *before* one even begins an investigation, a status-free of personal bias has been achieved such that the results, whatever they be, are *guaranteed*. This is what I call methodological objectivism, the reversal of the relationship of life and science. Thus when Rosenstock-Huessy is encountered, with his announcement that he stands on the earthquake of World War I and will not "demobilize",[97] the very premises of modern scholarship are called

95. Rosenstock-Huessy, *The Christian Future*, p. 10.
96. Rosenstock-Huessy, *The Christian Future*, p. 10.

into question.

Rosenstock-Huessy, however, takes what others might call the "accidents" of history as the very God-given context of one's calling, and failure to attend to those contexts is to turn one's back on one's cross of reality in favour of a disembodied reality that is certainly filled with obstract objects, but not with living human beings.

For Rosenstock-Huessy, the social thinker takes up his task in the midst of his generation and time, and seeks to render articulate the cross of its time and thereby to overcome the idiocy of every generation by linking this time and this cross with God's time, which is the making of humankind, the one process that goes on from the beginning to the end and in which we are a crucial link. However, the tendency of every generation to turn in upon itself and its own time requires thinkers to continue the never-ending task of remembering, re-membering, the past so that we can join our words to the one Word, and to evoking the future by sniffing out the imperatives that are presented to us as the necessities which need to be incorporated into our present. For Rosenstock-Huessy, the thinker finds himself in a situation which is shaped by events which precede him and by consequences beyond our reckoning which will emerge after him. Nonetheless, the Christian social thinker has a stance within that situation which is not value-free (that does not necessarily mean it is not true) but rather is grounded in a conviction of what is happening in history as humanity–in its several types and varieties–reproduces itself by passing the torch of its faith, hope, and love to the coming generation, and as God weaves the strand of this time and age into the fabric of His anthropurgy. Hence, Rosenstock-Huessy, is not captive to the present moment of time since he knows the times of others, nor is he the slave of a timeless present–the idol of the modern social thinker; but he seeks to serve the present by lifting it into the generations of humankind and the life of that One Spirit that continually renews the life of all from the end to the beginning of time.

Are we perhaps reluctant to deal with Rosenstock-Huessy as a Christian social thinker? Do we assume that that qualifies his work in a way that makes it parochial, as if to be a Christian is to be constrained by the interests of a particular sociological grouping? However, this is a peculiarly modern view of the Christian thinker which we would do well to question. To be a Christian social thinker is to be nurtured by an event and approach to reality that one holds

97. Rosenstock-Huessy, *Out of Revolution*, p. 5.

because one believes it to be true of reality as such. To speak of God–as Rosenstock-Huessy did, but not in the abstract terms of the philosopher–is to speak of that power of reality that places before us an imperative to live fully in the context of the whole human race. It is to know that the cross of reality is the context of human life in time, whether one be explicitly affiliated with a particular Christian group or not. In other words, Rosenstock-Huessy believed the cross of reality to be a true name of reality in time as such. And that is the case, whether one be a Christian, Jew, Hindu, Buddhist or whatever. For Rosenstock-Huessy, as for the great thinkers in the history of Christianity, the truth of faith opens out to the truth of reality; in his case, to a grammar of the spirit that expresses the truth of faith in social and temporal terms.

In Rosenstock-Huessy, then, we encounter a Christian social thinker whose many contributions to a grammar of the spirit in time we have yet to appropriate. Our sciences remain captive to space; they have yet to grasp the rhythms which make for social peace. But then Rosenstock-Huessy knew that he was speaking ahead of his time. Perhaps–just perhaps–we who have survived this century of transition will find in Rosenstock-Huessy an inspiration that can transform this ending age into a new beginning.

The Ever Growing Word

Bas Leenman

About 1970 a professor in Judaica from Dartmouth College, with some of his students, visited Rosenstock-Huessy at his home in Norwich, Vermont, and eagerly asked him about his encounters with Franz Rosenzweig. When leaving, one of the students who had not said anything took courage and asked what Rosenstock thought Franz Rosenzweig had added to life. The unexpected answer was: "Added to life? Franz Rosenzweig of course!" In this answer, the name itself is the new reality. Franz Rosenzweig's *life,* as incomprehensible as it may be, becomes pronounceable in his name. Yet the very work "pro-nounce" warns us that the act of pronouncing is still provisional.

As the reader may know, the Synagogue does not pronounce the name of God. Not until the last child is born will the Name become pronounceable. In the last child, the Name of names will have reached its final realization. Does this also count for human names?

In the countryside of New England, cemeteries are part of the land. One is easily attracted by such an open book of gravestones, and reading the pages one can hear the heartbeats of the body of Man: *NAMES* and *DATES!* Both are bestowed on the dead and carry them beyond their own reach. The names are given by lips other than their own; the dates carry them within a universal biography: the Christian Era. This universal biography was for the first time formally expressed by the Roman monk Dionysius Exiguus in about the year 525. He started a system of reckoning any event from the birth of Christ, the founder of one Body of Time for one Body of Man. In expressing it, Dionysius made it recognizable in the world.

What still remained unexpressed was the power by which it works: the language of languages whose vocabulary is PEOPLE! Otherwise the sentence "AND THE WORD BECAME FLESH" is up in the air, a comet that appeared and disappeared again. Christ, the founder of this language, made himself known in the vision of the apostle John as ALPHA AND OMEGA. We do not meet this name in the four gospels, but we repeatedly encounter it in the Book of Revelation. In the loneliness of Patmos, where John becomes the seer, the fullness of time is presented to him as a book opened by Christ, appearing like a lamb that is slain. Books have to do with language. As the key to this book, John hears four times the name ALPHA AND OMEGA, which is not merely "the beginning and the end," but SPEECH as the beginning and the end of all creation. ALPHA AND OMEGA, God's name and at the same time the reality of a living alphabet as *human* speech, pronounceable!

Still the Jew does not pronounce the Name.

I once spoke before the congregation of the liberal synagogue in Amsterdam, Holland, on the translation of the holy Name as revealed to Moses. Naively, I pronounced the Name and a shiver went through the listeners. One of the two rabbis present rebuked me. The other one, out of tolerance of the Christian way of speaking to God, defended me. Defended or not, a Jewish reverence for the Name was engraved in me then and there.

There is a secret in the different ways Christianity and Judaism relate to the Name, and this secret forbids us to take the difference as the mere Yes and No of two voices excluding each other. "The Third Millennium is the marriage of Judaism and Christianity," announced Rosenstock-Huessy in his speech at Columbia University in 1965. The two roads now cross. It is now the Yes and the No within the one conversation of the soul of man with the Spirit of the creation. Judaism leaves unpronounced the Name which comprehends all names, leaving the Name beyond the speech of men. The Name should not be translated from generation to generation. Judaism does not acknowledge generations. The voice of Judaism is the voice of the Fathers. It is only after Franz Rosenzweig and after the Holocaust that the Jews are becoming sons and daughters in a free conversation with the fathers. Until then, the righteous Jew was meant to be his fathers' voice, a bar mitsvah, a son of duty. As the one voice of the fathers, the Jew converses freely with the God of the Fathers, still wrestling with him as did Father Jacob, the very first Israel, at Peniel and still without any doubt about God's "conversableness." The Jews are the people of the ALPHA (the Jewish Era starts with the Creation) and of the OMEGA ("We, the Jews, we are already at the end," said Franz Rosenzweig). They converse freely with the ALPHA and the OMEGA, leaving the intermediate letters of the Name open as an eternal surprise.

Christianity is the opposite. Christianity is in the center, between Alpha and Omega. Faith in what Rosenstock-Huessy called God's "conversableness," in his openness in a conversation (as in his talks with Abraham, with Jacob, with Moses), is a weak point in

Christianity, a Christianity prone to misunderstanding the prayer "Thy will be done." But BETWEEN Alpha and Omega the conversation within Christianity is a free one, encompassing the living and the dead. Here we do not know beforehand which of God's dead will call, will teach, will comfort us tomorrow, and here none of the dead knows whether a new work of the living may call them on roads they had not gone before.

Peter, James, and John saw the appearance of Moses and Elijah, called by Jesus' prayer, conversing with him on the mountain, "speaking of the exodus which he should accomplish at Jerusalem." The conversation changed all three of them. Here the dead came to the living. But in Luke 3, the living visits the dead. Luke, the evangelist, converts (of the same root as "converse") all those fathers between Jesus and Adam, speaking them into sons of God, that is, into his and our conversation partners. Luke leads these pre-Christian fathers into the ever growing conversation between Alpha and Omega, in which every name is made a partaker in the open alphabet that constitutes the Name of names.

Within that ever-growing conversation, all names remain a surprise even after they have been chiseled in a gravestone, and new lives become new words beyond which Humankind cannot go back without causing a deficiency of speech. *Augustine* was such a new word, unknown to the first three centuries of Christianity. Can we still imagine what had been lacking before his name came in? And eight more centuries had spoken in this conversation of the growing Logos without knowing the key-word *"Francis"* as the entrance to a new stretch of the way of Life. In our own time, the name *Eugen Rosenstock-Huessy* has become a word in humankind's conversation, unknown a hundred years ago. Without his name as the key-word to a third millennium, the conversation between Alpha and Omega is under the threat of becoming idle talk.

The three names mentioned are only *three* new words in God's and humankind's still incomplete lexicon of the 144,000 living words seen by John, at Patmos, sharing the Name of names. 144,000! A thousand times the marriage of the twelve tribes of Israel with the twelve apostles of our Lord. The Logos grows, and in its conversation the creation continues, and even prayer and the Bible change.

Once Rosenstock-Huessy was asked by a shy voice whether he still prayed. The answer was: "May all my speaking be prayer!" Does prayer equal speech among men? From the Lord's Prayer from the lips of Jesus to the ocean of humankind's conversation, the river of prayer has broadened. It is the same spread as from the last written verse of the New Testament (John 21:25) to a world of writings reflecting the universal conversation of which John wrote the birth certificate. The conversation between Alpha and Omega is the religion of religions. Speech itself as the power of creation. Whose speech? The speech of those who have not spoken for themselves, but responded to what Saint Paul called "the groanings of the Spirit too deep for words." In their response the groanings became speech, human speech at the price of consuming the speaker. *Respondeo etsi mutabor.*

Human speech?

For long the Bible has been called the word of God. Now we recognize this same Bible as the beginning of the universal conversation of a new Humankind between Alpha and Omega. Within the living alphabet of this conversation, the word of God and the speech of Humankind have become indistinguishable. Therefore the speakers of the Third Millennium may freely move away from the Bible as the word of God, as long as the Synagogue bears witness to the Alpha and Omega of our speech, as long as the Church vouches for the incarnation of this same Alpha and Omega in the year 1, and as soon as we ourselves discover the four gospels as the cradle of the *universal* speech of Man, the gateway through which we all have come, even the pre-Christian people, whom Eugen Rosenstock-Huessy's *Sociology* (the Torah of the nations) ushers to their places in the conversation of Humankind.

For we are a conversation, from Adam to the last child, and it is carried on by the One who said from the midst of the burning bush: "It is me!"

Contributors

Harold J. Berman

Robert W. Woodruff Professor of Law, Emory University School of Law; James Barr Ames Professor of Law, *emeritus,* Harvard University School of Law, USA

M. Darrol Bryant

Associate Professor of Religion and Culture, Renison College, University of Waterloo, Canada

W. Thomas Duncanson

Visiting Lecturer in Speech Communication, University of Illinois at Urbana-Champaign, USA

Richard Feringer

Head, Graduate Program in Adult Education, College of Education, Western Washington University, USA

Clinton C. Gardner

President, US-USSR Bridges For Peace, Norwich, Vermont, USA

Cynthia O. Harris

M.D., Consultant to the Learning Clinic, Brooklyn, CT; Member Professional Staff, Gestalt Institute of Cleveland, USA

Hans R. Huessy

M.D., Professor Emeritus, Department of Psychiatry, University of Vermont, College of Medicine, USA

Raymond Huessy

Set Designer, Norwich, Vermont, USA

Dale T. Irvin

Ph.D. Candidate, Union Theological Seminary, New York; Adjunct Professor, New York Theological Seminary, USA

Stanley K. Johannesen

Associate Professor of American History, Department of History, University of Waterloo, Canada

Bastian Leenman

Doorwerth, the Netherlands

Patricia A. North

Ph.D., Cannery Worker, Pt. Adams Packing Co., Oregon, USA

Richard Shaull

Henry Luce Professor of Ecumenics, *emeritus*, Princeton Theological Seminary, USA

Terry Simmons

President, Humboldt Research Associates, Walnut Creek, California, USA

Harold M. Stahmer

Professor of Religion and Philosophy, University of Florida, Gainesville, USA

William C. Strickland

Professor of Philosophy and Religion, Appalachian State University, North Carolina, USA

Eugene D. Tate

Professor of Sociology, St. Thomas More College, University of Saskatchewan, Canada

INDEX

TORONTO STUDIES IN THEOLOGY